NORTHFLEET UNITED FOOTBALL CLUB

Set In Concrete

The History of Northfleet United Football Club, 1890–1946

Written by
Paul Harrison, John Jones & Ed Miller

Foreword by
Dr Abdulla Al-Humaidi

A lone Northfleet United forward climbs high as Erith & Belvedere defend against the reigning champions in this Kent League clash in 1937

First published in the UK in 2015
by Paul Harrison & Ed Miller

Acknowledgements
Many of these photos and illustrations come from the authors' own collections but the valuable help of Richard Ralph, Peter Jones, Bob Goodwin and the late Andy Porter in providing items from their own collections is also noted. Additional photos come courtesy of Topfoto, Getty Images and the Douglas Grierson Collection.

© Copyright 2015

Layout & design by:

Ed Miller / Last Word Creative Ltd.

ISBN: 978 0 9515001 4 9

Printed in the UK by Mixam Ltd.

Cover: The Northfleet United squad of 1924/25. Photo retouched and recoloured by Ed Miller

▮Contents▮

Foreword

It gives me great pleasure to introduce this first-ever complete history of the football club that preceded the present-day Ebbsfleet United.

When KEH Sports Ltd took over the club in 2013, it was clear with just one look around Stonebridge Road that the ground and the club was steeped in history, from the 110-year-old Main Stand around to the rows of terracing that supporters still stand on to this day.

So many great players have turned out in the red of the Fleet – that much is clear from the following pages – and it is my desire that this long tradition, stretching back 125 years, is maintained into the future.

As we move into that future, of the club that once called itself Northfleet Invicta (but is still very much 'the Fleet'), we do not do so without recalling the past and the foundations on which it is built.

As you delve into seasons past in this book, it is evident that the Fleet has always aspired to higher things. It is a club that has not been daunted by change or development but has embraced new opportunities.

It is my determintation that the future of the present club be assured and match the ambitions that its founders of 1890 might once have held. Our aim is to develop the current club as a focus for the whole community on the spot where so much of its history has been written.

Dr Abdulla Al-Humaidi,
Chairman, Ebbsfleet United Football Club
November 2015

● Stonebridge Road in 1932. The Main Stand and turnstiles/entrance are instantly recognisable. Both ends are as yet undeveloped and open to the elements, while the small curved stand situated by the roadside was acquired from Rosherville Gardens in 1909 and remained in situ until 1953. Compare the surrounding area to the picture on the previous pages where, save for a few buildings and cement wagons, the below scene is mainly marshland stretching back towards the Thames

From dust we came

As the autumn of 1890 set in across a stretch of the north Kent coast between Gravesend and Dartford, there was something in the air. It wasn't just the sharp, chill wind that heralded the arrival of a particularly severe winter. Nor was it the dry, pervading cement dust that snaked through the streets of Northfleet, emanating from the huge kilns and concrete plants that sustained much of the town's population.

It was, instead, the birth of an unremarkable football club, one like so many others formed in small towns and villages across England during the late 19th century – but one whose history can still be keenly felt to this day.

Little did the cricketers of Northfleet Invicta, from where the football team would derive its name, know what they had set in motion. Their new football club would go on to win 34 trophies in little more than the same number of seasons. It would blood several young men who would go on to win English football's biggest prize. And, despite an untimely demise, it would leave behind a powerful legacy that has enabled several more generations of football fans to pledge their allegiance to "the Fleet".

One hundred and twenty-five years on, we can now commemorate that football club for the very first time in published form.

A book can take anything from a week to a year to a lifetime to produce. This one certainly did since it has been 40 years in the making.

John Jones began his research into the club in the mid-1970s; it was a long-neglected part of local sporting history and a story that deserved to be told.

By the end of the decade he had produced the work that acted as a template for this book. Although unpublished, John presented the work to Gravesham Library where it has become a well-thumbed addition in the local studies section.

Now we move the story on 30 years and my feeling was that the story of the club needed to be told to a wider audience, embellished by photos and illustrations that were absent from the original.

Looking for a suitable date, the 125th anniversary seemed a suitable landmark. And so, in 2007, I marked the year 2015 as the ideal date... and promptly forgot

about it while producing books on first Gravesend & Northfleet and then Ebbsfleet United.

I gradually began to research further and the current Fleet programme editor Ed Miller showed his interest in the subject and came on board. His mastery of modern technology and know-how in gleaning information from obscure websites and online archives was a vital part of this book, enabling us to produce it ourselves without the need for a publisher or designer.

Northfleet United was closely linked to two clubs, Gravesend United (who they eventually amalgamated with) and Tottenham Hotspur, with whom they were associated throughout the inter-war years, an arrangement which provided mutual advantages for both clubs.

I was fortunate to count Andy Porter, the Tottenham club historian, as a good friend and he helped greatly with information about the club until his untimely death in October 2014. Fortunately, his family suggested another great Spurs fan in Bob Goodwin who could provide help and he stepped up to answer further queries and provide additional photos.

We have tried to obtain goalscorers from all Northfleet competitive matches and managed to track down 90% of them; often no goalscorers were mentioned – particularly at midweek games. Moreover, the opposition was sometimes a first-team, sometimes a reserve side or a mixture of both – so unless certain, we have simply named the club (teams most commonly in this scenario were Dartford, Folkestone, Gillingham and Margate).

The jigsaw of the inter-twining of local senior football history is now almost complete – only Gravesend United (1893–1946) remains, with preparations already under way for a book on their 125th anniversary in 2018.

This is likely to be the definitive Northfleet United book as it is unlikely that anyone in the future will have the time or inclination to better this effort, of which all three of us are proud.

We are delighted to be able to finally give due credit to a great club, one that brought so much joy to the local population in hard and troubled times and provided the solid foundation for the future Ebbsfleet United.

Paul Harrison, November 2015

● William Kennedy – a star forward of the treble-winning 1909/10 side, and who later played for West Ham United – died at the Battle of Loos in October 1915, almost exactly 100 years before publication of this history.
See page 59 for more.

> *This is what we expect*
> *of Northfleet, for the spirit*
> *and manhood of a town*
> *which can win laurels*
> *in the field of Kentish sports*
> *does not fail its country*
> *when laurels are to be won*
> *in a greater field...*

Kent Messenger, December 4, 1915

Club honours

Kent League (11): 1895/96; 1907/08; 1908/09; 1909/10; 1919/20; 1925/26; 1931/32; 1934/35; 1935/36; 1936/37; 1938/39

Kent Senior Cup (10): 1895/96; 1909/10; 1912/13; 1920/21; 1923/24; 1924/25; 1925/26; 1926/27; 1927/28; 1937/38

Kent League Cup (5): 1923/24; 1931/32; 1934/35; 1936/37; 1937/38

Kent Senior Shield (4): 1923/24; 1924/25; 1925/26; 1928/29

West Kent League (2): 1906/07; 1907/08

Thames & Medway Combination (1): 1909/10

Kent Junior Cup (1): 1894/95

Chapter One:
End of a century

● *Organised football leagues became commonplace in the 1890s, though the rules remained somewhat fluid. This undated artist's impression depicts a considerably more orderly match than would have often been the case. Goal nets, visible here, were not invented until 1891 and the crowd is somewhat larger than the early Northfleet club would have been used to*

1890-1900

It was the year Stan Laurel and Agatha Christie were born, that Vincent van Gogh and the Elephant Man died and the 54th of Queen Victoria's reign.

The Football League was just two years old, the first ever official County Championship cricket match had taken place that summer and the publication of Oscar Wilde's *The Picture of Dorian Gray* was causing a scandal.

Closer to home, Gravesend's Clock Tower had been completed and an electric tramline, the first in the south of England, had been laid down in Northfleet, from The Hill to Huggens College, which stood overlooking Stonebridge Road and what would become the town's football stadium.

As summer faded, and with it England's traditional summer sport, Northfleet's Invicta club cricketers convened a meeting for the autumn to determine interest among local youth in forming a football club.

Association football had been in existence as an organised sport for more than 20 years. In Kent, the county football association had been formed in 1881. A few miles up the road, Cray Wanderers FC had been going since 1860, Woolwich Arsenal since 1886, Dartford two years after that, while several clubs operated in neighbouring Gravesend.

Now it was Northfleet's turn.

The local paper had noted the increasing popularity of the game the year before, writing "football has gained much in popularity in the town and surrounds, and lovers of the game should now be sufficiently numerous to lend to any proposed clubs that support which is indispensable to the success of every institution."

The new club was destined to win its first league title at its first attempt and soon crossed swords with the best sides in southern England. But within the same decade, it would also be dormant, its short existence seemingly ended alongside the fading century in which it was created.

1890/91

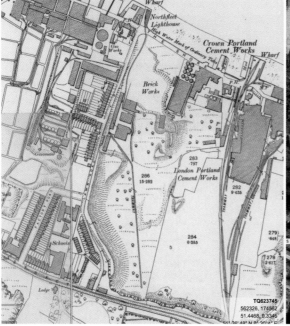

● 'Mr Northfleet' – Joe Lingham witnessed the first and last games of the club, first as a player in 1890 (above left) and finally, almost half a century later, as president in 1939 (above right)

As the autumn days grew shorter and the nights drew in, the teenagers of Invicta cricket club were preparing for a new venture – the founding of a football club to benefit the youngsters of Northfleet. The cricket club was a success and they were determined that the same might be true of a football club. While still in its infancy in Kent, the game of football was becoming ever more popular and was now the country's major winter sporting activity.

The club was officially founded in October 1890, as Northfleet Invicta FC, becoming the first football club in the town, although several were already formed in neighbouring Gravesend.

A committee of four was put in place: J.B. (Joe) Lingham was named chairman and would become the father figure and benefactor of the club down the years; first, as a player and administrator, then as chairman and president. He would also rise to a position of major influence within the Kent County Football Association (KCFA) and take up a role at the English FA.

The other officials tasked with getting the fledgling club off the ground were Edward D.

● Above left: Northfleet's first ground at Portland Meadows was in the region of the London Portland Cement Works, slightly to the east of Stonebridge Road and with the river to the north. Above right shows the same area today

Carrick as secretary and committee members F. Dabson and W. Ware.

Northfleet Invicta found a ground at Portland Meadows, later covered by the giant Blue Circle Cement Works before it was demolished. The local cement industry would become inextricably linked with the club and its ground(s) over the next 120 years, hence the nickname the 'Cementers' soon became established. Committee meetings were held in Church House, which stood on a site now occupied by Vicarage Road.

With few other teams to play, the first season produced a sparse fixture list, a state of affairs not aided by a severe winter that caused several postponements. The first match played – at Portland Meadows on 8th November, 1890 – was against a Gravesend club called Hotspur A who were based around the Canal Tavern area. The first ever Northfleet XI for this historic occasion was

J. Briggs; A.L Cole; W. Grant; F. Dabson; J. Nicholls; G. Dudney; P. Smith (captain); N. Shotton; J. Crane; Joe Lingham; W. Stables.

Invicta got off to a successful start with an impressive 5-2 victory over the Gravesend outfit, who were also beaten in the return game a couple of months later.

All the team, including the goalkeeper, wore red shirts adorned with the rampant white horse of Kent, with white knickerbockers and socks.

Football of the 19th century was, of course, a much more physical affair than today's game – which is of little surprise bearing in mind rugby and football had only gone their separate ways 25 years earlier and remnants of the other game were still to be found in both codes.

Hacking, scrimmaging, barging and occasionally punching were all still very much part of the scene. There were no penalty kicks and no restrictions on how a throw-in could be utilised.

Goalkeepers could be shoulder-charged, even when attempting a save, and they could do likewise to the opposition.

The control of games would normally be left to the good nature (or otherwise) of the two sides since 'umpires' (as they were generally referred to at this time) were few and far between.

As such, decisions had to be mutually agreed – something that was often impossible, even after much argument and, on certain occasions, physical violence.

In just seven games of Northfleet's first season, two of them ended with disputed results. But with five wins, it was a successful start for the fledgling club.

Results 1890/91

Date		Opponent	Venue	Result	
Nov	08	Hotspur A	home	**5-2**	
Dec	06	Chatham Albion	home	**2-2**	
	27	Wouldham Rovers	away	**4-0**	
Jan	03	Galley Hill	home	**7-1***	* disputed result
	31	Cliffe	home	**2-1***	* disputed result
Feb	21	Hotspur A	home	**3-1**	
	28	Chatham Albion	home	**1-2**	

1891/92

● *The earliest known photograph of a Northfleet side in existence, from 1891/92. Back row, from left: C Dear (referee), J Nicholls, A Cole, G Dudney, B Herbert, J Briggs, F Dabson, G Elford (linesman). Front row, from left: W Stables, J Lingham, E Shotton, J Crane, P Smith. The red, button-down shirts and white knickerbockers set a colour trend that exists to this day. One interesting point to note is the attire of the officials – one wonders if they officiated in such garb!*

The club managed to arrange twice as many fixtures as the previous season, no mean feat in an era of difficult travel arrangements and little finance to pay the expenses of the visiting team.

The Football Association had introduced further major changes to the laws of the game with the introduction of referees and linesmen to replace umpires. A 12-yard penalty kick was introduced for any infringement within this distance although at the time there was no penalty area or penalty spot. When a referee decided on a penalty being awarded, the kick could be taken at any point 12 yards from goal. Another innovation was the introduction of goal nets for the first time.

The standard of football continued to improve with the best performance coming in a 1-0 victory over Bexleyheath Rovers, ending their three-year unbeaten record. Against this Rochester Defiance had Invicta's measure, beating them home and away.

Several Invicta players featured in games for Northfleet & District with the key game being a match against Gravesend Ormonde on their Pelham Road ground, watched by a 3,000 crowd.

It was an attendance that encouraged local clubs and underpinned the notion that there existed a great enthusiasm for association football in the local community. The game itself ended in a hard-fought 1-1 draw with the clubs sharing a trophy for six months each.

Results 1891/92

Sep 26	Chatham Hill B	home	3-3
Oct 03	Gravesend Volunteers	home	4-1
14	Gravesend Ormonde	away	0-1
24	Dartford WMC Reserves	away	3-0
Dec 05	Rochester Defiance	home	1-5
12	Erith Avenue Reserves	home	3-3
19	Bexleyheath Rovers	home	1-0
26	Greenhithe Crusaders	home	9-0
Jan 02	Grays AAC	away	1-1
09	Gravesend Rangers	home	4-0
23	Chatham Albion	home	12-2
30	Rochester Defiance	away	0-2
Feb 06	Greenhithe	away	3-2
17	Parkhouse	away	3-0

> *A key game was the match against Gravesend Ormonde on their Pelham Road ground, watched by 3,000. It was an attendance that encouraged local clubs and underpinned the notion that there existed a great enthusiasm for association football in the local community...*

1892/93

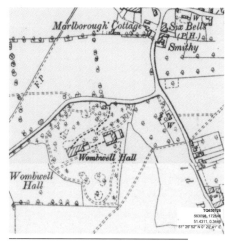

● *Right: the Six Bells pub at the turn of the century can be located at the top of the above map. Northfleet's latest home was situated between there and Wombwell Hall*

A season of further progress was marked by a new direction, with the club changing its name to plain and simple Northfleet FC.

The reason given for dropping the Invicta and focusing on Northfleet was to establish the club as the main player in the town. Since other clubs were beginning to appear, the Northfleet committee decided to protect its status and seniority in the area – so after two successful seasons, the name 'Invicta' was consigned to the history books.

There was not only a new name but a

There was not only a new name but a new ground as well – on the Wombwell Park Estate, close to the Six Bells public house. The pitch was roped off, a pay box erected and for the first time spectators were charged for watching the games at a price of one penny

new ground as well – on the Wombwell Park Estate, close to the Six Bells public house. The pitch was roped off, a pay box erected and for the first time spectators were charged for watching the games at a price of one penny.

After a comfortable victory at Snodland in the opening game of the season, Fleet's

debut on their new ground came against the cream of the Woolwich Alliance League – Clarence FC, who had lost just three games in as many years. Such a record was paid scant regard by the Cementers of Northfleet who won – narrowly – 3-2 in front of an encouraging crowd of 500.

Cup football also came to the club with entry into the Kent Junior Cup. After two fiercely contested games with Star Rovers in the opening round, a single-goal defeat on Rectory Field, Swanscombe, ended the club's interest at the second-round stage.

The first of several spats with the Gravesend club came in the Hospital Charity Cup when Northfleet were drawn out first and presumed themselves to be at home. Gravesend thought otherwise and felt the Bat & Ball venue would be more suitable. A neutral ground was suggested but, with Northfleet feeling hard done by, they decided instead to withdraw from the competition.

The club was now attracting plenty of support and some fans were recognisable by hats fitted with a white cardboard brim and suitably inscribed 'Play up Northfleet' in red letters, the headwear supplied by local Gentlemen's Outfitters A. Card.

The season ended earlier than expected after Northfleet were refused permission by the Wombwell Estate to play on their ground after 25th March, so they concluded the 1892/93 campaign by beating Snodland 3-0 in a benefit game for the Northfleet Temperance Band.

Results 1892/93

Date		Opponent	Cup	Venue	Score
Sep	17	Snodland		away	**8-2**
	24	Clarence		home	**2-3**
Oct	01	Royal Engineers E Company		away	**6-1**
	08	Little Thurrock		home	**10-0**
	29	Horton Kirby		away	**2-2**
Nov	05	Stone		away	**3-1**
	12	Star Rovers	KJC1	away	**2-2**
	19	Star Rovers	KJC1 *replay*	home	**2-0**
	26	Chatham Ormonde		away	**0-0**
Dec	03	Woolwich Trinity		home	**6-0**
	10	Gravesend Ormonde		home	**0-2**
	17	Swanscombe	KJC2	away	**0-1**
Jan	14	Falcon		away	**3-0**
	21	Gravesend St Andrews		home	**7-1**
	28	Mr Lilley's X1		home	**3-0**
Feb	04	Gravesend Ormonde		away	**4-3**
	11	Clarence		home	**4-0**
	18	Stone		home	**3-0**
	25	New Brompton		home	**2-3**
Mar	11	Leicestershire Regiment		home	**1-4**
	25	Snodland		home	**3-0**

1893/94

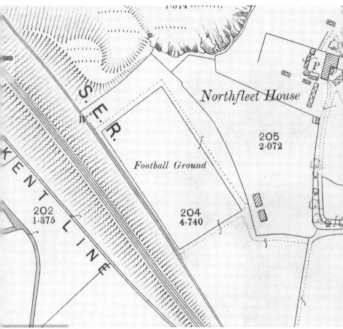

For the club's fourth season, a third ground was used after it became clear the Wombwell Estate would not allow football beyond the middle of March.

Fortunately the club had already anticipated the problem and negotiated a move to Collins Meadow – which is now occupied by Huntley Avenue – running parallel to the main railway line between Northfleet and Gravesend. It was owned by Mr H. Evans, a director of the Portland Cement Company, and while the quality of soil and grass was good, the pitch sloped badly towards the railway line and was known as 'The Roof' by unhappy opponents who were quick to claim it gave the hosts an unfair advantage.

Despite this, two-thirds of the games were played on the ground as the club were able to tempt visitors with generous financial guarantees because of Northfleet's fast-growing fan base – and just two of 23 home games were defeats. By the time the first game was played, the ground was enclosed by fencing and a club house and dressing rooms erected. Later in the season was lighting and a gas-heated bath were installed and water was obtained from a well in the south-west corner of the ground.

Season tickets were priced at /6d plus a 2/- club membership fee – while the regular price was d for men, half price for ladies and 1d for children.

Unfortunately for the club, the ground was overlooked by a high bank (now, appropriately enough, Bankside – the curved line to the

● *Northfleet's third ground, Collins Meadow, can be seen labelled on this Ordnance Survey map from the 1890s. Today, the houses of Huntley Avenue stand where the pitch (white outline) once was. The railway line running parallel travels north-west to Northfleet Station*

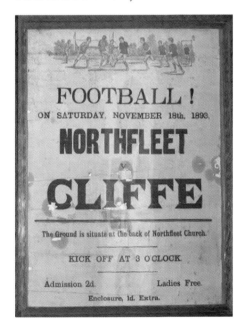

FOOTBALL !
ON SATURDAY, NOVEMBER 18th, 1893,
NORTHFLEET
v
CLIFFE
The Ground is situate at the back of Northfleet Church.
KICK OFF AT 3 OCLOCK.
Admission 2d.   Ladies Free.
Enclosure, 1d. Extra.

right of the pitch, above left) which enabled a free view for spectators, despite valiant attempts by club stewards to dissuade them.

This problem continued well into the season when it was decided desperate measures were needed and, at the cost of 7/6d, the redoubtable local policeman PC Cladingbowl was successfully employed as a deterrent and the problem ceased.

Whilst the Fleet had teething problems with the new ground, their first trip to Dartford was something of an eye-opener: the ground at Summers Meadow, Lowfield Street, was described as a bumpy swamp surrounded by water-filled ditches from which the ball had to be constantly retrieved. And in the days when the ball easily retained water, it soon became almost impossible to kick it more than a few yards. The Darts fans were not described favourably either, the local correspondent – perhaps with a hint of bias – accusing them of being "uncouth louts who constantly abused the referee".

Continued over page ➔

● *A contemporary poster advertising a home game against Cliffe in November 1893. Ground directions and admission details are visible... as is the generous offer of free admission for ladies! At 2d admission for everyone else, it was value for money as Northfleet won the game 7-1. The "Northfleet Church" referred to on the poster is St Botolph's Church, pictured left after the First World War. Northfleet's Collins Meadow would have been situated roughly in the direction the arrow indicates*

1893/94 *(continued)*

Another new rival came in the shape of Gravesend United, who Northfleet played for the first time on Boxing Day at the Fairfield ground on the Overcliffe, drawing 2-2.

The only competitive football was again the Kent Junior Cup and once more Swanscombe prevented progress at the second-round stage, this time after a

● *Northfleet played twice in a day on March 26, 1894. It didn't help their second set of opponents, the Scots Guards pictured here in the same year, who lost the afternoon game 3-0*

Results 1893/94

Sep 02	White Hart		home	**3-1**
09	Clarence		home	**0-0**
16	Bostal Rovers		away	**1-5**
23	New Brompton		home	**1-2**
Oct 07	Border Regiment		home	**1-0**
14	Dartford		away	**1-3**
21	Chatham Hill		home	**3-0**
28	Swanscombe		away	**1-3**
Nov 04	Polytechnic	KJC1	home	**3-0**
11	Rochester Defiance		home	**7-2**
18	Cliffe		home	**7-1**
25	Polytechnic		home	**2-1**
Dec 02	Royal Oak		away	**6-0**
09	Greenhithe		away	**1-1**
16	Swanscombe	KJC2	home	**1-1**
26	Gravesend United		away	**2-2**
30	Woolwich Ramblers		home	**1-0**
Jan 13	Swanscombe	KJC2 *replay*	away	**0-4**
20	Greenhithe		home	**2-1**
27	Bow		home	**3-1**
Feb 03	Erith Avenue		away	**2-0**
10	Stratford Town		home	**5-0**
17	Royal Ordance Reserves		home	**2-1**
24	Chatham Reserves		home	**2-0**
Mar 10	Swanscombe		away	**3-1**
17	St Marys Vale		home	**0-0**
23	Bostal Rovers		home	**2-0**
24	Pickwicks		home	**4-1**
26am	Gravesend United		away	**0-1**
26pm	Scots Guards		home	**3-0**
31	Ordnance Store Corporation		home	**3-0**
Apr 07	Clarence		home	**1-1**
14	Plaistow		home	**6-0**

January replay. In March, Fleet took their revenge with a 3-0 win in a benefit game for widows and orphans although it hardly echoed the benevolence of the occasion.

In a hard, physical game, Fleet's Pat Cullen was constantly given rough treatment by Markham, the Swans' no-nonsense centre-half, and after one blatant late tackle left the unfortunate Cullen writhing in agony, the referee gave Markham the choice of either being sent off or (as it was a fundraising game) to leave the field voluntarily. Unsurprisingly, he chose the latter.

There was a murky tale (see newspaper cutting below) to be had towards the end of Northfleet's first season at Collins Meadow when a grisly discovery was made one Thursday morning in early April 1894. The grim find of the body of a man with his throat cut was made by labourers, close to the entrance to the football ground. Foul play was initially suspected but upon a spot of detective work by Inspector Hoare of north Kent's finest, it was found the man had cut his own throat with a pocket knife found on his person.

Such ghastly events often held the Victorian public in thrall and their grim preoccupation with death extended to a new fad amongst football supporters. This was the season when keen rivalries between the local clubs began to develop, with the tradition of mock funerals coming to the fore. This suprisingly well-organised show of gallows humour involved groups of supporters assuming the role of pall bearers; they would enter the ground bearing a coffin in the colours of the opposition and proceed to carry it around the ground before the game. Thereafter, they would hand out memorial cards to the watching crowd!

Football – along with its off-field rivalries and peculiarities – was indeed beginning to take a major hold on the North Kent public.

● *From the South Eastern Gazette, April 1894*

1894/95

Progress was rapid in many areas through the season and there was a first honour for Northfleet as they collected the Kent Junior Cup. The club also turned professional, became affiliated to the Football Association, gained exclusive tenancy of Collins Meadow and, at the end of the season, was accepted into the Kent League for the 1895/96 season.

An impressive series of on-field performances resulting in 34 victories from 42 games and 186 goals scored rapidly enhanced the reputation of the club, attracting larger attendances. That enabled Northfleet to offer generous guarantees to provide a better quality of opponent, with 33 of the games being played on their own ground including against such teams as Queens Park Rangers and Fulham, two fledgling clubs with the same ambitions as Northfleet. Both were put to the sword in emphatic fashion.

Many of the defeated clubs complained that the slope was worth at least a three-goal lead to the home team in a vaguely concealed display of sour grapes.

The first 12 games of the season were played at Collins Meadow and were all victories, the spell only broken when the Kent Junior Cup came around. After receiving a bye and a walkover in the first two rounds, subsequent wins over Greenhithe, Woolwich Poly and Holmesdale took Fleet into the final and a match with Chatham Reserves at Rectory Field, Swanscombe. A crowd of 1,000 saw Fleet win by 2-0 with goals from Smith and Moody.

Although this was a major success for the club, the main highlights of the season were the eagerly anticipated meetings with local rivals Gravesend United on Boxing Day and Easter Monday.

The team went into special training for weeks before the Christmas clash and the rivalry was strained by the Shrimpers' attempt to get their local rivals to amalgamate with them, a request immediately turned down by the Fleet. The game was played on Gravesend's Overcliffe ground and watched by 4,500 people paying 6d each – many of them watching from wagonettes placed around the ground to provide better viewing.

A keenly contested game went the Fleet's way by 2-1 but the Shrimpers, with what was described as a childish attitude, refused to play the return game at Collins Meadow. So Northfleet again visited the Overcliffe for the Easter return where an even bigger crowd of 5,000 watched as Gravesend gained their revenge by a 2-0 margin.

With professionalism being approved by the KCFA in January, Northfleet were quick to register the entire first team as professionals with payments of between 10 and 12 shillings a week (50p to 60p). The club was keen to step up a grade and with the Kent Junior Cup won, Fleet applied to join the second division of the Kent League which required a test match with another applicant – Folkestone Harveians – to be played at Faversham. Fleet romped to a comfortable 7-1 win and so impressed were the Kent League that they accepted the club into the First Division rather than the Second.

After five years of progress, the club was now among the elite of Kent football and ready for the challenge.

Results 1894/95

Date		Opponent		Venue	Score	Scorers
Sep 01		Royal Ordnance Reserves		home	**6-1**	
	08	Bostal Rovers		home	**5-1**	
	15	Garfield		home	**12-0**	
	22	Pickwicks		home	**7-0**	
	29	Millwall Reserves		home	**2-1**	
Oct 06		Stanley		home	**4-0**	
	13	Upton Park		home	**2-0**	
	20	Royal Warwick Regiment		home	**3-2**	
	27	Greenhithe		home	**6-0**	
Nov 03		Park Grove		home	**4-0**	
	10	3rd West Kent Volunteer Regt		home	**4-0**	
	17	Grenadier Guards		home	**4-1**	
	24	Greenhithe	(KJC3)	away	**5-1**	Smith, King, Moody, Hills, Lingham
Dec 01		Woolwich Ramblers		home	**7-1**	
	05	HMS Pembroke		home	**3-0**	
	08	1st Coldstream Guards		home	**9-3**	
	15	Woolwich Poly	(KJC4)	away	**6-1**	Moody 2, Hills 2, Cullen, Smith
	22	North Woolwich		home	**7-0**	
	26am	Gravesend United		away	**2-1**	
	26pm	Chatham Hill		home	**8-2**	
	29	Park Grove		home	**4-1**	
Jan 05		Grays Town		home	**3-0**	
	12	8th Hussars		home	**5-2**	
	19	Luton Town Reserves		home	**4-4**	
	26	Fulham		home	**6-0**	
Feb 16		Chesham Town		home	**8-4**	
	23	Royal Scots		home	**1-6**	
Mar 02		Holmesdale	(KJC SF)	at Maidstone	**6-0**	Wright 3, Hills, Moody, OG
	09	Dartford		home	**2-3**	
	16	Royal Warwick Regiment		home	**5-0**	
	23	Grays Town		away	**2-0**	
	30	Chatham T Res	(KJC Final)	at Sw'combe	**2-0**	Smith, Moody
Apr 03		Royal Scots Guards		home	**2-3**	
	06	Queens Park Rangers		home	**5-1**	
	12	Woolwich Arsenal Reserves		home	**1-3**	
	13	Matlock Swifts		home	**3-2**	
	15am	Gravesend United		away	**0-2**	
	15pm	Royal Scots		home	**1-3**	
	20	London Caledonians		home	**5-0**	
	24	1st Warwick Regiment		home	**3-3**	
	27	Folkestone Harveians	(KL Test)	at Faversham	**7-1**	Cullen 3, Smith 3, Wright
	30	Dartford		away	**5-1**	Moody 2, Hills, Smith, Russell

1895/96

After tasting their first success with Kent Junior Cup victory the new season offered exciting possibilities with entry into the Kent League. To step up to the challenge a limited company was formed in May 1895 entitled Northfleet Athletic Company Limited under the chairmanship of Mr J. Shotton and much of the £750 raised was spent on the improvement of Collins Meadow.

Five feet of soil was excavated from the top of the considerable slope and moved to the bottom of the ground to level the pitch off and end the perceived advantage the Fleet took into every home game. The ground was enclosed by a high fence with two turnstiles installed and a grandstand, with a seating capacity of 400, was erected on the northern side of the ground.

This stand also incorporated changing rooms and was installed by G.W. Harbrow and Co. of South Bermondsey. They arrived on site on 12th October, 1895, at 08.30 and by 15.30 – just seven hours later – the stand was complete, enabling an FA Cup game with Dartford to kick off. The club also obtained a 21-year lease on the ground and decided to drop the Collins Meadow name and rename it the Northfleet Athletic Ground.

The management of the football club was a separate section and

● *The Northfleet side of 1895/96 were Kent League champions in their first competitive league season. Players as follows – back row from left: W. Ware, S. King, J. McGregor, T. Beveridge, J. Walker, E. Hills. Middle row: R. Cotter (trainer), E. Bundock, T. Grieves, A. Wright, A. Russell, P. Cullen, J. Lingham (secretary). On ground: W. Ferguson, J. Moody*

was under the chairmanship of Mr William C. Treen, with the familar name of Joe Lingham as secretary. This period also marked his election to the Kent County Football Association where his influence would run throughout the club's life.

Two new rules were introduced for the season: both hands had to be used for

throw-ins and goalkeepers could only be charged when playing the ball or obstructing an opponent. Previously, shoulder charges could be administered against players even if they did not have the ball. If a goalkeeper caught the ball, he could be barged over the line (see photo, above right). As a result, they tended to punch the ball a great deal.

With most of the players remaining from the previous campaign it was soon evident that the team would be more than capable of holding their own. Both club captain Teddy Bundock and J. Moody – who lived near to the Fleet's future ground on Stonebridge Road – played for Kent in prestigious county games.

The FA Cup was entered for the first time and after the satisfaction of sneaking past local rivals Dartford in a replay, Fleet found themselves well beaten at Botany Road by Sheppey United. The Sheerness club would prove to be their main challengers for the Kent League title. In that, the Fleet got off to a flyer with five wins and a draw, while having

● *Northfleet could have made it a treble of silverware but New Brompton (left) beat them in the then-prestigious Chatham Charity Cup. It was Fleet's first competitive set of games against the club that would become Gillingham in 1912*

● *A rule change to protect goalkeepers was brought in during the 1895/96 season but the practice of barging them over the goalline continued for a while longer*

to replay a home game with Sittingbourne. The original was abandoned to fog after 80 minutes with the men in red leading 6-0; there was little hangover, however, as Fleet promptly won the rearranged game just over a fortnight later to the tune of 8-0.

December saw something of a stutter with successive 3-2 home defeats by Chatham and Woolwich Arsenal before Fleet roared back to form with a 5-1 Christmas Day victory in a friendly with Gravesend United in front of 5,000 spectators.

The Chatham Charity Cup was a major trophy of the period and victories over Bromley and Sheppey put Fleet in the final against New Brompton (later to become Gillingham FC). The first game at Sheerness ended 2-2 in front of 4,000 but the replay at Chatham, in front of another 4,000 gate, went the way of New Brompton who won 2-0. By then, however, Fleet had claimed the Kent League with a decisive 2-0 victory at Sheppey completing a strong run of 10 league games since February with just one defeat – a narrow 1-0 reverse at arch-rivals Gravesend United.

To celebrate the club's success, which also included the Kent Senior Cup – issued automatically and rather strangely to the Kent League champions at this time – a celebration was held at the Factory Hall on 13th May, 1896, where medals were presented to the following members of the successful team: Auld, Bundock, Cottam, Cullen, Fergusson, Grieves, Hills, McGregor, Moody, Ware, Walker and Wright.

The success of the team had seen a doubling of gates but, despite this, the Kent League had proved expensive with trips to Folkestone, Ashford and Sheppey stretching the purse strings and ensuring a deficit at the end of the season.

The club was forced to distribute circulars appealing for donations. In hindsight, this should have ensured caution but instead it was decided to apply to join the Southern League where, instead of meeting the cream of Kent, it would be the elite of southern England coming to Northfleet and the Athletic Ground.

Results 1895/96

Date	Opponent	Competition	Venue	Score	Scorers
Sep 07	Grays Town	Friendly	away	5-2	
14	Royal Artillery	Friendly	neutral	7-0	*at Gravesend
21	Royal Scots	Friendly	neutral	1-3	*at Swanscombe
28	Royal Engineers T.B	KL	away	6-1	
Oct 05	3rd Grenadier Guards	Friendly	home	4-0	
12	Dartford	FAC 1Q	home	3-3	Bundock, Taylor, Moody
16	Dartford	FAC 1QR	away	3-2	Bundock 2, Moody
19	Folkestone	KL	away	1-0	Grieves
26	Dartford	KL	away	1-1	
Nov 02	Sheppey United	FAC 2Q	away	1-4	Grieves
09	Sittingbourne	KL	home	8-0*	*Abandoned (fog), 80min
13	Bromley	CCC1	away	3-2	
16	Ashford United	KL	home	5-0	
23	Gravesend United	KL	home	4-3	Moody, Wright, Hills, Grieves 2
27	Sittingbourne	KL	home	8-0	
30	Swanscombe	KL	home	8-0	Wilson 3, McGregor 2, Moody 2, OG
Dec 07	Woolwich Arsenal Res	KL	home	2-3	Bundock, Moody
21	Chatham	KL	home	2-3	Hills, Wilson
25	Swanscombe	Friendly	home	5-2	
26am	Gravesend United	Friendly	away	5-1	Grieves 5 (Attendance: 5,000)
26pm	Greenhithe	Friendly	home	2-2	
28	Sheppey United	KL	home	5-0	
Jan 04	Royal Ordnance	Friendly	home	2-2	
11	Royal Scots	Friendly	home	2-2	
18	Ashford United	KL	away	5-1	Moody 2, Grieves 2, OG
25	Woolwich Arsenal Res	KL	away	0-7	
Feb 01	Reading	Friendly	away	0-1	
05	New Brompton	KL	away	4-0	
08	2nd Coldstream Guards	Friendly	home	7-1	
15	Folkestone	KL	home	4-0	
22	Gravesend United	KL	away	0-1	
29	Dartford	KL	home	7-3	
Mar 07	Sittingbourne	KL	away	8-3	Connor 2, Wright 2, Russell, Bundock, Allen, OG
11	New Brompton	KL	away	5-3	Connor, Wright (three missing)
14	Royal Engineers TB	KL	home	4-2	Moody 2, Ferguson 2
18	Chatham	KL	away	0-0	
21	Woolwich Arsenal Res	Friendly	home	5-2	
25	Sheppey United	CCC SF	home	4-1	
28	Swanscombe	KL	away	4-0	Moody 2, Grieves, Russell
Apr 03	Leicester Regiment	Friendly	home	6-1	
04	Stockton	Friendly	home	5-2	
06am	Swanscombe & District	Friendly	home	3-0	
06pm	Liverpool League	Friendly	home	8-0	
11	Wellingborough	Friendly	home	2-1	
14	Sheppey United	KL	away	2-0	
18	Barking	Friendly	home	7-0	
25	New Brompton	CCC Final	neutral	2-2	(Attendance: 4,000)
29	Royal Scots	Friendly	home	2-3	
30	New Brompton	CCC Final R	neutral	0-2	(Attendance: 4,000)

1896/97

After almost unbridled success in Northfleet's early seasons, entry into the Southern League provided a complete reversal of the previous successes.

Instead of Sittingbourne and Swanscombe it was Southampton and Spurs in opposition. From teams with similar support and resources, the club had boldly left its comfort zone to take on the cream of southern England, most of their new rivals sporting far superior resources and funding. On reflection the results were inevitable.

The side that had been so successful in the previous season was rightly given the opportunity to continue that success but an opening 4-0 defeat at old rivals Chatham – who along with Gravesend and Sheppey had also decided to vacate the Kent League – was a sign of things to come. Although Fleet held their own into the autumn with a point a game from the first six matches (in the days of two points for a win), the next five games secured just a single point from a draw with Swindon Town.

The team did well in the FA Cup, reaching the fifth round, before being drawn away at Millwall Athletic in Northfleet's first visit to the Lions' home. A local clergyman had described the area around the football club as "badly lighted, astonishingly foul, inconceivably smelly, and miserably bare and lifeless." Millwall's then-home was on East Ferry Road by the docks and close by was a dumping ground where mud dredged from the river would be left. It was said to "stink terribly" and a Corinthian player once declared of the club's ground that he "did not mind playing there but he objected to falling down on it because the smell wouldn't come off for weeks."

It clearly affected the Fleet's performance as they found themselves on the end of one of their heaviest defeats of the season, exiting the FA Cup to the tune of 6-1. (A further 5-0 drubbing followed at Millwall in March and Fleet then lost a test match on the same ground [see below] so clearly something had got up their noses!)

The Thames & Medway Combination was also entered, Northfleet finishing third of six in a round-robin tournament, while there was also competition in the form of the Sevenoaks Charity Cup and the Chatham Charity Cup. The Kent Senior Cup, meanwhile, was still awarded to the winners of the Kent League.

The best results came in the Sevenoaks competition where victories over Swanscombe, Folkestone and New Brompton put Fleet in the final. They were hot favourites to beat RETB (Royal Engineers Training Battalion) but after leading at the interval they slumped to a 4-2 defeat. In the T&M Combination the team finished third while there was a shock exit to Swanscombe in the opening round of the Chatham Cup.

Discipline was a problem on and off the field with both Bundock and Grieves being sent off in games and the club being reported to the Football Association after a 4-0 home defeat by Swindon in February. The referee had four specators removed from the ground for abusive behaviour towards him and the Swindon players. At the enquiry

• William J Moody, who lived on Stonebridge Road, was the club's top scorer for three seasons

a local police inspector was called as a witness – the first policeman to ever be called to an FA enquiry… he would not be the last.

The club was severly censured, ordered to pay the expenses of the enquiry and post warning notices around the ground about supporters' behaviour.

The gloom surrounding Northfleet was lifted on 6th March when high-flying Tottenham Hotspur arrived in town and were promptly sent home with their tails between their legs as Fleet produced their best result of the season by winning 2-0.

Despite this Northfleet could only manage to finish ninth of 11 and were thus one of three teams forced into test matches with the top three of the second division.

They were paired with the Southampton-based club Freemantle and lost 3-0 on neutral ground (Millwall's East Ferry Road) and thus relegated. Good fortune for the club had been in short supply through the season but they found some when it was discovered Freemantle had fielded an ineligible player.

Northfleet lodged a protest about the footballer in question – Phillips – who had played most of his season with Royal Artillery Portsmouth. A week later, a meeting of the league found that Phillips had signed Southern League forms for both Northfleet and Freemantle; although he had already played for Freemantle and had made no appearances for Northfleet, his transfer had never been applied for.

Rather than play the game again, the committee ruled that Freemantle be deducted two points, dropping them to fourth and that both sides involved in the test match should remain in their original divisions – thus sparing Northfleet from relegation

Financially, the season had been costly with 9,000 fewer spectators coming through the turnstiles, causing a deficit of £129 and prompting serious financial concern. A proposal that an amalgamation with Gravesend United – a topic that would crop up annually over the next three years – would be advisable was rejected by the commitee.

• The Millwall Athletic team that knocked Northfleet out of the FA Cup at a ground that was "inconceivably smelly"

Results 1896/97

Date	Opponent	Comp	Venue	Score	Scorers	Att
Sep 03	Royal Warwick Regiment	Friendly	home	**7-0**		
05	Chatham	SL	away	**0-4**		
12	Sheppey United	SL	away	**2-1**	Moody, Grieves	1,000
16	Millwall Athletic	SL	home	**2-2**	Moody, Richardson	
19	Reading	SL	away	**0-1**		
23	Chatham	TM	home	**2-4**	Richardson, OG	1,500
26	Gravesend United	SL	home	**1-1**	Moody	4,000
Oct 03	Wolverton	SL	away	**3-0**	Cullen, Gilchrist, Moody	
10	Leyton	Friendly	home	**5-3**		
17	Swanscombe	Friendly	home	**2-0**		
21	New Brompton	TM	away	**3-1**	Grieves, Moody, Richardson	
24	Southampton St Mary's	SL	home	**1-2**	Grieves	
31	Civil Service	FAC1Q	home	**8-0**	Cullen 2, Grieves 2, Allen, Richardson, Moody, Wright	500
Nov 07	Gravesend United	TM	away	**1-1**	OG	
14	Royal Ordnance	Friendly	home	**6-1**		
18	Swanscombe	SCC1	away	**4-1**	Moody, Grieves, Bundock, OG	
21	Dartford	FAC2Q	away	**4-1**	Moody 2, McGregor, Grieves	
28	Chatham	SL	home	**1-3**	Moody	
Dec 05	Sheppey United	TM	home	**3-0**	Moody, Allen, Bundock	
12	New Brompton	FAC3Q	home	**3-1**	Pennington, Quinn, Bundock	300
19	Swindon Town	SL	away	**2-2**	Wright, Richardson	
26	Dartford	TM	away	**5-3**	Moody 2, Grieves, Bundock, McGregor	
28	Tottenham Hotspur	Friendly	away	**0-4**		
Jan 02	Millwall Athletic	FAC4Q	away	**1-6**	Wright	
09	Sheppey United	TM	away	**3-5**	Moody 2 (1 pen), Richardson	
13	Folkestone	SCC2	away	**1-1**		
16	Clapton	Friendly	away	**3-1**		
23	London Caledonians	Friendly	away	**2-3**		
30	New Brompton	SL	home	**2-4**	Grant, Moody	
Feb 03	Folkestone	SCC2 R	home	**4-2**		
06	Swindon Town	SL	home	**0-4**		
10	Chatham	TM	away	**1-4**		
13	Tottenham Hotspur	SL	away	**0-5**		
17	Swanscombe	CCC1	home	**0-4**		
20	Gravesend United	TM	home	**0-6**		
27	Swanscombe	Friendly	away	**2-3**		
Mar 03	New Brompton	TM	home	**1-0**	Gentle (OG)	
06	Tottenham Hotspur	SL	home	**2-0**	Moody, Bundock	
13	Southampton St Mary's	SL	away	**2-6**		
20	New Brompton	SL	away	**0-2**		
22	Millwall Athletic	SL	away	**0-5**		
27	Reading	SL	home	**2-2**	Bundock, Moody	
Apr 03	Gravesend United	SL	away	**0-1**		
05	New Brompton	SCC	neutral	**1-0***	*Abandoned, poor light 80 minutes*	
10	Sheppey United	SL	home	**3-1**	Bundock, Carver, Hancock	
14	New Brompton	SCC SF	home	**1-0**	Hills	
16	Wolverton	SL	home	**1-0**	Moody	
17	Gravesend United	Friendly	away	**1-0**	Moody	
19	Dartford	TM	home	**4-0**		
24	Swanscombe	Friendly	home	**2-0**		
26	Freemantle	SL (Test)	at Millwall	**0-3**		
30	Royal Engineers TB	SCC Final	neutral	**2-4**		

1897/98

This was to prove a very gloomy season indeed for the club during which relegation from the Southern League became almost inevitable, especially considering it took until 27th December to register a first league win of the season (a 3-2 victory over New Brompton at the Northfleet Athletic Ground).

The season had started on a bad note with a 7-0 thumping in a friendly at Chatham, followed by a trip to Thames Ironworks for another friendly. This saw Northfleet play the first ever game at the Memorial Recreation Ground, a new venue for the ambitious Thames Ironworks club headed by the owner of the company Arnold Hills, who modestly stated of the new ground: "It will have a capacity of 120,000 and will be good enough to hold the English cup final."

The game hardly tested the alleged capacity with fewer than 200 attending the 1-1 draw. After a few years, Hills' dislike of professionalism saw the club split, with the result being the formation of West Ham United, who moved to the Boleyn Ground in 1904.

Despite struggling in the Southern League, the team did well in the less exacting Thames & Medway Combination and they looked likely winners until a trip to Dartford on 26th March sent an already disappointing season over the edge.

Leading by a comfortable 3-0 margin with less than 20 minutes to play, Fleet had wing half Fred Cook sent off for persistent misconduct. Cook, rather than accepting the decision, remonstrated with referee Runacas and then to the amazement of everyone punched the referee to the ground, causing a pitch invasion by irate supporters that had to be quelled by calling in the police.

When the game was replayed, Dartford turned the tables, winning 3-1 and Fleet

GRAVESEND.

PROPOSED AMALGAMATION OF FOOTBALL CLUBS.
—The proposed amalgamation of the Gravesend and Northfleet Football Clubs bids fair to become an accomplished fact. Representatives of the two clubs have met, and on Tuesday evening a tacit understanding was arrived at, subject to confirmation by general meetings of members of the respective clubs

ASSAULTING A REFEREE.

At the Dartford Police Court on Saturday last; before Major Frobischer, Fred Cook, of Plumstead, a member of Northfleet Football Club, was charged with grossly assaulting Mr. Runacus, the referee in the Thames and Medway contest between Dartford and Northfleet on the previous Saturday. Cook had been ordered off for kicking Stevens, the Dartford centre, and accepted this decision by striking Mr. Runacus a severe blow in the face. The Bench regarded the case very seriously, but were disposed to deal leniently with prisoner, this being the first case of this description. Prisoner would be fined £3 including costs, a decision which created immense surprise. Mr. Clinch, in an able speech, although appearing for the prosecutor, requested that prisoner would be most leniently dealt with.

A London contemporary thus refers to the case :—"A subscription will probably be got up for Frederick Cook, a professional footballer, playing for the Northfleet Club. During a match Mr. Runacus, the referee, was indiscreet enough to caution Cook for foul play, and finally ordered him off the ground. No self-respecting paid footballer could put up with this interference with his rights and privileges, and Cook promptly retaliated by striking the referee in the face, knocking him to the ground. It is absolutely a fact that the magistrates have, for this trivial performance, fined Cook £3 or fourteen days' hard labour! It is the inalienable right of every player to use the referee as he likes, and this decision will considerably affect a large body of deserving people with large feet.

consequently slumped to fourth in the table. Had the original result stood, they would instead have won the league by a point.

Cook, for his sins, was given the choice at the local magistrates court of a £3 fine or

● Above: the South Eastern Gazette of 22nd March, 1898, reported the likelihood of a Gravesend and Northfleet merger. It failed to materialise and the idea was shelved little more than six weeks later. A coming together of the two clubs would be another 48 years away...

● Left: a report of Fred Cook's assault on the referee in a match at Dartford and his subsequent punishment

seven days hard labour. It was little surprise that he opted for the former.

Northfleet had already been drummed out of the Kent Senior Cup for fielding an ineligible player in their victory over Dover, sending the club further into the doldrums. By the end of the season just four of 22 Southern League games had been won, pushing Fleet into two test matches: although Warmley of Bristol were beaten, Royal Artillery (Portsmouth) proved too strong and Fleet were relegated.

This proved of little consequence because an extraordinary general meeting had already been arranged for 6th May, 1898, where treasurer Mr Fredrick R. Barkway announced a deficit of £360 and stated that all games – other than matches with Gravesend, Chatham and New Brompton – had been played at a financial loss.

Chairman William Treen proposed that the club depart the Southern League and return to the Kent League, a motion that was unanimously carried.

At the same meeting a proposal from Gravesend United to amalgamate was rejected (an earlier meeting in March had initially been receptive to the idea) and it would be a further 48 years before the inevitable happened – and a further 30 before Northfleet ventured into the Southern League again.

● Left: Northfleet moved in illustrious circles, mixing it with Southampton and Tottenham Hotspur (left) who during this season wore a strip of chocolate brown and gold stripes

Results 1897/98

Date	Opponent	Comp	Venue	Score	Scorers	Att
Sep 01	Chatham	Friendly	away	0-7		
02	Thames Ironworks	Friendly	away	1-1		
04	Thames Ironworks	Friendly	home	1-0		
08	Sheppey United	TM	home	1-0	Moody	
11	Grays United	TM	home	3-0	Moody 2, Neale	
18	Gravesend United	SL	away	0-3		
25	New Brompton	FAC1Q	home	1-3	Nicholl	
27	Millwall Athletic	SL	away	0-4		
Oct 02	Wolverton	SL	away	1-5	Moody	
09	Chatham	SL	home	0-1		
16	Maidstone	Friendly	home	1-3	Hoare	
23	Bristol City	SL	away	2-3	Nicholl 2	
Nov 03	Chatham	TM	home	1-4	Nicholl	
13	Gravesend United	TM	home	1-3	Moody	
20	Dartford	Friendly	away	4-2		
27	Brentford	Friendly	away	3-2	Cook 2, Nicholl	
Dec 01	New Brompton	TM	away	3-2	Nicholl 2, Groves	
04	Chatham	SL	away	1-2	Cook	3,000
11	Swanscombe	Friendly	home	0-1		
18	Sheppey United	SL	away	1-5	Campbell	
25	Dartford	TM	home	5-0		
27	New Brompton	SL	home	3-2	Grieve, Campbell, og	2,000
Jan 01	Swanscombe	Friendly	away	1-2		
08	Swindon Town	SL	home	1-2	Stuart	
15	Tottenham Hotspur	SL	home	0-4		
22	Grays United	TM	away	2-0	Campbell, Cook	
29	Dover	KSC1	away	2-1	* disqualified - ineligible player	
29	Swindon Town	SL	away	2-7	Grieves, Cook	
Feb 02	New Brompton	TM	home	2-1	Moody 2	
05	Queens Park Rangers	Friendly	away	1-1		
12	Reading	SL	away	1-1	Nicholl	
16	Reading	SL	home	1-1	Nicholl	
19	Tottenham Hotspur	SL	home	1-3	Nicholl	
26	Gravesend United	TM	away	3-0	Nicholl 2, Moody	2,500
Mar 02	Sheppey United	SL	home	3-2	Bundock, Grieve, Moody	
05	Bristol City	SL	home	1-4	OG	1,000
09	Chatham	TM	home	0-2		
12	Royal Scots Fusiliers	Friendly	home	4-0		
16	RETB	TM	home	5-0	Bundock 2, Grieve, Nicholl, Wright	
19	New Brompton	Friendly	away	1-5		
23	Millwall Athletic	SL	home	2-3	Moody, Bundock	
26	Dartford	TM	away	3-0	* match abandoned	
30	Wolverton	SL	home	4-1	Moody 2, Wright, Grieve	
Apr 06	RETB	TM	away	3-1	Nicholl 2, Wright	
08	New Brighton	SL	away	1-1		
09	Gravesend United	SL	home	3-1	Nicholl 2, Moody	
11	Southampton	SL	away	1-3	Nicholl	
16	Southampton	SL	home	0-2		
18	Warmley	SL (Test)	home	3-1	Moody, Nicholl, Campbell	
25	Dartford	TM	away	1-3	Grieve	500
27	Royal Artillery (Portsmouth)	SL (Test)	home	1-3	Wolfe	
30	Royal Artillery (Portsmouth)	SL (Test)	away	0-1		1,500

> BRISTOL CITY v. NORTHFLEET.—This Southern League match will be played at St. John's-lane to-morrow afternoon. His Worship the Mayor and the Mayoress will be present, and it is announced that the Bristol South band will make a collection for the Mayor's Convalescent Home Fund. The following teams have been selected:—Bristol City Monteith, goal; Davy and Milligan, backs; Mann, Higgins, and Hamilton, half backs; Wyllie, Carnelly, Caie, O'Brien, and Russell, forwards. Northfleet: Clare, goal; Weaver and Bagnall, backs; Wright, Bundock, and Bailey, half backs; Cook, Wolfe, Nicholls, Moody, and Campbell, forwards.

1898/99

As the 19th century entered its death throes, so too did Northfleet. The club was in a serious position financially. The decision to leave the Southern League had given Northfleet the opportunity to reduce costs by returning to the Kent League but with a serious deficit running at nearly £400, supporters were left in no doubt that the club faced a severe crisis that threatened its very existence. It was made clear that unless it was supported at the turnstiles and by donations, the club was unlikely even to reach the new century. Such a warning proved to be prophetic.

With the standard of football reduced, and in a bid to encourage more people to come through the turnstiles, admission was reduced from 6d to 4d but it mattered little and gates were soon settling at around 500. The novelty with senior football had apparently ended and the crowds stayed away despite dire warnings of the consequences.

A sound start on the field was made, with the Fleet going unbeaten in the first four games, a mix of Kent League and Thames & Medway Combination matches. Some heavy defeats followed but also a couple of big Kent League wins – 9-0 over Faversham and 5-1 against Bromley. Despite this the committee was becoming increasingly frustrated at the lack of support. When just 400 fans turned up for the local derby with Dartford, it proved to be the last straw and the committee voted to disband the club.

Five members of the committee, although outvoted, strongly disagreed with this decision and felt the only honourable way to discharge its debts was the old chestnut of amalgamating with Gravesend United – something the Shrimpers had long been in favour of. On 14th November, 1898, the five – Messrs J. Grieves; William Treen; W. Waller; G. Williams and, significantly, Joe Lingham – agreed on the terms. The proposed amalgamated club would continue to be called Gravesend United playing at the Overcliffe ground in red and green, with the Fleet members having a minimum of two seats on the committee of Gravesend United with a place on management at the first vacancy. Collins Meadow, or the Athletic Ground as it was also known, would be closed and any fundraising by the enlarged committee would be shared – two-thirds to Gravesend and one-third towards the debts of Northfleet United. Fleet players Bagnall and Bright would also sign for the Shrimpers.

The local press was pleased with the result, hoping that past differences would be forgotten and the challenge would be met by the committee as all were respected local businessmen.

But the Kent County Football Association was not as impressed and on 7th December, 1898, they set up a special commission to examine the debts of Northfleet United and the proposed amalgamation with Gravesend.

The report into the investigation was published on 18th January, 1899, stating that no regulations were broken and that the amalgamation was "fair and honourable". However, it ruled that those members of Northfleet who had not joined Gravesend United would be banned from football until all the club's debts were paid. They also decreed that of the one-third that Northfleet would receive from fundraising, this would be split. One half would go towards the club's debts and the other to the KCFA as compensation to the clubs who would lose gate money by Northfleet not fulfilling their fixtures.

It looked likely to be a sad end for the club… but was it?

The state of play

The turn of the century marked a watershed for many of Kent's clubs. Northfleet's eagerness to progress had perhaps made them jump the gun in the mid-1890s and the result, closure of the debt-ridden club in 1899, ultimately saw them fall behind a host of other clubs at Southern League level who went on to eventually feature in the Football League – and continue to do so to this day.

As the 20th century dawned, Gravesend United were soon to follow Northfleet into a period of dormancy, as too did Dartford.

Chatham resigned from the Southern League in 1900/01 and played as Chatham Amateurs for a year. Like Gravesend, they couldn't keep pace with expanding clubs such as Crystal Palace, Tottenham, Southampton, Portsmouth, Fulham, QPR and Bristol Rovers and would revert to a more local outlook in the early years of the new century.

Yet spurred on by Joe Lingham, who was still to hang up his boots, Northfleet's first chapter was not to be its final one.

Results 1898/99

Date		Opponent	Comp	Venue	Score	Scorers	Att
Sep	03	Cray Wanderers	KL	home	3-3	Marsden, Hills, Bundock	600
	10	Woolwich Arsenal Res	KL	home	4-4	Mann, Marsden, Bundock, Hills	
	17	Royal Engineers TB	TM	away	3-2	Hills, Reader, Bundock	
	21	Grays United	Friendly	home	3-1		
	24	New Brompton	TM	away	0-8		
	28	Chatham	TM	away	1-6		
Oct	08	Bromley	KL	away	4-3	Hills 2, Mann, Wright	1,200
	12	Royal West Kent Regiment	KL	home	0-1		
	15	Faversham	KL	home	9-0	Wright 4, Bagnall, Richardson, Mann, Hills, Cullen	
	22	Bromley	KL	home	5-1	Richardson 2, Wright 2, Bagnall (pen)	
	29	Ashford United	KL	away	1-7		
Nov	02	Gravesend United	KL	away	2-5	Davis, Richardson	
	05	Dartford	KL	home	1-2	Bagnall (pen)	

League Tables

● *Southampton St Mary's, Southern League winners in 1896/97. They defeated Northfleet home and away. The Saints were able to sign several players who were keen to earn more money in the Southern League as there was a maximum wage cap in the Football League*

Kent League Division 1 1895/96

FINAL TABLE	PL	W	D	L	F	A	Pts
Northfleet	22	16	2	4	85	31	34
Woolwich Arsenal II *	22	16	1	5	76	30	31
Folkestone	22	12	4	6	46	34	28
Chatham	22	12	3	7	49	30	27
Sheppey United	22	9	5	8	48	42	23
RETB Chatham	22	9	5	8	47	39	23
New Brompton	22	9	3	10	36	42	21
Gravesend United **	22	10	4	8	46	44	20
Dartford	22	8	3	11	52	69	19
Sittingbourne	22	4	5	13	40	73	13
Swanscombe	22	3	3	16	34	69	9
Ashford United	22	3	3	16	34	69	9

* –2pts ** –4pts

Southern League 1896/97

FINAL TABLE	PL	W	D	L	F	A	Pts
Southampton St Mary's	20	15	5	0	63	18	35
Millwall Athletic	20	13	5	2	63	24	31
Chatham	20	13	1	6	54	29	27
Tottenham Hotspur	20	9	4	7	43	29	22
Gravesend United	20	9	4	7	35	34	22
Swindon Town	20	8	3	9	33	37	19
Reading	20	8	3	9	31	49	19
New Brompton	20	7	2	11	32	42	16
Northfleet	20	5	4	11	24	46	14
Sheppey United	20	5	1	14	34	47	11
Wolverton LNWR	20	2	0	18	17	74	4
Royal Ordnance Factories	7	0	0	7	8	46	0

Thames & Medway Combination 1896/97

FINAL TABLE	PL	W	D	L	F	A	Pts
Chatham	10	9	1	0	36	4	19
Gravesend United	10	5	4	1	28	11	14
Northfleet United	10	5	1	4	23	24	11
Sheppey United	10	3	2	5	18	28	8
New Brompton	10	2	0	8	21	31	4
Dartford	10	1	2	7	17	40	4

Southern League 1897/98

FINAL TABLE	PL	W	D	L	F	A	Pts
Southampton	22	18	1	3	53	18	37
Bristol City	22	13	7	2	67	33	33
Tottenham Hotspur	22	12	4	6	52	31	28
Chatham	22	12	4	6	50	34	28
Reading	22	8	7	7	39	31	23
New Brompton	22	9	4	9	37	37	22
Sheppey United	22	10	1	11	40	49	21
Gravesend United	22	7	6	9	28	39	20
Millwall Athletic	22	8	2	12	48	45	18
Swindon Town	22	7	2	13	36	48	16
Northfleet	22	4	3	15	29	60	11
Wolverton LNWR	22	3	1	18	28	82	7

Thames & Medway Combination 1897/98

FINAL TABLE	PL	W	D	L	F	A	Pts
Gravesend United	14	10	1	3	35	14	21
Chatham	14	10	1	3	42	15	21
New Brompton	14	9	2	3	33	15	20
Northfleet United	14	10	0	4	33	18	20
Dartford	14	6	0	8	27	40	12
Sheppey United	14	5	1	8	37	31	11
Grays	14	2	1	11	16	56	5
Royal Engineers TB	14	1	0	13	16	49	2

Play-off: Gravesend United 3-1 Chatham Town

Chapter Two:
Mobilising the Fleet

● *Back to being top dogs in Kent, the Northfleet side of 1909/10 earned a significant treble of Kent League (shield in middle), Kent Senior Cup (trophy on right) and Thames & Medway Combination (trophy on left). This line-up included future West Ham player William Kennedy (middle row, centre) who was killed in action during the First World War (see page 59)*

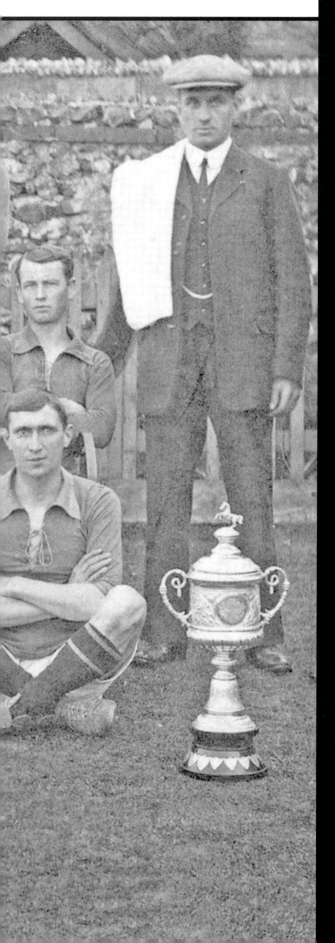

1899–1914

As the Victorian era finally came to an end, Edwardian England witnessed football and sport in general go from strength to strength – even if the state of the game in north Kent at the time was anything but promising.

The Boer War was in full swing and sport – like society at large – was increasingly a matter of national concern. Organised sport expanded rapidly across all classes and while society's hierarchical structure was still rigidly adhered to, male working-class influence increased in football. Commercialisation of the game, while still in its infancy, began to expand as the numbers of spectators increased.

Locally, however, it was a downward spiral. Away from football, Rosherville Gardens – the once-grand Victorian tourist attraction situated between Northfleet and Gravesend – was put up for auction but there were no bidders and it was closed for a time in 1901. This was the same year in which there was no senior football across Gravesend, Northfleet or Dartford, leading the committee at Swanscombe FC – sandwiched in between those three clubs – to note, during its AGM, that "owing to the unfortunate collapse of Gravesend, Northfleet and Dartford there is a total lack of rivalry".

Things did improve slowly, however, and once back on their feet, Northfleet United began to plot their return to the summit of Kent football. A new ground at Stonebridge Road and continual improvements to it leading up to 1914 saw the construction of an impressive main stand that would gain the club the label of having a "proper" non-league ground well into the 21st century.

By 1909, five-figure crowds were flocking to Maidstone to see the Cementers vie for the coveted Kent Senior Cup and county rivalry with the likes of Gravesend, Chatham and Maidstone was in full swing. Players including future England international Charles Buchan and Tottenham's Second Division-winning goalkeeper Bill Jacques graced the Stonebridge Road pitch and, though there were a few bumps along the way, the Northfleet club was on a high heading into the year that would change everything – 1914.

1899–1903

Northfleet was now in its wilderness years: no team, the ground mothballed and the committee splintered, with the influential half now backing Gravesend United while simultaneously determined to wipe out debts incurred by the Fleet.

The Fleet's hardcore support had dwindled from a couple of thousand to a few hundred and had been the main cause of the club's demise but the good form of Gravesend in the Southern League ensured crowds were up for them as, begrudgingly, Fleet fans starved of good football and encouraged by the Northfleet share of the committee made the trip to the Overcliffe.

Sadly, Gravesend's success was not to last and with the Southern League getting ever stronger, the Shrimpers struggled badly in 1900/01. The quality of the league could be judged by the fact that member club Tottenham Hotspur won the FA Cup in this season and remain the only non-league winners of the competition (Gravesend indeed famously recorded a league victory over Spurs during that season).

The Northfleet committeemen further reduced the debt on their old club with a series of their own fundraising activities as well as others held in tandem with Gravesend United. They also sold their main stand at the Athletic Ground/Collins Meadow but by 1901 the debt was still just over £200.

At the end of the 1900/01 season Gravesend United decided to leave the Southern League – heavily in debt, their crowds had dwindled with poor results and the Christmas Day gate receipts against Woolwich Arsenal Reserves had amounted

to just over a pound, with the Gunners expenses amounting to £3. The committee decided to end the amalgamation and for the 1901/02 season there was no senior football played by either local club, although both maintained a committee.

On 10th December, 1902, a meeting of influential local sportsmen was arranged at the Factory Club in Northfleet High Street to discuss the lack of senior football in the locality and attempt to resurrect the name of Northfleet. With this in mind a game was arranged for Boxing Day between a Northfleet XI and a team under the banner of Old Swanscombe to be played at the Athletic Ground.

In the meantime a further meeting on 15th December agreed to call the new club Northfleet United – with Mr J. Wilson as chairman and Mr Charles Veevers as secretary. A 14-strong committee (which

only included Joe Lingham from the five who had split from the original club to attempt the amalgamation with Gravesend United) was also established.

The Boxing Day game proved a great success with more than 2,000 attending and paying the 3d admission, bringing back memories of the great days of the mid-1890s. The gate receipts were donated to Northfleet Samaritans and Swanscombe Nursing Home.

The Northfleet United side won a keenly contested game 2-1 and featured several of the old favourites in the following team: Walker; Shotton; Cullen; Povey; Ware; Henry Lingham; Joe Lingham (captain); Hills; Herbert; Bundock; Wright.

After the game both sides were entertained with lunch at Ye Olde Leather Bottle. Northfleet football was very much alive again.

● *Back in business – Northfleet reconvened at Christmas 1902 for a friendly – and captain Joe Lingham took the post-match celebrations a short distance from the Athletic Ground to Ye Olde Leather Bottle*

1903/04

Northfleet United, as they were now titled, were back but it was a far cry from the glory days of the mid-1890s. Instead of the Southern League it was the West Kent League and, although they were still able to use the Athletic Ground, the well-appointed home they had left five years earlier was now an empty shell lacking a grandstand, changing rooms and turnstiles which had all been sold to help erase the club's considerable debts before the end of the 19th century.

That said, there was plenty of good news, too, with no wages to pay – as the club had

The public of Gravesend is not enthusiastic over the prospects of football for the coming season, and although a team is being arranged it will again participate in minor matches only, and in Dartford and District League games. They have lost several of their last season's players, who have signed on for the new Northfleet Football Club. This team, which will be run on amateur lines and will compete in the West Kent League, will provide the best football of the district. The Managers are making a last effort to revive the interest in football, but it is questionable whether they will receive the support necessary to carry on even an amateur team. The matches will be played on the old team's ground, this having been greatly improved. The Managers have prevailed upon the best talent in the district to assist them and have hopes of winning a high position in the league table. The first match will be played against Woolwich Arsenal on Thursday, when Northfleet's strongest team will be placed in the field.

● *Left: relations between Northfleet and Gravesend remained a little frosty in September 1903 as the Fleet prepared to kick off the 20th century – a few years late – against Woolwich Arsenal, having appropriated several of their neighbour's players. Nonetheless, the South Eastern Gazette was not convinced Fleet could "carry on even an amateur team"*

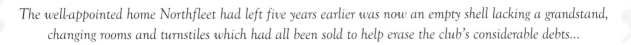

> *The well-appointed home Northfleet had left five years earlier was now an empty shell lacking a grandstand, changing rooms and turnstiles which had all been sold to help erase the club's considerable debts...*

everted to amateur status – and funds were further boosted courtesy of a donation from Associated Portland Cement Manufacturers to help get the club on a solid financial foundation. This was the start of a long-term arrangement with the cement makers.

A couple of home friendlies began the new campaign and the lack of changing facilities was temporarily alleviated by making use of a room used by the local Northfleet Silver Band until new dressing rooms were erected in January 1904.

The team that turned out for the opening game on 3rd September, 1903, included several former Gravesend United players – Obee, Mitchell, Shotton and Lingham – while former Fleet hero Teddy Bundock, captain of

the treble-winning team a decade earlier, was also a regular in the autumn months until he broke his wrist. The club also managed to recruit former trainer Tub Handley but were beaten 4-1 in that opening game, with the team lining up as follows: Obee; Packham; Shotton; Lingham; S. Kirby; Sandford; Day; Howell; James; J. Kirby; Mitchell. After the game both teams were entertained with a "Meat Tea" at Ye Olde Leather Bottle.

The West Kent League consisted of just eight clubs but at least it provided matches once again with old rivals Dartford, Gravesend and Swanscombe while a reserve side was entered into the Dartford & District League.

The season was hard going, with the Fleet winning only one league game and also going out in the opening round of the FA and Amateur cups – but at least they were back and better times were just around the corner.

● *The boys are back in town – old favourites Shotton, Lingham and Bundock were back playing in the red shirt for the West Kent League campaign of 1903/04*

Results 1903/04

Sep 03	Woolwich Arsenal	Friendly	home	1-4	Shotton (pen)	
12	London Welsh	Friendly	home	4-1		
19	New Brompton	FACPr	home	0-2		
26	Eltham	WKL	home	3-7		
Oct 03	Cray Wanderers	WKL	home	1-3	Packham	
10	RE Service Battalion	FAACPr	home	1-1	Lingham	
17	RESB	FAACPr R	away	3-3		
24	Eltham	Friendly	home	3-1		
28	RESB	FAACPr 2R	away	0-5		
31	Swanscombe	WKL	home	1-1	Pettitt	
Nov 07	RETB	Friendly	home	1-0	Lingham	
14	Crayford Athletic	WKL	away	0-3		
21	Dartford	WKL	away	0-1		
Dec 25	London Devonians	Friendly	home	2-1		
26	Swanscombe	WKL	away	0-6		
Jan 02	Harmsworth Athletic	Friendly	home	3-0		
09	New Brompton Reserves	Friendly	away	0-6		
23	RETB	Friendly	home	6-0		
30	Eltham	WKL	away	1-1		
Feb 06	Woolwich Orient	Friendly	home	5-2	Paine 3, Harris, Hills	
13	Crayford Athletic	WKL	home	1-1	Ford	
20	5th Fusiliers	Friendly	home	2-0		
27	Grays Town	Friendly	home	1-0	Harvey	400
Mar 05	Gravesend United	WKL	home	2-1	Harris, Baker	1,300
12	New Brompton Reserves	Friendly	home	0-6		
19	Dartford	WKL	home	0-2		800
26	Gravesend United	Friendly	away	3-1	Gray 2, Baker	1,200
Apr 02	Cray Wanderers	WKL	away	0-3		
04	Swanscombe	Friendly	home	2-4	Hills 2	1,500
09	Gravesend United	WKL	away	1-2	Gray	1,500
16	Woolwich Poly	Friendly	home	2-1	Hills, Paine	
30	London Devonians	Friendly	home	5-2	Baker 2, Gray, Packham, Handley	

1904/05

● *A familiar view, even now. The Plough public house stands at the bottom of Stonebridge Hill (which ascends to the right of the photograph). In the foreground is the pond (here empty) which was fed by the Ebbsfleet river and emptied into nearby Robin's Creek. The sluice gates are visible on the left, where the turnstiles and stadium entrance now exist. This picture was taken in around 1905, at the time that Northfleet United were setting up camp at their new home*

A second season in the West Kent League offered better prospects than the previous one with 11 rather than seven clubs taking part. The newcomers were the eventual champions Catford Southend along with Homesdale, Prices Athletic and Lewisham Montrose.

Once again the FA and Amateur cups proved disappointing, with the club failing to win a game in either competition for the second season running.

Crowds were similar to the previous season, averaging 800, although the old rivalry with Gravesend United was clearly still there when more than 3,000 flocked to Pelham Road for the March league fixture.

Most of the excitement came off the field when APCM, the local cement manufacturers, agreed to lease "a nice piece of level ground at the bottom of Stonebridge Hill" to the club and this meant the Athletic Ground at Collins Meadow would be phased out as the club's base.

On the field Fleet finished a modest 8th of 11 in the league, though celebrated a record 11-0 win over Cray Amateurs in a friendly before receiving a taste of their own medicine when Catford Southend recorded victory by the same margin and clinched the title into the bargain. The most successful player proved to be centre forward 'Rudder' Gray who hit 21 goals during the season.

The close season, meanwhile, would prove to be a busy one as the club prepared for their new venture at the bottom of Stonebridge Hill.

> *Most of the excitement came off the field when the local Associated Portland Cement Manufacturers agreed to lease "a nice piece of level ground at the bottom of Stonebridge Hill" to the club...*

● *Zooming out from the photo above, this earlier scene from 1890 – the year Northfleet Invicta was founded – shows the pond in full view in the centre of the photograph. Where the stadium itself now stands, to the left of this photograph, would have been water meadows and marshland stretching down to the River Thames*

Results 1904/05

Sep 03	Luton (Chatham)	Friendly	home	**2-1**	Gray, Harris	400
10	Sheppey United	FAC Pr	home	**0-1**		500
17	London Welsh	Friendly	home	**6-1**	Handley 3, Gray 2, Harris	
24	Cray Wanderers	WKL	away	**1-4**	Donnelly	
Oct 01	New Brompton Amateurs	FAACPr	home	**3-4**	Gray 2, OG	
08	Woolwich Orient	Friendly	home	**2-1**	Gray 2	
15	Gravesend United	WKL	home	**1-3**	Chidley (pen)	1,100
22	Crayford Athletic	WKL	home	**0-1**		
29	Orpington	WKCC 1	away	**4-2**		
Nov 05	Eltham	WKL	away	**0-5**		
12	Catford Southend	WKL	away	**1-0**	Gray	
19	Swanscombe	Friendly	home	**3-1**		
26	Prices Athletic	WKL	away	**3-1**	* match abandoned, fog	
Dec 17	Dartford	WKL	away	**4-2**		
26	Swanscombe	WKL	away	**2-1**		
31	Crayford Athletic	WKCC 2	home	**0-1**		
Jan 07	Cray Amateurs	Friendly	home	**11-0**	Fowle 3, Scollard 3, Gray 2, Hills, Regan, Lewis	
14	3rd KGA Volunteers	KSC 3	away	**2-0**	Gray, Fowle	
21	Lewisham Montrose	WKL	home	**5-0**	Gray 2, Scollard, Fowle, OG	
28	Prices Athletic	WKL	home	**6-3**		
Feb 04	Crayford Athletic	KSC 4	home	**1-0**	Gray	
11	Prices Athletic	WKL	away	**1-1**	Gray	
18	Holmesdale	WKL	away	**1-3**	Gray	
25	Eltham	KSC 5	home	**0-2**		
Mar 04	Crayford Athletic	WKL	away	**2-2**	Hills, Kearns (pen)	
11	Holmesdale	WKL	home	**6-1**	Cairns 2, Harris 2, Fowle 2	
18	Gravesend United	WKL	away	**0-2**		3,000
25	Dartford	WKL	home	**2-1**	Gray, Harris	
Apr 01	Cray Wanderers	WKL	home	**1-2**	Harris	
08	Lewisham Montrose	WKL	away	**1-3**	Fowle	
15	Catford Southend	WKL	home	**0-11**		
22	Eltham	WKL	home	**3-3**	MacNamara 2, Regan	
24	Swanscombe	WKL	home	**0-2**		3,000
25	Gravesend United	Friendly	away	**1-1**		3,000

● *Northfleet had defeated champions Catford Southend (left) on their own turf but suffered an 11-0 humiliation on one of the last ever matches staged at the Athletic Ground/ Collins Meadow, in April 1904*

1905/06

Preparations for the move to the new ground at Stonebridge Road – or the Northfleet Sports Ground as it was called at the time – were completed just in time for the new season. A seven-foot fence was built to enclose the ground, along with two changing facilities, a room for match officials, a small shelter and a tea bar. The ground had been kindly provided at a peppercorn rent by APCM while Russell's Brewery supplied the tea bar – whether they also provided their famous "Shrimp" Brand Beers from their thriving West Street brewery is unknown.

September 2nd, 1905, was the historic day for the opening game against East Ham Athletic in a relatively low-key friendly fixture won by the Fleet with a single goal netted by Chapman. The first Northfleet team to play at Stonebridge Road was Bowie, Brown, Hillery, Attwood, Bremner, Lewis, Chapman, Slender, Gray, Croucher, Thomas.

The club again entered the West Kent League which was down to nine clubs from the previous season's 11, with some of them, including local rivals Gravesend, moving up to the Kent League. But having been seriously damaged in the previous decade by the step up to the Southern League while not sufficiently financed, Northfleet were now taking a much more cautious strategy.

An early blow came when chairman Jack Grant died in the first month of the season. He was replaced by Joe Lingham, by now an influential member of the KCFA as well.

Transport to away games was often undertaken by train – with road transport still almost non-existent – and the London, Chatham & Dover railway was used for the games into metropolitan London. For the trip to Orpington in the Kent Senior Cup, faith in

WEST KENT LEAGUE.

NORTHFLEET v. CRAY WANDERERS.

Northfleet United were at home to Cray Wanderers in a West Kent League fixture on Saturday, and had to acknowledge defeat by three goals to one. The new ground was in fine condition considering the weather, but rain fell heavily throughout the match, with the result that the ball became terribly greasy and made accurate football impossible.

the railway company proved to be misplaced. The trip required a journey to London Bridge and then a change to connect on a service back out to Orpington. The kit hamper was sent on ahead in the care of the railway only for club officials to find on their arrival at Orpington that it was nowhere to be seen!

Desperate wires were sent to find out what had happened to the kit and eventually it was found in the lost-property office at London Bridge, by which time Fleet had kicked off in a variety of shirts and "knickerbockers" of all colours, shapes and sizes that had

● Left: the first competitive game at Stonebridge Road and the newspapers commented that the "new ground was in fine condition"

been borrowed from the opposition and bystanders. They must have looked a pretty sight but nonetheless managed to earn a replay in all the confusion.

The season was a moderate one, with Fleet coming fifth of nine sides in the league and failing once again to win a cup competition. The performances were not helped by the loss of goalkeeper Butler and wing-half Alfred Scollard to Woolwich Arsenal, but new signing from Swanscombe Eddie Newman proved effective, top scoring with 13 goals – one ahead of Albert Chitty, another newcomer who had moved up from Dorset.

The new Stonebridge Road ground had proved successful and a level pitch was a luxury after the steep slope at Collins Meadow.

● Northfleet held on to forward Rudder Gray (above) who had been top scorer in 1904/05 but lost winger Alfred Scollard (left) to Woolwich Arsenal. He also played for Croydon Common before moving to St Johnstone in Scotland. He served in the Royal Garrison Artillery in the First World War and died in London in 1925

Stonebridge Road : a place to call home

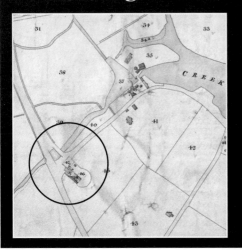

Stonebridge Road (formerly Fisherman's Hill) derived its name from the 'stone bridge' of the previous century which had spanned the Fleet (or Ebbsfleet) river as it flowed into the creek and nearby Thames. A previous bridge across the river at Northfleet is mentioned in 1451 and it was still tidal and used for shipping into the 16th century.

The stone bridge was built in 1634 and replaced by a brick one around 1790. In between those two events, the area also witnessed the Battle of Stonebridge Hill during the English Civil War when, on 1st June 1648, a force of 600 Royalists was

Results 1905/06

Date	Opponent	Competition	Venue	Score	Scorers
Sep 02	East Ham Athletic	Friendly	home	**1-0**	Chapman
09	Cray Wanderers	WKL	home	**1-3**	
16	Prices Athletic	WKL	home	**5-0**	Newman 2, Hills, Gray, Chapman
23	Plumstead	Friendly	home	**2-0**	Brown, Hills
30	Orpington	KSC1Q	away	**2-2**	Lewis, Gray
Oct 07	Swanscombe	WKL	away	**1-1**	Newman
11	Orpington	KSC1Q R	home	**1-3**	
14	Woolwich Argus	WKL	home*	**2-1**	Newman, Gray
21	Eltham	WKL	home	**0-6**	
28	East Ham Athletic	Friendly	home	**2-0**	Newman, Draper
Nov 04	Rochester **	GCC1	away	**3-6**	Whitty 3
11	Crayford	WKL	away	**2-1**	Newman Neale
18	Woolwich Argus	WKL	home*	**4-0**	Draper 2, Hills, Whitty
25	London Caledonians	Friendly	home	**4-2**	Newman 3, Brown
Dec 02	Cray Wanderers	WKL	away	**1-3**	Whitty
09	New Brompton Amateurs	Friendly	home	**6-0**	Newman 3, Spreadbury, Chapman, Lewis
23	Orpington	WKL	home	**0-2**	
25	Swanscombe	Friendly	home	**0-0**	
26	Gravesend United	Friendly	away	**2-0**	
30	Brighton & Hove Reserves	Friendly	away	**1-5**	Newman
Jan 06	Swanscombe	WKL	home	**0-2**	
13	Luton (Chatham)	Friendly	home	**6-1**	Hills 2, Parker, Draper, Gray, OG
20	Orpington	WKL	away	**0-3**	
27	Dartford	WKL	home	**1-0**	Parker
Feb 03	Rochester **	GCC1 R	home	**3-0**	Newman 2, Hills
10	Swanscombe	Friendly	home	**1-1**	Parker
24	Gravesend United	GCC SF	away	**2-4**	Draper, Whitty
Mar 03	Prices Athletic	WKL	away	**1-0**	Hills
10	Eltham	WKL	away	**2-3**	Spiers, Parker
24	Dartford	WKL	away	**1-1**	Parker
31	Old Holloway Collegians	Friendly	home	**3-0**	Hills 2, Whitty
Apr 07	Crayford	WKL	home	**2-0**	Parker, Whitty
14	Cranbrook Park	Friendly	home	**6-0**	Whitty 3, Parker 2, Neale
16	Gravesend United	Friendly	home	**5-0**	Parker 2, Spreadbury, Hills, Brown (pen)
28	Gravesend League	Friendly	home	**5-1**	

*Both WKL games with Woolwich Argus played at home / ** Northfleet complained about the condition of Rochester's ground and with Rochester found to have fielded ineligible players, the game was ordered to be replayed, Fleet winning the rematch*

efeated by 400 Parliamentarians in a kirmish by the stone bridge.

Plough Pond (now the area of the tadium entrance), which can be seen in he photographs on the previous page, was riginally a sheep wash constructed around 775 where the turnpike road began. It ell into disuse the following century nd became a pond before being filled towards the end of the 19th century probably after the 1890 date on the earlier hotograph). The Ebbsfleet river was then iverted beneath the road via a pipeline.

Other landmarks in the immediate area urrounding Stonebridge Road included he grand Huggens College, the site of the resent-day Wallis Park, situated behind the Plough End. Its spires can be seen in several photographs of the Northfleet United and early Gravesend & Northfleet eras until it was demolished in 1968.

Behind the opposite goal (now the Swanscombe End) was the Black Eagle Pub (also demolished in 1968, *pictured right*), and that part of the ground was referred to as the Black Eagle end in Northfleet's heyday. It was still visible in photographs from the 1950s, in the corner by Stonebridge Road, before the present stand (earmarked for replacement in 2016) was built.

Opposite the ground, where the petrol station and other outlets are currently situated, was Plough Marsh. This had

another pond called the 'mud hole' where several drownings occurred until cement workers filled it in around 1890. During the Second World War a barrage balloon was sited here and it was undeveloped marshland well into the 1950s.

1906/07

● *Reconquering Kent, bit by bit, Northfleet captured the West Kent League title in 1906/07. Back row, from left: Unknown, J Wilson, F Cornford, W Mattheson, F C Johnson, M Elliott, W H Harris, Joe Lingham. Third row: Henry Lingham (Joe's brother), P Smith, J Wood, W Gray, F Hills, J C Walsh, J Quayle, H Nettingham, F Reynolds, E Hills (treasurer), Herbert Lingham (another of Joe's brothers), A Walker. Seated: A Church, A Williams, T Cannon, F Lee, T Smith. Front: T Caulfield, T Mays, S Harris. Both Caulfield and Mays went on to captain Northfleet in Kent Senior Cup finals*

Despite competing in both the West Kent League and Kent League, the season proved very successful with Fleet winning the former and finishing as runners-up in the latter.

The move to Stonebridge Road had brought with it much fortune and with the help of a winning team, crowds averaged 2,500. At 4d each for admission, the club was able to announce a profit at the end of the season and had at last wiped out the crippling debt incurred when it had resigned from the Kent League in 1898/99.

Much of the credit for the turnaround was due to the work of the committee under the guidance of Joe Lingham.

It had decided (see newspaper cutting, right) to engage several professional players – despite being fully aware of the financial dangers this entailed – and by entering two leagues, the thinking was that the provision of a generous helping of competitive football would be more attractive than friendly games which were fast losing their appeal.

The new players blended in well with the group of amateurs already at the club and the pick of the new men

was 19-year-old Ted Cannon from Woolwich Arsenal who led the front line with vigour and skill, finishing as top scorer. He was helped considerably by his powerful shooting ability, equally devastating from either foot.

Other pro signings included inside forward Albert Williams and centre-half Tom Caulfield, both from Sittingbourne, and Tommy Mays – a utility player stepping up from local football and judged as a player of potential.

THE NORTHFLEET CLUB.

An effort is to be made this year to restore North-fleet to the position it once occupied as a club to be reckoned with among the strong combinations. This season Northfleet will compete in the Kent League, and this move has necessitated the introduction of new talent amongst the players. Childs, the Cray Wanderers' half-back, and "Nutty" King, who has also represented the same team and Southern United, have been secured, and other new-comers are Gibbard, who last year played on more than one occasion for the London Juniors, and Barratt, who played some fine games at outside right for Grays United. Many old members have re-signed, including Bowie (goal-keeper), Brown and Gray (backs). Spreadbury will again be seen at centre-half, and Knight at left-half, vice Lewis, who is giving up football owing to the exigencies of busi-ness. In addition to the county league, the club will again seek honours in the West Kent League.

The West Kent League, consisting of 11 clubs, appeared to be going the way of Metrogas who visited Stonebridge Road with a huge 12-point lead on 2nd April for their final game of the season (although Fleet still had a chance with seven games in hand and a busy schedule ahead). Fleet won 2-0, forcing Metrogas to wait while they caught up on their fixture backlog.

Three victories were attained in convincing fashion over Northumberland Oddfellows, Orpington and Foots Cray before Fleet slumped to a shock home defeat against Crayford.

In the days of two points for a win, it meant at least two of the final three games needed to be won and Fleet left nothing to chance by winning all three to take the title, while simultaneously finishing runners-up to Sheppey United in the Kent League.

The club was now firmly back on track.

● *Left: Northfleet meaning to do the business in 1906. Their colourful backs of Brown and Gray were re-signed while the addition of King from Cray Wanderers was made all the more intriguing for his nickname – hitherto unexplained – of 'Nutty'*

Results 1906/07

Sep 01	Orpington	WKL	away	**1-0**	Smith	
08	Gravesend United	Friendly	home	**1-4**	Parker	
15	RN Depot	KL	away	**0-2**		
22	Cray Wanderers	KL	away	**4-2**	Williams, Mays, Neale, Parker	
29	RN Depot	KL	home	**1-0**	Williams	
Oct 06	Ashford United	FAC1Q	away	**3-2**	Williams 2, Hills	
13	Maidstone Church Institute	KL	away	**2-3**	Williams 2	
20	Sittingbourne	FAC2Q	away	**2-1**	Neale, Williams	
27	Gravesend United	KL	home	**1-2**	Williams	
Nov 03	Gravesend United	FAC3Q	away	**2-2**	Mays, Smith (pen)	
07	Gravesend United	FAC3Q R	home	**4-2**	Smith 2, Neale, Williams	
10	Northumberland Oddfellows	WKL	away	**2-1**	Neale, Smith	
17	Swanscombe	WKL	home	**5-1**	Williams 3, Smith, Curtis	
24	West Norwood	FAC4Q	away	**1-6**	Curtis	
Dec 01	Swanscombe	KSC1	away	**0-1***	*Swanscombe played ineligible players; eliminated from cup*	
08	Faversham	KL	away	**0-2**		
15	Argyll & Sutherlanders	KSC2	away	**2-0**	Smith, Hills	
22	Dartford	WKL	away	**1-4**	Caulfield	
25	Swanscombe	GCC1	home	**4-1**	Neale 2, Cannon, Smith	1,200
Jan 05	Callenders Athletic	WKL	away	**3-0**	Smith, Cannon, Neale	
12	Cray Wanderers	WKL	away	**0-0**		
26	Sheppey United	KSC3	home	**1-1**	Cannon	500
30	Sheppey United	KSC3 R	away	**2-6**		
Feb 02	Foots Cray	WKL	home	**6-2**	Williams 3, Cannon, Caulfield, Smith	
09	Callenders Athletic	WKL	home	**5-1**	Cannon 2, Williams 2, Caulfield	
16	Metrogas	WKL	away	**2-2**	Hills, Harris	
23	Dover	KL	home	**6-0**	Cannon 2, Mays, Neale, Smith, Williams	
27	Cray Wanderers	WKL	home	**9-1**		
Mar 02	Sheppey United	KL	home	**2-0**	Williams, Caulfield	
06	Gravesend United	GCC SF	away	**2-4**	Griffiths, Cannon	
09	Faversham	KL	home	**2-0**	Cannon, Neale	
13	Swanscombe	WKL	away	**0-4**		
16	Maidstone Church Institute	KL	home	**5-1**	Cannon 3, Williams, Smith	
23	Crayford Athletic	WKL	away	**6-0**	Cannon 2, Griffiths 2, Williams, Neal	
29	Sheppey United	KL	away	**0-3**		
30	Dartford	WKL	home	**5-1**	Caulfield, Williams, Cannon, Mays, Griffiths	
Apr 01	Metrogas	WKL	home	**2-0**	Harris, Cannon	
02	Dover	KL	away	**2-1**	Mays, Cannon	
06	Northumberland Oddfellows	WKL	home	**6-2**	Neale 3, Williams 2, Knight	
10	Orpington	WKL	home	**11-1**		
13	Foots Cray	WKL	away	**4-1**	Griffiths 2, Cannon, Williams	
17	Crayford Athletic	WKL	home	**1-3**		
20	Gravesend United	KL	away	**3-2**	Cannon 2, OG	
24	Eltham	WKL	home	**3-0**	Cannon, Caulfield, OG	
27	Cray Wanderers	WKL	home	**4-2**	Parker, Williams, Cannon, Neale	
30	Eltham	WKL	away	**2-0**	Humble, OG	

NORTHFLEET.

Despite inclement weather, a large gathering attended the annual athletic sports, arranged by the Committee of the Northfleet United Football Club, which were held on Whit-Monday on the Sports Ground, Northfleet. Flat racing was the principal feature of the afternoon, and the donkey races provided good fun. The Northfleet Silver Prize Band, under the conductorship of Mr. J. Jackson, was in attendance, and played delightful music during the proceedings. At the close the prizes, valued at £40, were distributed by Mrs. S. Sargeant.

GRAVESEND.

Upwards of four thousand spectators were present at the sports meeting promoted by the United Football Club, held at the Sports Ground, Gravesend, on Whit-Monday The programme was varied, and the events were keenly contested.

● *Even in the close season Northfleet and Gravesend were rivals, with both holding well-attended sports meetings on their respective grounds on the same day in 1907*

1907/08

The great success achieved in the previous season enabled the momentum to continue into the new one. Every player was retained with the exception of goalkeeper Bowie who had moved out of the area. Six new players were signed to bolster the squad still further (the most notable being former Woolwich Arsenal full-back James Quayle) and most of the squad were now once again professionals for the first time in a decade.

Off the field, the still-basic Stonebridge Road was improved by a willing band of volunteers who laid tons of ashes around the perimeter of the ground to form shallow banking for easier viewing. A new fence was erected around the pitch and the enclosure on the north side of the ground was extended. Negotiations also began to bring an ornate grandstand from the formerly grand tourist attraction of Rosherville Gardens to hold more than 300 people for the Stonebridge Road side of the ground.

When the season began, the players had one important new law to quickly come to grips with – the offside rule had changed to the effect that a player could only be offside in the opponents' half and not anywhere else as was previously the case.

Once again the club entered into two leagues: the West Kent League had 11 entries once more as Northfleet defended their title while the Kent League – where the club hoped to go one better than runner-up – was nine-strong.

The season began badly with a 6-0 thrashing at Bromley in the FA Cup but other than two successive defeats by Gravesend United and Orpington in early November, the West Kent League was retained in emphatic fashion.

In the Kent League, Fleet looked like going the season undefeated until losing the penultimate game to Royal Scots – by which time the title had already been won.

The only other defeat during an impressive season came against Sheppey United in a marathon first-round Kent Senior Cup tie that went to three games before the Fleet lost out in a third game at neutral New Brompton.

Once again Ted Cannon and Albert Williams would score the bulk of the goals. Cannon got his reward by re-signing for Woolwich Arsenal, but sadly it would have no happy ending with his tragic death after a short bout of typhoid fever in 1910. Arsenal played a memorial game in his honour in the same year.

Results 1907/08

Date	Opponent	Comp	Venue	Score	Scorers	Att
Sep 07	Gravesend United	Friendly	home	1-6	Smith	
14	Crayford Athletic	Friendly	home	2-0	Lee 2	
21	Bromley	FACPr	away	0-6		
28	East Ham Athletic	Friendly	home	10-1	Williams 4, Cannon 2, Caulfield, Lee, Smith, Neale	
Oct 05	Metrogas	WKL	away	2-1	Lee (pen), Caulfield	
12	Foots Cray	WKL	home	5-1	Williams 2, Lee 2, Neale	
19	Royal West Kent Regt	KL	away	4-2	Cannon, Lee, Hills, Mays	
26	Cray Wanderers	WKL	away	7-1	Williams 4, Cannon 2, Lee	
Nov 02	Gravesend United	WKL	home	3-5	Smith, Williams, Neale	
09	Orpington	WKL	away	1-6		
16	Charlton Albion	WKL	home	6-1	Williams 3, Cannon 2, Lee	
23	RN Depot	KL	home	4-2	Cannon 2, Smith, Williams	
30	Faversham	KL	away	7-1	Williams 3, Cannon 2, Lee, Neale	
Dec 07	Coldstream Guards	Friendly	home	3-0	Williams, Cannon, Mays	
14	Sheppey United	KL	away	4-0		
21	Cray Wanderers	KL	home	6-1	Williams 3, Cannon 2, Church	
25	Gravesend United	KL	home	3-0	Cannon, Caulfield, Harris	3,000
26	Gravesend United	WKL	away	2-0	Church, Cannon	2,500
28	Maidstone CI	KL	away	3-1	Cannon 3 (1 pen)	
Jan 04	Crayford Athletic	WKL	away	5-0	Cannon 2, Lee 2, OG	
11	North Woolwich	WKL	away	2-2	Cannon 2	
18	Dartford	WKL	away	3-5*	Cannon 2, Lee *abandoned 70 minutes, fog	
25	Northumberland OF	WKL	home	6-1	Cannon 3, Lee 2, OG	
Feb 01	Faversham	KL	home	4-0	Williams 2, Lee, Cannon	
08	North Woolwich	WKL	home	3-0	Lee 2, OG	
15	Orpington	WKL	home	7-0	Cannon 3, Lee, Caulfield (pen), Williams, Mays	
22	Sheppey United	KL	home	1-0	Cannon	
26	Dartford	WKL	home	6-1		
29	Foots Cray	WKL	home	5-1	Cannon 3, Williams, Caulfield (pen)	
Mar 07	Sheppey United	KSC1	away	3-3	Williams 2, Smith	
11	Sheppey United	KSC1 R	home	2-2	Williams, Caulfield (pen)	
14	Dover	KL	home	3-3	Harris, Church, Lee *Attendance: 2,000*	
18	Sheppey United	KSC1 R2	neutral*	1-2	*at New Brompton	
21	Royal West Kent Regt	KL	home	5-0	Burridge 3, Cannon 2	
25	Royal Scots	KL	home	1-0	Cannon	
28	Northumberland OF	WKL	away	1-1	Caulfield	
Apr 04	Dover	KL	away	4-0	Cannon 2, Lee, Mays (pen)	
11	Crayford Athletic	WKL	home	4-1	Williams, Burridge, Mays, Cannon	
17	Gravesend United	KL	away	1-0	Mays *Attendance: 4,500*	
18	RN Depot	KL	away	2-1	Williams 2	
20	Metrogas	WKL	home	6-1	Cannon 3, Smith, Burridge, Lee	
22	Royal Scots	KL	away	0-1		
25	Maidstone CI	KL	home	8-2	Cannon 3, Williams 2, Lee, Hills, Smith	
27	Charlton Albion	WKL	away	4-1		
28	Dartford	WKL	away	2-1	Caulfield, Wallis	

1908/09

● *Kent League champions for the second successive season. Back row: S Sargeant (treasurer), Joe Lingham (chairman), Dr Sells (president), H Griffiths, G Benson. Third row: W B Harris, W G Harris, F Martin, G Bailey, F Hills, Thomas Holmes, James Quayle, W Gray, J Wood, W Busbridge. Seated: B Johnson, A Crowhurst, Albert Williams, Albert Court, John Grant, Edwin Myers, J Martin (trainer). Front: Tom Caulfield, Tommy Mays, Sid Harris*

Basking in the glory of a highly successful 1907/08 season it was soon time for Northfleet to defend their Kent League and West Kent League titles. Despite the successful season just behind them, five new players were signed – three of them teenagers in Albert Crowhurst, John Grant and Edwin Myers – and the average age of the side that usually took the field was just 21.

The stand rescued from Rosherville Gardens was now in place on the Stonebridge Road side of the ground. That would remain there until 1953 when it was dismantled to make room for a much larger construction that eventually became the Liam Daish stand, before it too was earmarked for replacement by further improvements in 2016.

The season began with a friendly against a new local club, Gravesend Amateurs, who rather ambitiously entered the Southern League Division Two and played on a ground in Grange Road. The team changed their name in November to Gravesend Athletic

and turned professional but soon ran into financial difficulties and disbanded in February, failing to complete even a single season of a rather foolhardy enterprise.

A sparkling start to the season saw an unbeaten 11-match run before Northfleet came to grief in spectacular fashion at Tunbridge Wells Rangers, losing 7-0.

A good FA Cup run saw Fleet reach the fourth qualifying round and a home tie with Croydon Common that attracted a best-of-the-season crowd of 4,100 – but Croydon grabbed a draw and won the replay to end Fleet's interest despite the bait of a game against Football League side Bradford Park Avenue for the winners.

By the turn of the year Northfleet were again setting the pace in the Kent League but had played just one West Kent League game of a scheduled 20!

A good run in the Kent Senior Cup saw Fleet gain some good fortune when, after losing to Dartford, they were reinstated following the discovery of the Darts fielding ineligible players. The club duly moved through to the final where they were beaten 4-2 by Maidstone United. It was a big day for the Fleet with more than 1,000 supporters plus the Northfleet Silver Band travelling to the county town. Tommy Mays gave Fleet an early lead from the penalty spot but Maidstone soon took a firm grip on the game and led 3-1 until Grant scored a Fleet second with just six minutes left. This saw Fleet pile on the pressure in a bid for an equaliser but it was the Stones who secured the cup with a fourth goal after a mix-up in the Fleet defence.

Continued over page →

ENGLISH CUP.
CROYDON OUST NORTHFLEET AT SECOND ATTEMPT.

Splendid weather prevailed at Selhurst yesterday, where about 3,000 spectators gathered to witness the replayed English Cup tie between Croydon Common and Northfleet. A hard-fought game was again the outcome of the meeting of these two teams, victory resting with the Common by the odd goal in seven.

The previous game ended in a draw of one goal each, and it looked as though yesterday's event would also end indecisively, for there was little or nothing to choose between the teams.

Croydon lacked the services of Barnfather, Colyns, Lewis, and Spottiswood. The football was fast and exciting, but rather wild. The Northfleet forwards played in dashing style, and in the opening few minutes they had the better of the exchanges.

Still, Croydon Common were the first to score, Toal easily beating Etherington after eight minutes' play.

But the visitors continued to work splendidly, and one of the Common backs was penalised for handling, and from the free kick Mays equalised.

Even play followed until nearing the interval, when Northfleet gained the mastery and obtained the lead through Williams, but Hayward at once put Croydon level.

Shortly after this Lee was carried off the field, stunned through a collision with Gardner, and was still unconscious when the teams changed ends.

On resuming Northfleet again played well, and after twelve minutes Williams gave them the lead. Subsequent to this Lee returned, and the play became very fast, both ends were visited in turn.

At the end of seventeen minutes' keen play McDonald again made the rising level. From then until the close both sides fought hard for a winning goal. It fell to Croydon Common, Hayward scoring a capital point.

Though the visitors tried hard to get on terms, all their efforts proved futile, and the end came with Croydon Common narrow winners.

● *Northfleet made national headlines for their cup exploits. This Daily Express report praised their "dashing" forwards in a hard-fought game. Perhaps that was a literal interpretation as Northfleet's Lee spent much of the first-half and half-time unconscious following a collision with Croydon's full back David Gardner – a former Newcastle player and Scottish international*

1908/09

(continued)

Retaining the Kent League made up for the disappointment of losing the cup and that was secured with a clear-cut 3-0 win at Dover.

Unfortunately Fleet were unable to complete their West Kent League games despite being in a strong position – with a record of 10 wins from 12 games – leaving eight games unplayed and, much to the club's chagrin, thus handing the title to old rivals Dartford.

With the Kent League becoming more powerful it was decided to terminate the West Kent League. With most clubs moving over to the former, that would make it an even harder challenge as Fleet aimed for three titles in a row for the following season.

● *What passed for a media frenzy in 1909 as the county's newspapers devoted plenty of space to the Kent Senior Cup final*

Fleet's 1909 cup runners-up

The *South Eastern Gazette* of 13th April, 1909, published the biographies of the Northfleet players as follows with some colourful descriptions of players who include a former fortune- hunter, a right half with "good capacity for punting" and another fond of using his "nether extremities" for defensive duty...

THOMAS HOLMES – It is a coincidence that the keeper of the Northfleet fort was formerly in the opposite camp, being last season captain of Maidstone United. A man of happy temperament, who can adapt himself to any company.

TOM CAULFIELD – The skipper of the side. This is his third season with Northfleet, but he has indulged in the game at Rochester and Sittingbourne. His real position is right half, but he takes the place of Hills, who was injured in the semi-final. His form at back is practically unknown. A good all-round player who with a long stride and plenty of vitality has a penchant for outstepping the man in possession. Should have good capacity for punting.

JAMES QUAYLE – One of the stalwarts of the eleven. Went straight from Faustience School, Blackheath, into the Woolwich Arsenal Reserves three years ago, but Northfleet developed him. A fine kick, resolute and reliable; never more happy than when in the thick of the fray. Has the entire confidence of his club and the respect of his opponents. A genial soul.

GEORGE BAILEY – The only serviceman in the side, being attached to the 1st Duke of Cornwall's Light Infantry. When stationed at Woolwich, looked upon as one of the finest halves in the district. First played for the Cementers in the semi-final against Sittingbourne. Has the characteristic style of the Northfleet team and fitted himself to the position as though it had been specially reserved for him. Rapid on his feet, with a pace that is deceptive; has rare facility for feeding his forwards.

SID HARRIS – A purely local product, and a credit to his native heath. First chased a ball for Swanscombe. A man of dogged determination, who sticks to his opponent like a leech. The forward who outshines him is a forward indeed. Probably the finest of the trio of halves and rarely plays an indifferent game. A very regular member of the side. "Consistency" is his motto.

TOM MAYS – The "father" and doyen of the eleven; more popularly known as "Day-worker" because of his deliberate methods. Although seeming not to exert himself, Mays gets through a wonderful amount of work and finishes as fresh as a daisy. As the ideal centre-half should do, he seems to spread-eagle the field; uses his head as well as his nether extremities; is clever at trapping the ball; and is rarely minus a smile. Tried fortune-hunting in Canada, but prefers hunting the bouncing ball. Fond, too, of drily humorous sallies.

ALBERT CROWHURST – The budding rose of the club. Discovered in a trial match last autumn, previous to which he had not played in senior football. Aged 19, and his home is Northfleet. A lad with splendid turn of speed and a gift for centring the ball at the right moment. Has an eye for accuracy and a foot that planks the leather goalwards at a high speed. Goalkeepers require to vigilantly watch Crowhurst.

ALBERT WILLIAMS – A player on the light side; races like a hare and has a remarkable knowledge of the geographical position of a net. Has scored more goals than any other man in the team during the last three years. He is a clever dribbler and has a knack of wriggling past any number of halves and backs. The most capable of the quintet. Is never satisfied unless he scores at least once in a game. Formerly played for Grays.

ALBERT COURT – A great favourite in the cement district. The light of publicity has shone fiercely upon him this season but he has not turned a hair. Thus the secret of his popularity. Has had one or two tempting offers to stray to pastures new but he has shown unserving loyalty to his present club. Has played for Sheppey United, Faversham, Sittingbourne, Maidstone and New Brompton but did not receive due recognition until he went to Northfleet. He just gives the balance to the forward line which makes it effective. "Paws" the ball neatly and shoots hard. Familiarly known as "Dimple".

JOHN GRANT – Son of a former treasurer of the Kent Football Association. Eighteen years old and a Northfleet lad bred and born. Went to Ireland two years ago and last year, straight from school, played for Cliftonville. Returned to the old country in January and was immediately found a place in the team. Has undoubted ability and shapes somewhat after the Corinthian style. Unselfish, unassuming and altogether a happy lad but not more happy than when he has vanquished a goalkeeper.

EDWIN MYERS – Popularly known as 'Micky', another 18 years' colt. "Colt" is not an incorrect term for he is on the ground staff at the Oval as a left-hand trundler but has a Kent birth qualification. A very speedy footballer with a thorough command of the ball. His shots from a position far away near the touchline are notable for their force and accuracy of aim.

F HILLS – Was injured in the semi-final. Looked upon by Northfleet as a great back and is a serious loss to the team. Speedy, fearless and is a fine "clearance" man with either foot.

Results 1908/09

Date		Opponent	Competition	Venue	Score	Scorers	Attendance
Sep	05	Gravesend Amateurs	Friendly	home	**5-0**		
	12	Dover	KL	home	**4-0**	Williams, Court, Caulfield, Lee	
	19	Charlton Albion	WKL	home	**7-1**	Court 2, Mays (2 pens), Lee, Williams Crowhurst	
	26	Sheppey United	KL	away	**3-2**	Crowhurst 2, Wilkinson	
Oct	03	Plumstead St Johns	FAC1Q	home	**5-2**	Court 2, Crowhurst, Caulfield, Williams	
	10	Maidstone Athletic	KL	away	**3-1**	Court 2, Mays	
	17	Dartford	FAC2Q	home	**5-2**	Court 3, Lee, Mays (pen)	2,000
	24	Faversham	KL	home	**7-0**	Court 6, Mays (pen)	
	31	Plumstead St Johns	KSC1	home	**4-1**	Mays 2, Caulfield, Lee	
Nov	07	Royal Engineers Depot Battalion	FAC3Q	home	**1-1**	Court	
	12	Royal Engineers Depot Battalion	FAC3Q R	away	**3-1**		
	14	Tunbridge Wells Rangers	KL	away	**0-7**		
	21	Croydon Common	FAC4Q	home	**1-1**	Lee	4,100
	25	Croydon Common	FAC4Q R	away	**3-4**	Mays, Williams (2)	3,000
	28	Sheppey United	KL	home	**2-1**	Court, Mays	
Dec	05	Maidstone Athletic	KL	home	**5-0**	Caulfield 3, Lee, Myers	
	12	Dartford	KSC2	home	**1-2***	Griffiths *Match awarded to Northfleet*	
	19	RN Depot	KL	home	**5-2**	King 3, Caulfield, Crowhurst	
	25	Gravesend United	KL	away	**1-1**	Crowhurst	
	26	Gravesend Athletic	Friendly	home	**2-1**	Griffiths, OG	
Jan	02	Crayford	WKL	home	**3-1**	Court 2, Mays (pen)	
	09	Gravesend United	KSC3	away	**3-1**		
	16	Gravesend United	WKL	home	**4-0**	Court 2, Williams, Mays	
	23	Woolwich Poly	WKL	home	**2-1**	Williams, Court	
	30	Northumberland Oddfellows	WKL	away	**1-1**	Myers	
Feb	06	Woolwich Poly	WKL	home	**3-0**	Williams, Court, Grant	
	13	Gravesend United	WKL	away	**2-3**	Grant, Myers	
	20	Tunbridge Wells Rangers	KL	home	**4-1**	Mays, Williams, Myers, Court	
	27	Faversham	KSC4	home	**4-0**	Mays, Crowhurst, Grant, Williams	
Mar	13	Royal West Kent Regiment	KL	home	**5-2**	Williams 2, Crowhurst 2, OG	
	17	Crayford	WKL	away	**6-0**	Crowhurst 2, Mays (pen), Grant, Court, Williams	
	20	Dartford	WKL	home	**4-1**	Mays, Myers, Court, OG	
	27	Sittingbourne	KSC SF	neutral	**3-0**	Court 2, Crowhurst	
Apr	03	Royal West Kent Regiment	KL	home	**1-2**	Myers	
	09	Gravesend United	KL	home	**4-2**	Grant 2, Court, Williams	
	10	Bexley	WKL	home	**2-1**		
	12	Maidstone United	KSC Final	away	**2-4**	Mays (pen), Grant	8,125
	15	Faversham	KL	away	**3-0**	Mays, Court, Grant	
	17	Orpington	WKL	home	**6-0**	Crowhurst 2, Mays 2 (1 pen), Williams, Caulfield (pen)	
	19	RN Depot	KL	away	**2-1**	Crowhurst, Grant	
	24	Cray Wanderers	WKL	home	**4-2**		
	29	Dover	KL	away	**3-0**	Court 2, Grant	

MAIDSTONE'S HOLIDAY PROGRAMME.

THE EASTER MONDAY SURPRISE.

HOW THE CUP WAS WON.

THE VALUE OF EXPERIENCE.

● *Just to prove that partisanship isn't confined to more modern football, Maidstone's Gazette newspaper correspondent, going by the pen name of "The Old 'Un", was far from magnanimous in victory, seeming to revel in Northfleet's defeat. He wrote, "The Cup has come to Maidstone. No wonder other clubs in the county get a bit jealous. There is not much doubt that the result was a big surprise, more so to the losers than to the winners. Northfleet – and their supporters – were so confident of winning that wherever you went on Monday morning it appeared to be only a question of how many goals Northfleet would win by... Northfleet played schoolboy football – Sittingbourne must have been in a bad way to allow such a team to defeat them in the semi-final. I expected to see a dashing set of forwards, backed up by a worrying set of halves and a resolute pair of backs. But they never gave me the slightest reason to believe that they are one whit above average Kent League class. Diplomacy to one side, there were no men in the Northfleet team last Monday who were above the run of ordinary players." He was eating those words a year later...*

1909/10

As if to confound their critics who, despite Northfleet's achievements, still referred to them as "that lucky village team", the Fleet excelled themselves with a dazzling series of successes taking the Kent League, Kent Senior Cup and Thames & Medway Combination to complete a magnificent hat-trick.

The already strong team was further galvanised by goalkeeper Bill Jacques arriving from Northumberland Oddfellows. He would go on to have an outstanding career, first with Coventry City and later Tottenham Hotspur. Don Sharp came from Maidstone to stiffen the defence while young forwards William Kennedy and Frank Jecock

● Taken either just before or after the photograph on page 26 (the entrance to St Botolph's Church is visible behind the wall), this version sees the club committee members lining up alongside the successful team. The players are as follows – back row: Rogers, Bill Jacques, James Quayle. Middle row: Albert Crowhurst, Albert Williams, William Kennedy, Fred Jecock, Sid Harris. Front row: Bill Nash, Tommy Mays, Don Sharp. The trophies are, from left, Thames & Medway Combination, Kent League and Kent Senior Cup

would add a lethal cutting edge up front with Kennedy scoring more than 50 goals to earn a transfer to West Ham.

Midway through what was clearly going to be a successful season a disillusioned youngster just released by Woolwich Arsenal was snapped up – Charles Buchan – who would become one of the footballing legends of the first half of the 20th century. His trickery helped make the Fleet's forward line an even more lethal unit.

In the Kent League, Sittingbourne set

the pace for most of the season with Fleet close behind – strangely, Fleet's first two league games were against the Brickies in an ill-balanced programme that saw the club paired with six teams in successive games in the first half of the season, albeit because of coincidental cup clashes.

Once Buchan arrived in January, Fleet stormed to 11 successive victories, taking them into the Kent Senior Cup Final and gaining a stranglehold on the two league titles. Fleet confirmed both of those in fine

● Fleet were once again knocked out of the FA Cup by Croydon Common, who won via a replay once again after a 2-2 draw at The Nest, Selhurst. The postcard, left, shows The Nest at that time – which became Crystal Palace's ground for a while after the First World War

THAMES AND MEDWAY COMBINATION.

MAIDSTONE UNITED
v.
NORTHFLEET.

"The Champions of the County," so-called, entertained Maidstone this afternoon.

Play ruled in favour of Northfleet at the start, but their work in front of goal was very poor. After some desultory play, Buchan had an open goal, but missed the ball altogether, and the Maidstone backs were able to clear.

● *Some grudging praise from the Maidstone correspondent... and Charles Buchan proves he's only human by missing the ball entirely!*

style in April with a 7-1 win over Royal Navy Depot to take the Kent title and then a highly satisfying 5-0 drubbing of old rivals Gravesend to take the T&M title.

By this stage, Northfleet had already collected the Kent Senior Cup with a hard-fought 2-0 win over Chatham in front of a 7,000 crowd at Maidstone. It was a doubly sweet triumph as Fleet had beaten old rivals Dartford in a crunch semi-final on the Pelham Road ground of Gravesend United.

The final saw Northfleet in almost complete command against Chatham, with former Fleet goalkeeper Holmes forced to produce a fine display before Kennedy headed a 40th minute opener – just as the large Fleet support were wondering if a goal would ever come. Albert Williams scored a second to secure the cup for a second time (although on the first occasion it was simply presented to the club as Kent League winners, which occurred for three successive seasons before reverting to the more satisfactory format of a knockout competition). The Northfleet Silver Band, which was a regular backer of the club on major occasions, struck up a tune as delighted skipper Tommy Mays received the cup from Alderman Billings.

The three trophies were officially presented to the club on 2nd June, 1910, at the Factory Hall, Northfleet, by KCFA President Frank Griffiths. The club also received the Dampier Palmer Cup to commemorate the success of the "old team in days gone by" and Ned Shotton – team captain from 1892 – accepted the trophy on behalf of the club. Despite the great success of the season just gone, the club made only a wafer-thin profit of £9 15s 11d, proving that finances throughout the non-league game were and would continue to be a problem, even for the most successful clubs.

For results, see over page ➔

Fleet's 1910 cup runners-up

For the second consecutive season, the *South Eastern Gazette* published player biographies, little knowing in Jacques, Buchan and Kennedy they had future Football League stars.

BILL JACQUES – Regarded as one of the most trusty keepers of a fort that Northfleet has ever possessed. This is his first season in senior football and he has come through the baptism of fire well. Has a wonderfully true eye, as well as a sure fist and foot. A boilermaker by trade.

G ROGERS – Age 24, came into the team from Fulham but is in reality a product of Woolwich Polytechnic. Untilthis season he figured as half-back but full-back is undoubtedly his right position. Kicks hard and clean; remarkably speedy of foot and has fine "recovering" capacity. Is an all-round sportsman and possesses an almost countless array of medals. Has held the swimming championship of Woolwich and is occupied in the chemical research department of the Arsenal.

JAMES QUAYLE – Migrated from Woolwich Arsenal to Northfleet, where his best work has been shown. And in spite of this "history" is still only 20 years of age. One of the genial giants of the team, weighing well over 13 stone. A fine lad in many respects, with a tendency to be over-condifent at times. Is, however, a resolute defender with any amount of pluck. Has a penchant for seeing the droll side of things.

BILL NASH – Probably the best of the trio; young, full of vitality and very tenacious. Played last season with Southend Reserves but was really trained at Grays. He has, however, received his polishing at Northfleet. Nash, who is 21, knows no fear; tackles grandly and feeds his forwards well.

DON SHARP – Formerly of Tunbridge Wells Rangers, Leyton Reserves, Metrogas and Maidstone. Infuses a little more fire into his play sometimes than his opponents like. Is a stiff tackler and has a ready command of the ball.

TOMMY MAYS – The captain of the Northfleet club is probably the most popular player it has ever had – popular that is with both spectators and players. As a footballer he has greater experience than any man in the team. A perfect artiste, he figures at centre half and has a happy knack of being seen to advantage against a man physically his superior. He was formerly with Queens Park Rangers. He has also just been appointed Assistant Secretary of the club.

ALBERT WILLIAMS – A mishap early in the season kept him out of the team for a time but on his return he was given the outside right position in preference to the inside, where he was one of the great goal-getters of the eleven. Speedy and a clever dribbler, possessing a knack of wriggling past any number of the opposition.

CHARLES BUCHAN – Is barely 18. Last autumn he had two games with Arsenal Reserves, and he was selected as reserve to the premier Woolwich Arsenal team for their English Cup tie. But Buchan had ambitions and joined Northfleet to be in the fuller glare of the limelight. Is a trifle slow on the ball but has undoubted ability and passes beautifully. He is a teacher of botany under the LCC.

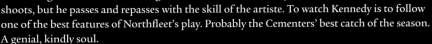

WILLIAM KENNEDY – The sharpshooter of the Cementers. In the scholastic profession at Grays. He came to Northfleet as a diamond in the rough. He could do nothing but shoot. Now he not only shoots, but he passes and repasses with the skill of the artiste. To watch Kennedy is to follow one of the best features of Northfleet's play. Probably the Cementers' best catch of the season. A genial, kindly soul.

FRANK JECOCK – Another youth, aged 20, introduced to senior football this season. Tried his skill during the practice matches and took the eye of the critics. Has a neat style of play and is regarded as the most unselfish man in the team. By trade a pattern-maker, with Erith as his domicile.

EDWIN MYERS – One of the stars of the side. Sometimes brilliant. At other times does not show the sparkle that he is known to possess. Is speedy and has a wonderful command of the ball. Often sends in a swinging shot from the touchline with just sufficient "screw" to curl in and deceive. Follows cricket in the summer, being on the ground staff at the Oval, and may be Surrey's slow bowler.

ALBERT CROWHURST – Has been standing down, through illness, for some weeks. Purely a local product, but one who promises well. Is a rapid shot and knows the geographical position of the net. Quite a favourite at home.

SID HARRIS – A keen, consistent player, both in attack and defence, but hardly so fast as of yore. Unselfish, unassuming and altogether a happy lad.

GORDON HOARE – The international who has also represented Kent specially desired to play in the final, but the Committee did not feel justified in changing the team, even for the inclusion of so brilliant a player – preferring to win, or lose, with an eleven of regular players.

Results 1909/10

Date		Opponent	Comp	Venue	Score	Scorers	Att
Sep	04	Woolwich Poly	Friendly	home	8-0	Kennedy 3, Sharp, Williams, Jecock, Nash, Crowhurst	
	11	Sittingbourne	KL	home	4-2	Kennedy 2, Williams, Myers	
	18	Dartford	FAC Pr	away	2-2	Nash, Williams	
	22	Dartford	FAC Pr R	home	2-1	Kennedy, Myers	
	25	Sittingbourne	KL	away	3-3	Kennedy 2, Mays (pen)	
Oct	02	Sheppey United	FAC1Q	home	6-5	Kennedy 4, Mays (pen), Williams	
	09	Sheppey United	KL	away	0-1		2,000
	16	Royal Engineers Depot Battalion	FAC2Q	home	5-1	Mays 2 (1 pen), Jecock, Kennedy, OG	
	23	Royal Engineers Depot Battalion	KL	away	3-1	Kennedy, Mays, Jecock	
	30	Maidstone United	KL	away	5-1	Kennedy 3, Crowhurst, Jecock	
Nov	06	Chatham	FAC3Q	away	4-1	Jecock 2, Mays (pen), Kennedy	4,000
	13	Chatham	KL	home	1-0	Mays (pen)	2,300
	20	Croydon Common	FAC4Q	away	2-2	Jecock, Mays	3,000
	24	Croydon Common	FAC4Q R	home	1-3	Jecock	
	27	Dartford	KL	away	1-1	Jecock	
Dec	04	Chatham	KL	away	1-2	Kennedy	
	11	Bromley	KSC2	home	4-2	Jecock 2, Mays (pen), Kennedy	1,100
	18	Maidstone United	KL	home	4-2	Kennedy 2, Mays, Crowhurst	
	25	Gravesend United	KL	home	2-1	Kennedy, Mays (pen)	3,000
	26	Gravesend United	TM	away	3-2	Kennedy, Quayle	
Jan	01	Sheppey United	KSC3	home	3-2	Jecock 2, OG	
	08	RN Depot	KL	away	3-1	Myers, Kennedy, Mays	
	15	Dartford	TM	home	0-0		
	17	New Brompton Reserves	KL	away	2-1	Williams, Hoare	
	22	Rochester	KL	away	5-1	Kennedy 3, Buchan, Jecock	
	29	Maidstone United	TM	away	3-1	Kennedy 2, Buchan	
Feb	02	Sheppey United	TM	away	3-2	Jecock 2, OG	
	12	Dartford	KL	home	4-2	Kennedy 2, Jecock, Myers	
	19	Dartford	KSC SF	neutral	1-0	Myers * at New Brompton	
	26	Rochester	KL	home	3-1	Mays, Jecock, Kennedy	1,500
Mar	02	Sittingbourne	TM	home	2-1	Kennedy, Mays	
	16	Metrogas	KL	home	7-1		
	19	New Brompton Reserves	KL	home	6-1	Kennedy 2, Mays, Williams, Myers, OG	3,000
	25	Gravesend United	KL	away	4-2	Kennedy 2, Buchan 2	3,000
	26	Sittingbourne	TM	away	1-1	Kennedy	
	28	Chatham	KSC Final	at Maidstone	2-0	Kennedy, Williams * at Maidstone	7,000
Apr	02	Sheppey United	TM	home	5-2	Buchan 3, Kennedy 2	
	06	Sheppey United	KL	away	1-2	Crowhurst	
	09	Dartford	TM	away	1-0	Jecock	2,000
	13	Chatham	TM	home	3-0		
	16	Royal Engineers Depot Battalion	KL	away	4-2	Mays 2, Rogers, Jecock	
	20	Gravesend United	TM	home	5-0		
	23	RN Depot	KL	home	7-1	Buchan 3, Jecock 2, Kennedy, Crowhurst	
	25	Metrogas	KL	away	3-2	Williams, Quayle, Buchan	
	28	Chatham	TM	away	1-2		
	30	Maidstone United	TM	away	0-0		

● *Newspaper cuttings including a hat-trick for 50-goal Kennedy, the derby game v Gravesend and a big signing in January 1910*

1910/11

After a run of almost unbroken success, the loss of several key players resulted in a moderate season. Full backs Quayle and Rogers were off to Woolwich Arsenal, while three key forwards also left – Myers to Crystal Palace, Jecock to Coventry and, the biggest blow, 50-goal leading scorer William Kennedy to West Ham. Another setback was the loss through injury of Tommy Mays, an inspiring skipper who played just a few games in an injury-hit season before retiring. And Charles Buchan had moved to Leyton, before his big move to Sunderland materialised a short time later.

The previous seasons of success had allowed some improvements to the ground: a dip at the south-east corner was filled in and levelled, the seats in the stand on the Stonebridge Road side (previously all situated at one level) were rearranged into tiers while on the north side a small covered enclosure without seats was erected, making the ground superior to nearly all of its rivals.

The team never really settled with so many changes to the playing staff and a preliminary round home defeat to Dartford in the FA Cup got matters off to a bad start. And there was plenty of controversy in the Kent Senior Cup (see newspaper cutting, right) which saw Fleet visit Rochester in an ill-tempered game.

Tom Buchan, a brother of Charles who had signed in the summer, was struck by a Rochester defender, who was rightly sent off, but home officials proved to be poor losers.

They accused well-regarded Fleet official Joe Lingham – by now, as mentioned, a major KCFA figure – of influencing the referee. Rochester submitted an official report and protest on the matter, while Fleet players were forced to make a rapid exit from the ground as local urchins took the opportunity to throw stones at the fleeing team.

Lingham initially resigned his KCFA post but unsurprisingly – being one of the most

A HAPPY ENDING

NORTHFLEET AND ROCHESTER UNPLEASANTNESS.

COMMISSION'S REPORT WITHDRAWN.

Those who take an active interest in the game in the county will be glad to learn that the little unpleasantness which arose out of the Rochester and Northfleet Christmas matches is to have a happy ending. It will be remembered that a Commission was appointed to enquire into certain allegations and counter-allegations arising out of the matches between the clubs, and after a protracted hearing the Commission "severely censured" Mr. Lingham, the County Treasurer, and Chairman of the Northfleet Club, for "interfering with the referee in his conduct of the game," and the Rochester club were "cautioned and warned to see that their supporters conducted themselves properly in future." Mr. Lingham felt that this was a serious reflection on his conduct, and at once resigned his position on the K.C.F.A., and, feeling that only one side of the facts had been placed before the Commission, took legal opinion with a view to refuting the reflection which had been cast upon him. It now appears that the Commission as formed had no status to deal with the dispute, and, further, it is said that the mistake arose through the absence of Mr. Lockwood, who, unfortunately, was prevented from attending through illness. Mr. Lockwood has since taken steps to put matters right, and Mr. Lingham has accepted the explanation given, and has withdrawn his resignation for the time being.

● *There was a very different kind of visitor to Stonebridge Road in 1910 when battleships USS Georgia (pictured) and USS Rhode Island anchored off Gravesend. It was chairman Joe Lingham's idea to stage the American football game between them at Stonebridge Road*

● *"Northfleet are but a relic of last year's champions' side," said the South Eastern Gazette after a 7-2 trouncing at Maidstone in November 1910. It was little surprise, with players of the quality of Kennedy, Grant, Rogers and Mays all on their way out. Goalkeeper Bill Jacques (far right) played through the season but stepped up a level with Coventry in May 1911*

popular characters in Kent football – he was vindicated as to his behaviour at a subsequent enquiry and Fleet moved on to a second-round marathon with local rivals Gravesend United. It took four games before the Shrimpers triumphed 3-1 at Chatham in a third replay that at least helped boost the coffers of both clubs.

Form in the Kent League deteriorated badly in the new year with the last 15 games securing just one win and two draws – ensuring a miserable 13th-place finish from 14 teams.

The Thames & Medway Combination proved a farce with the six teams split into two groups. Fleet had Gravesend and Dartford for company, leaving a hardly exacting four games to play. This proved beyond them, with both the Darts and Northfleet withdrawing from the competition with games still to play and being fined £5 each for their trouble.

Gravesend, who were leading the league, were livid, having prepared their ground and printed bills for the Dartford game, while Maidstone were none too impressed, accusing Northfleet and Dartford of "acting as they pleased in the matter".

With crowds averaging a modest 1,100, the club finished the season with a deficit of £11 4s 3d.

As an aside, Stonebridge Road witnessed a strange new sport during the season when American football came to the ground on 14th December, 1910. A 4,500-strong crowd witnessed a game played by two teams from a visiting US Naval Squadron anchored off Gravesend. The two teams, USS *Rhode Island* and USS *Georgia*, met in an ill-tempered challenge match that the *Georgia* won 11-0. *For results, see over page* ➔

Results 1910/11

Sep 03	Gravesend United	Friendly	home	**5-0**	Williams 2, Hoare 2, Jecock	
10	Sittingbourne	KL	away	**1-3**	Spreadbury	
17	Dartford	FAC Pr	home	**0-1**		
24	Royal Engineers Depot Battalion	Friendly	away	**2-2**	Buchan 2	
Oct 01	Woolwich Poly	Friendly	home	**0-0**		
08	Millwall Reserves	KL	home	**2-0**	Saward, Buchan	
15	Nunhead	Friendly	away	**4-1**	Buchan 2, Saward 2	
22	Chatham	KL	home	**2-1**	Anderson, Saward	
29	Crystal Palace Reserves	KL	home	**2-1**	Saward, Williams	3,000
Nov 05	Peel Institute	Friendly	home	**5-1**	Goad 2, Saward (pen), Anderson, Williams	
12	Maidstone United	KL	away	**2-7**	Saward 2	
19	Metrogas	KL	home	**1-1**	Goad	
26	Grays Athletic	Friendly	home	**1-1**		
Dec 03	Orpington	KL	away	**4-2**	Anderson 2, Axcell, Buchan	
10	Maidstone United	KL	home	**2-1**	Steel 2	
17	Sheppey United	KL	home	**0-5**		
24	Gravesend United	KL	away	**2-1**	Buchan, Saward	
26	Gravesend United	TM	home	**0-3**		
27	Rochester	KL	home	**1-2**	Williams	
31	Rochester	KSC1	away	**2-1**	Anderson, Williams	
Jan 07	Chatham	KL	away	**1-2**	Saward	
14	Metrogas	KL	away	**3-6**	McCourt, Dixon, Goad	
21	New Brompton Reserves	KL	home	**2-4**	Axcell (pen), Hills	
28	Gravesend United	KSC2	home	**1-1**	Harris	3,000
Feb 01	Gravesend United	KSC2 R	away	**1-1**	Williams	1,200
04	Royal Irish Rifles	KL	away	**1-5**	Mays (pen)	
08	Gravesend United	KSC2 R2	at Dartford	**1-1**		
11	Dartford	KL	home	**0-1**		
15	Gravesend United	KSC2 R3	at Chatham	**1-3**	Saward	
25	Millwall Reserves	KL	away	**1-2**	Axcell	
Mar 04	Rochester	KL	away	**1-3**	Johnson	
11	New Brompton Reserves	KL	away	**0-3**		
18	Orpington	KL	home	**4-1**	Axcell (pen), Robinson, Anderson, Williams	
25	Dartford	KL	away	**1-1**	Ferrier	
Apr 01	Sittingbourne	KL	home	**0-0**		
08	Sheppey United	KL	away	**2-2**	Clark, Johnson	
14	Gravesend United	TM	away	**1-1**	Williams	
15	Crystal Palace Reserves	KL	away	**0-3**		
17	Gravesend United	KL	home	**1-3**	OG	
22	Royal Irish Rifles	KL	home	**2-4**	Williams, Mays (pen)	

In the fast gathering darkness Maidstone tried hard to equalise, and although in the last ten minutes Northfleet were reduced to nine men through Goad, who was injured in a collision, having to be carried off the field, they did not succeed.

The game furnished another instance of weak refereeing, the decisions throughout being very peculiar. There was a bit of a demonstration towards the referee at the close. Result:—

NORTHFLEET 2
MAIDSTONE 1

• *Referees on the receiving end of harsh words in the Northfleet-Maidstone game (above) while the Fleet were not making too many friends in the Thames & Medway Combination league (right)*

THAMES AND MEDWAY COMBINATION AFFAIRS

THE CUP WITH-HELD.

HEAVY FINES IMPOSED ON DARTFORD AND NORTHFLEET.

As was reported last Saturday night in the "Football Gazette," matters in the Thames and Medway Combination are not in a very healthy state, due principally to the fact that the clubs in Section A have not been keen on fulfilling their engagements. Through the action of the Dartford and Northfleet clubs in not carrying out the order of the Council of the Competition and playing off their remaining fixtures by last Monday, so that the champion-

1911/12

This was to be a better campaign than the previous one but still a long way from the success of just two seasons earlier. The club finished off preparations with a six-a-side tournament at Maidstone on August Bank Holiday weekend, finishing as runners-up to Ashford Railway Works.

Tom Buchan, like brother Charles before him, went to Leyton while goalkeeper Bill Jacques had moved to Coventry City over the summer. Don Sharp also made the short trip to Gravesend for a season, though he was to return to Northfleet to defeat the Shrimpers in the 1913 Kent Senior Cup final.

With so many of their free-scoring forwards now departed, Fleet desperately searched for a successor and found him in teenager Arthur Seccombe who would become a Fleet legend over the course of the next 15 years. Credit had to go to Joe Lingham and his management committee for persuading Arthur to come to Stonebridge Road when Fulham and other large clubs were showing an interest in signing him.

The West Kent League was revived after a two-year gap, although only five teams were entered; 15 clubs meanwhile entered the Kent League.

The season started in a sweltering 85° F for the home game with Orpington, which Fleet won comfortably to get the West Kent League season off to an impressive start. The heat aside, that game was notable for goalkeeper William Gooda finding himself on the scoresheet, though the exact details of his unlikely feat are not known. All four games in this competition before Christmas were won to put Fleet in pole position.

Unfortunately the Kent League proved a tougher proposition after an indifferent start and a 2-1 defeat at Bromley in early December sent Fleet to the bottom of the table. Another new signing saw the return of Northfleet-born John Grant, who had originally played for the club from 1908–10. He had moved north to turn out for Southport Central for a time and found his shooting boots for the Fleet in the second half of the season. After beating league leaders Millwall Reserves 2-0 in February, Fleet went on an impressive run that pushed them up to a final position of eighth.

On 30th March, Grant produced an outstanding performance to score an amazing 11 goals in the 15-0 demolition of Catford Southend, who fielded what amounted to a reserve side because of interests in both the Kent Senior and Kent Amateur cups – and they paid a heavy price for their decision.

Despite this superb result against Catford, Northfleet's West Kent League hopes gradually slipped away and were not helped by a 5-0 thrashing at Dartford and a 4-1 loss to Gravesend United in the final game, which saw the Fleet slip to third.

It had also been a disappointing cup season going out of both the FA Cup and the Kent Senior Cup in the opening rounds.

Financially, the club had been badly hit

● Arthur Seccombe, a Northfleet club legend in the making

by a strike in the cement industry that lasted for months and affected attendances, as supporters felt the financial squeeze and were forced to stay away. This turn of events put the Fleet back in the financial doldrums and only a generous payment from Joe Lingham to clear the debts saved the club from the sort of full-blown crisis that had resulted in closure once before.

Results 1911/12

Date		Opponent	Comp	Venue	Score	Scorers
Sep	02	Orpington	WKL	home	4-1	Lee 3, Gooda
	09	Crystal Palace Reserves	KL	away	1-3	Seccombe
	16	Ashford Railway Works	FAC Pr	away	1-2	Lee
	23	Metrogas	KL	home	4-1	Seccombe 3, Lee
	30	Orpington	WKL	away	3-0	
Oct	07	Royal Dublin Fusiliers	Friendly	home	3-4	
	14	Gravesend United	WKL	home	3-2	
	21	Royal Irish Rifles	KL	away	1-2	
	28	Maidstone United	KL	home	1-2	Williams
Nov	04	Rochester	KL	away	1-2	Fairman
	11	Royal Irish Rifles	KL	home	2-1	Williams 2
	18	Metrogas	KL	away	1-4	
	25	New Brompton Reserves	KL	home	1-1	Seccombe
Dec	02	Bromley	KL	away	1-2	
	09	Chatham	KL	home	2-3	
	16	Gravesend United	WKL	away	2-1	
	23	Sittingbourne	KL	away	0-3	
	25	Gravesend United	KL	home	3-1	
	26	Dartford	KL	away	2-2	
	30	New Brompton Reserves	KL	away	0-3	
Jan	06	Millwall Res	KL	away	0-1	
	13	Sheppey United	KL	away	0-0	
	20	Sheppey United	KL	home	3-0	Seccombe, Williams, Seager
	27	Sittingbourne	KSC1	away	2-3	
Feb	03	Chatham	KL	away	0-2	
	10	Dartford	WKL	away	0-5	
	17	Millwall Reserves	KL	home	2-0	Grant, Seager
	24	Crystal Palace Reserves	KL	home	1-1	
Mar	02	Cray Wanderers	KL	away	0-3	
	09	Cray Wanderers	KL	home	2-1	
	23	Bromley	KL	home	5-2	
	30	Catford Southend	WKL	home	15-0	Grant 11
Apr	05	Gravesend United	KL	away	1-1	Seager
	06	Maidstone United	KL	away	0-4	
	08	Dartford	WKL	home	5-0	
	09	Dartford	KL	home	5-2	
	13	Sittingbourne	KL	home	4-1	
	20	Rochester	KL	home	4-0	
	27	Gravesend United	WKL	home	1-4	

1912/13

● *Possibly the earliest photograph of the Plough End – or the College End as it was known – in existence, this 1912 shot shows an entirely uncovered end separated from the pitch by a small fence. Over the shoulder of Joe Lingham (far right) can be seen The Plough public house and to the left, in the background, the spire of Huggens College where Wallis Park now stands. Players in this photograph include George Goodhind, Henry Balding, Bill Nash, Don Sharp, W Tyler, Dick Goad, Arthur Seccombe and Edwin Myers*

The match that all local fans had been wishing for since the formation of the local clubs at last took place – a Kent Senior Cup final between the two great rivals.

The whole of North Kent seemingly made their destination Maidstone on Easter Monday, 1913, as a record 10,000 crowd packed into the Athletic Ground.

Hours before, boisterous fans had taken over Maidstone in the red and green favours of Gravesend United and the red and white of Northfleet United.

The game proved an exciting one that saw every viewing place occupied both within and outside the ground. One overloaded tree gave way as a branch snapped and its human cargo was dumped on to the roof of the grandstand where they were able to scramble away, albeit having lost their lofty viewing position. Although the Shrimpers started well, it was Northfleet who took the lead with a wonderful individual goal from Arthur Seccombe finishing a 40-yard run with a rocket shot.

And when Bill Lawrence added a second goal in the second period the game appeared secure... but Armitage reduced the leeway with 15 minutes left, ensuring a nail-biting finish before the Fleet could celebrate.

The team that won the day was Henry; Mason (captain); Goodhind; Nash; Sharp; Tyler; Blackburn; Seager; Lawrence; Seccombe; Myers.

This was the icing on the cake in a promising season during which the side finished third in a strong Kent League, won for the third successive season by Millwall Reserves. The club had lost goal-hungry John Grant – he of the 11 goals in a single game – to Woolwich Arsenal (Grant went on to score three goals in four games for Arsenal and 41 in 28 appearances for Genoa!) but welcomed back winger Edwin 'Micky' Myers from Crystal Palace, who also provided ex-Dartford full back George 'Sonny' Goodhind, half back W Tyler and ex-amateur international Bill Lawrence. Mason, the solid Chatham defender, was meanwhile secured as captain.

The club also entered the West Kent League but not for the first time this competition was marred by fixture congestion and failed to be completed.

Plans for the development of the ground continued with an impressive design for a grandstand announced and planned by Joe Lingham and his building company. Lingham also used his place on the KCFA board to raise the matter of railway fares, with a view to action being taken for better terms for clubs and their supporters.

During the season it became apparent that betting was going on at Stonebridge Road. The club originally stated the matter was to be "left to the police to deal with". Later in the season, however, a threat was issued that the club would shut down if gambling continued, strongly condemning it as "evil".

Midway through the season, an advertisement for new players was placed in the local newspaper and committee members were exhorted to "go in search of talent" themselves.

Goalkeeper Henry Balding broke his leg in the game with Chatham in March and as the sole support for his widowed mother, he was granted 10 shillings per week and also awarded a Kent Senior Cup winner's medal (which the club had to pay for!), having played in all games except the final.

Although crowds were slightly up on the previous season, a deficit of £39 6s 4d was incurred which was wiped out by a donation of £40 by Mr Lingham. In the final minutes' entry for the season, "it was suggested that several outside gentlemen be approached with a view to strengthening the committee" as finances continued to be an issue.

● *Scenes of many a Northfleet triumph in the Kent Senior Cup. Northfleet Station was traditionally thronged by travelling supporters and the conquering team as they returned to large assembled crowds. From the station a triumphal procession was usually led by the Northfleet Silver Band (above) who would proceed to the top of the town at The Hill and then return to the Factory Club (left), a building synonomous with Northfleet United. It was there that the club was mothballed in 1914 and resurrected in 1919 and where so many decisions about its future were made by committee. It was also where, in April 1946, Northfleet United officially died and Gravesend & Northfleet was created. To this day it is a Grade II listed building and was recently a night club known as Portland's*

For results, see over page ➜

"Northfleet went mad" *From a contemporary report*

WILD ENTHUSIASM AT NORTHFLEET!

With the added "charm of the cup" imparted to the keen local rivalry that exists between Northfleet and Gravesend, it was small wonder, that, in spite of the dull threatening weather, huge crowds from both towns proceeded to Maidstone, there to see the final fight for possession of the trophy take place. The great majority made the journey by rail and the gate which amounted to £215 is a record for the cup ties at the Maidstone ground.

Bells and other musical instruments galore were on evidence everywhere, while other paraphernalia in the form of coloured hats, umbrellas, favours, etc, were freely be-sprinkled amongst the huge crowd. All points of vantage were made use of and some excitement was caused when a branch of a tree broke and precipitated the occupant on top of one of the stands, fortunately for him, without injury.

Northfleet may well be proud of their brilliant achievements in the football world, for with a scattered population of about 14,000 to draw from for support, the continued success that marks their efforts must surely be phenomenal for so small a town and speaks volumes for the businesslike way in which the work of the club

is conducted by Councillor J B Lingham, vice chairman KCFA and chairman of the club, whose name is almost synonmous with football and whose devoted labour and interest in the popular pastime has had no small part in the club's many successes. Meanwhile, the social side of the club is greatly helped by a Ladies' Committee.

The train with the conquerors in streamed into the Northfleet station soon after 9pm and here crowds had assembled to welcome them back, while the Northfleet Fire Brigade and engine were also waiting. Mounting the engine surrounded with the team, the chairman held the cup aloft and then began a triumphal procession, headed by the Northfleet Silver Band playing suitable airs through the main streets to the Hill returning to the Factory Club (headquarters) where the cup was filled and passed merrily around.

The population gave vent to their great joy in many ways, which baffle description; in fact, for the time being, Northfleet went mad.

Results 1912/13

Sep 07	West Norwood	Friendly	home	**6-1**	Seccombe 2, Calvert 2, Baker 2	
14	Cray Wanderers	KL	away	**2-2**	Calvert 2	
21	Sheppey United	KL	home	**3-1**	Sharp 2, Calvert	
28	Sittingbourne	FAC Pr	home	**4-1**	Blackburn, Myers, Sharp, Calvert	
Oct 05	Millwall Reserves	KL	home	**1-3**	Cleland	
12	Sheppey United	FAC 1Q	home	**0-1**		
19	Bromley	KL	home	**2-0**		
26	Rochester	KL	away	**1-3**	Seccombe	
Nov 02	Maidstone United	KL	away	**4-2**	Lawrence 2, Seager, Blackburn	
09	Dartford	KL	away	**3-1**	Lawrence 3	
16	Rochester	KL	home	**3-1**	Lawrence 3	
23	Metrogas	WKL	away	**1-2**	Seager	
30	Maidstone United	KL	home	**3-0**	Seccombe, Lawrence, Nash	
Dec 14	Dartford	KL	home	**1-2**	Myers	
25	Gravesend United	KL	home	**1-0**	Lawrence	
26	Gravesend United	WKL	away	**4-2**	Blackburn, Seccombe, Sharp, OG	
28	Sittingbourne	KL	home	**4-1**	Seager 2, Seccombe 2	
Jan 04	Gillingham Reserves	KL	away	**3-3**	Lawrence 2, Seager	
11	Clapton	Friendly	home	**2-2**	McCahey, Seager	
18	Millwall Reserves	KL	away	**0-4**		
25	Ashford	KSC1	home	**8-0**	Lawrence 4, Mason 2 pens, Seccombe, Sharp	
Feb 01	Sittingbourne	KL	away	**4-3**	Lawrence 2, Blackburn, Myers	
08	Crystal Palace Reserves	KL	away	**3-1**	Lawrence 2, Seager	
15	Sittingbourne	KSC2	away	**2-0**	Seager, Lawrence	
22	Gillingham Reserves	KL	home	**1-3**	Lawrence	
Mar 01	Chatham	KL	away	**3-2**	Seccombe, Blackburn, Mason	
08	Tunbridge Wells Rangers	KSC SF	Chatham	**2-0**	Lawrence, Seager	
15	Bromley	KL	away	**4-2**	Seccombe 2, Lawrence, Tyler	
21	Gravesend United	KL	away	**1-1**	Buckingham	
22	Crystal Palace Reserves	KL	away	**0-4**		
24	Gravesend United	KSC Final	Maidstone	**2-1**	Seccombe, Lawrence	11,000
29	Sheppey United	KL	away	**1-2**	Seager	
Apr 05	Chatham	KL	home	**5-2**	Lawrence 2, Seager, Tough, Seccombe	1,200
09	RN Depot	KL	away	**0-6**		
12	Cray Wanderers	KL	home	**2-2**	Tyler, Tough	
16	RN Depot	KL	home	**0-0**		
19	Metrogas	KL	home	**3-1**	Seccombe 2, Lawrence	
23	Metrogas	KL	away	**0-3**		
26	Gravesend United	WKL	home	**6-1**	Lawrence 3, Seccombe 2, Sharp	

● *Frederick Calvert, who had played a handful of games for Woolwich Arsenal, scored six goals in the opening four games of the season*

● *George Goodhind played a handful of gam~ for Crystal Palace after joining them in 191~ following five seasons at Dartford. He was wounded in action during the First World Wa~*

● *Goalkeeper Henry Balding, who arrived from Crystal Palace the previous season for £30, broke his leg just before the Kent Senior Cup final*

1913/14

There were wholesale changes to the playing staff for the new season with just Nash, Seccombe, Myers and Tyler remaining, the latter being named as captain. With goalkeeper Balding still injured from the previous season, he was made a gift of a season ticket. Full back H Tough remained as well, but he resigned only two weeks into the new season, while former captain Mason departed for Sittingbourne in November. After a trial match in August, the string of newcomers included goalkeeper J.Joel from Millwall and defender George Green, while Ernest Harber and George Taylor were recruited locally, from Sutton-at-Hone.

The blend of old and new proved effective and once more Fleet were among the contenders for the Kent League, eventually finishing fourth, while another strong challenge in the Kent Senior Cup saw a narrow defeat to Maidstone in the final.

The other two cup competitions proved disappointing with defeat at home to amateurs New Crusaders in the FA Cup by a humiliating 7-2 margin, a result put into context by the fact Gravesend United beat them 3-0 in the next round.

That game was also remarkable for chairman Joe Lingham's diplomatic strengths being brought to bear when one of the opposing players, the Reverend Barnfield, accused Northfleet spectators of failing to show him enough reverence on the field of play. Lingham explained that the Fleet supporters were rough but good-hearted people who meant no offence to him and they were targeting him only with good-natured abuse!

The Kent Senior Shield was entered for the first time and saw an opening-round defeat by Chatham. The competition had been instigated by Gravesend MP Sir Gilbert Parker and limited to eight clubs selected by the KCFA as the best in the county.

The club also investigated purchase of a

● *The Kent Messenger goes for a visual medium in January 1914 to analyse each club's chances in the battle for the county's blue-riband prize*

THE KENT CUP.

"motor conveyance" to save money on train fares but eventually shelved the idea.

The highlight of the league season was beating eventual champions Crystal Palace Reserves home and away, showing what might have been with slightly more consistency.

Soon after at last becoming full members of the Football Association in February 1914, the club was hauled in front of it charged with fielding two ineligible players in a Kent League game with Chatham. The reason for the players' ineligibility was the dastardly crime of playing Sunday football – outlawed at the time by the FA. The players involved – Woodmason and Fincham – were banned for the rest of the season and the two points from the 2-0 victory were rescinded... meaning a fourth-place finish rather than third.

The Kent Senior Cup saw victories over Margate and Sittingbourne; the replay against the latter in Round 2 was remarkable for the "unsportsmanlike spirit" in which it was played after it "became apparent that both sets of players had lost their heads." Just before half-time, Seccombe was forced off with an injury after a terrible tackle by Sittingbourne's Smith. The resulting penalty was saved after a controversial rush off his line by the goalkeeper, who received a kick in the face for his troubles. Northfleet's George Green was cautioned for a challenge and then Seccombe, back in the fray, was ordered off for gaining a measure of revenge on Smith for his earlier challenge.

It degenerated from there and the *Kent Messenger* takes up the sorry tale: "This was the signal for further disorder. The players simply forgot the laws of the game, and were apparently out for other sport. Smith promptly struck the Cementers' Church and in a couple of seconds a spectator had leaped the ropes and deal the Sittingbourne man a smashing blow in the face. Church framed up to defend himself from a further attack by Smith but

For results, see over page ➔

FOOTBALL.

Northfleet Players Disqualified.

KENT LEAGUE BUSINESS.

The much-talked-of protest lodged by Chatham against Northfleet on the ground that Northfleet's team on March 14th included men who had taken part in Sunday football, was also heard. The evidence showed that Woodmason and Fincham played in a match for a Sunday League club on February 22nd, and also that Woodmason (under the name of A. Leyton) played on February 15th. On that day a photo of the team was taken, and it was now produced, showing Woodmason and Fincham sitting among the players. The Committee sustained Chatham's protest and declared Woodmason and Fincham ineligible for Kent League football. Northfleet were ordered to lose two points (which should be deducted from the table on page 3) and to pay £2 2s. fine.

(This latter decision is quite contrary to the finding of the Cup Committee, who considered a protest on the same grounds in the cup-tie between the clubs. The Chatham club however, we understand, can take no further proceedings in the matter, but on the face of ties present finding Northfleet are certainly fortunate to be allowed to compete in the cup final at Maidstone on Easter Monday. In fairness to the Cup Tie Committee it should be added that they could have come to no other decision than they did on the evidence before

THE MAIDSTONE TEAM.

instantly the crowd swarmed on the field and for several minutes there was great disorder. After a time the referee, with the help of Northfleet officials, managed to get the ground cleared and Smith was ordered off. Both sides were given time to cool down before proceeding to the conclusion."

The semi-final was a tamer affair and Chatham were despatched to qualify for another clash with old rivals Maidstone on the county town's Athletic Ground before a 7,907 crowd. Neither side was at full strength, with Northfleet missing the suspended Woodmason and Fincham, while the veteran of two previous cup finals, Myers, was injured. The supporters were emblazoned in their usual riots of amber or red colours and "made no attempt to conceal their partisanship – they never do. On the contrary, they revelled in it to the point of aggressiveness."

The usual highly competitive game was deadlocked until the 82nd minute when Northfleet goalkeeper Joel collected a cross only to then drop it at the feet of the grateful Marsh, who tapped it into the empty net for the winner.

Despite this disappointment the club was now on a solid foundation, making a profit of £32 1s 5d – the first profit since 1910 – with average gates of 1,800 and a top crowd of 4,000 for the clash with local rivals Gravesend United.

Fleet's 1914 cup runners-up

The *South Eastern Gazette* of 14th April, 1914, published its usual array of biographies for a Kent Senior Cup final. Here is the last set of Northfleet players before the war erupted four months later...

J JOEL – Played for Millwall for three years. Standing 6ft tall, he is quick and resourceful, with a liking for close shots. Very fond of punching a ball. Is in the first flight of Kent goalkeepers.

GEORGE TAYLOR – Right back. Came from Sutton-at-Hone in October last. Has played for no other club of prominence. Very steady and can be relied on. Exceptionally fair and plays quite a high-class game.

GEORGE GREEN – Left back. Has played no senior football of any note before. Was secured from Bexley Heath. The best back Northfleet has ever possessed. A fine, strong kick, and is very agile. Plays quite a 'Corinthian' game and if he rightly develops should secure his English cap. Leaves for Southampton, for which he has signed on, directly the game is over. He looks well after himself and is quite a genial character. Was badly injured in the game with Chatham.

DOUGLAS McWHIRTER – Right half. Has played from time to time for Northfleet. Is an international amateur in the Olympic games at the Stadium. Has been associated more with Bromley and Leicester Fosse. Plays a clean, cleaver game. A pleasant personality.

W NASH – Centre half. Has played a stong fearless game for Northfleet for six seasons. Has an almost inexhaustible supply of energy. In temperament typically English. Is regarded as a pattern by youngsters in the team. This is his third final and he revels in cup-tie football. His proper position is right half.

W TYLER – Left half. Played for Crystal Palace for some years, but this is his third final with the "Reds". Has represented Essex County on a number of occasions. A clean, sterling player. He is just a nice weight for a half. He is captain of the side and is probably the cleverest half the club has ever had.

CHURCH – Outside right. Another player with final experience. Has formerly appeared for Sheppey, Chatham and Maidstone. Last year, Gillingham was his club. Very reliable and fast. Rather too much inclined to shoot at goal instead of centering the ball.

ARTHUR SECCOMBE – Inside right. Until quite lately, the boy of the team. Is undoubtedly clever. What he lacks in height and weight he makes up in speed. Is remarkably quick and has a happy facility for threading his way through a sea of legs and shooting a goal. Never known to play a bad game. A great favourite with the Northfleet crowd.

ALBERT WILLIAMS – Centre forward. The veteran of the side. Has been with Northfleet seven or eight years. Has played little this season. Is brought in owing to the team being disturbed. His intelligence far above the average and this may compensate him for his lessened speed. Is a great "general" and may do much to guide the younger members. A good deal depends upon him.

ERNEST HARBER – Inside left. Another player hailing from Sutton. This is his first appearance in a final. In the early part of the season was brilliant, but his play has since been marred by an accident. He is now gradually returning to form. Very fast, strong, and has a good eye for the net. He may prove a first class man.

HARRY SECCOMBE – Outside left. Another boy brought into the team at the last minute owing to an accident to E Myers. Shows excellent style for a youth. Resembles his brother in most respects. Moves over the turf well and may have a good future.

F B TREADWELL – Reserve. A fair-haired product of Northfleet. Has plenty of vigour and with training should prove a player of great capacity. If he plays Northfleet will confidently look to him to do well.

Once again Arthur Seccombe was outstanding, top scoring with 29 goals. And breaking into the team also was his younger brother Henry (or 'Harry' as he was called), who was predicted to have a bright future.

1914 was the year when much of the ground was transformed, with the main stand work completed while a permanent tea stall was erected, a bar area concreted and extended and the local Russell's

Brewery asked to stock it. In the wider world, although there was much talk and rumour about a European conflict, nobody really could have foreseen that this would be the last completed Kent League season for six years... and that the world was about to change forever.

The cost to Northfleet United was not just in its closure, but also in the blood that a number of its young men shed for king and country.

Results 1913/14

Date		Opponent	Comp	Venue	Score	Scorers	Att
Sep	06	Tunbridge Wells Rangers	KL	home	2-1	Nash, Stewart	
	13	Ilford	Friendly	home	7-0	Mason 4, Seccombe 2, Harber	
	20	Millwall Reserves	KL	away	1-3	Seccombe	
	27	Ramsgate	FAC Pr	away	4-0	Mason, Hubard, Seccombe, Baxter	
	30	Chatham	KSS1	home	0-2		
Oct	04	Bromley	KL	home	6-1	Seccombe 2, Harber, Myers, Baxter, Sayc	
	11	New Crusaders	FAC1Q	home	2-7	Somerville 2	
	18	Woolwich	KL	home	0-5		
	25	Sheppey United	KL	away	5-2*	*abandoned, bad light	
Nov	08	Southend Reserves	KL	away	2-2	Harber 2	
	15	Southend Reserves	KL	home	2-1	Seccombe, Green	
	22	Maidstone United	KL	away	3-3	Woodmason, Harber, Seccombe	
	29	Sittingbourne	KL	home	5-0	Woodmason 4, Seccombe	
Dec	06	Bromley	KL	away	1-0	Tyler	
	13	RN Depot	KL	home	0-1		
	20	Dartford	KL	away	0-2		
	25	Gravesend United	KL	home	4-2	Seccombe 2, Myers 2	4,000
	26	Gravesend United	KL	away	1-1	Seccombe	
	27	Rochester	KL	away	5-2		
Jan	03	Woolwich	KL	away	3-2	Woodmason, Seccombe, Harber	
	10	Sheppey United	KL	away	1-1	Harber	
	17	Margate	KSC1	away	3-0	Woodmason, Harber, Seccombe	
	24	Chatham	KL	away	2-1	Harber, Woodmason	
	31	Maidstone United	KL	home	2-3	Knapp, Seccombe	
Feb	07	Millwall Reserves	KL	home	1-5	Myers	
	14	Sittingbourne	KSC2	away	2-2	Seccombe, Green	
	18	Sittingbourne	KSC2 R	home	5-3	Woodmason 2, Seccombe, Green, Harber	800
	21	Sheppey United	KL	home	2-1	Woodmason, Seccombe	
	27	Sittingbourne	KL	away	0-2		
Mar	07	Dartford	KL	home	2-0	Myers (pen), Woodmason	
	14	Chatham	KSC SF	at Gravesend	2-1	Nash, Seccombe	2,900
	21	Chatham	KL	home	2-0	Seccombe, Church	
	28	Royal Dublin Fusiliers	KL	home	1-0	OG	
Apr	04	Crystal Palace Reserves	KL	home	2-0	Church, Dunn	
	10	Royal Dublin Fusiliers	KL	away	2-2	Harber, Seccombe	
	11	Tunbridge Wells Rangers	KL	away	2-6	Harber 2	
	13	Maidstone United	KSC Final	at Maidstone	0-1		7,907
	18	RN Depot	KL	away	2-1	Taylor (pen), Church	
	25	Rochester	KL	home	4-0	Seccombe 2, Harber, Ansell	

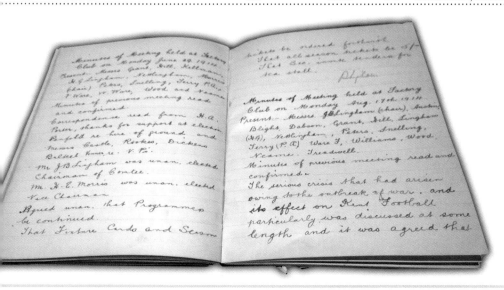

● *This Northfleet United minutes' book remains in good condition today – the set of notes, covering 1912 up to the outbreak of war in 1914, with an appendix for 1919, is for the most part fairly mundane but offers a fascinating insight into the mindset of the club leading up to war. Written mainly by Joe Lingham, or brother Henry, it covers subjects ranging from team selection to transfers to the choice of tea lady!*

1914/15

The lamps were going out all over Europe, Foreign Secretary Sir Edward Grey was supposed to have remarked, and with war declared on 4th August, 1914, the authorities decided – for the time being – to allow football to continue. The Kent League was expected to go on as usual but a wave of patriotism across the country was summarised by the *Gravesend Reporter*, which stated "As the county has no use for idle young men who cluster around a football ground at such time as the present, the paper has no time for stories of bravery on the football field,and during the war there will be no football news in the *Reporter*."

And they were as good as their word, making the results of any matches played very difficult to find. The FA Cup did continue and all Northfleet's competitive games were played in this competition, with the club eventually losing in their fifth game to the old rivals, Dartford.

At the outbreak of war, Northfleet were, unsurprisingly, forced to turn down a planned Christmas tour of Spain – including a game against Barcelona – given the agitation in Europe. But the club continued to plan its ground rental agreements with local sides, its ground improvements and its fixture-card and ticket-printing requirements. Players were re-signed, trial dates mulled over.

Club president Mr T Church had remarked earlier that summer, somewhat ironically given what was to follow, that the club "met under the most happy circumstances of any year since its inception for they were in the happy and he believed unique position for Northfleet of having a balance in hand." Joe Lingham was presented with a "smart fitted dressing case" which left him "deeply moved and he thanked the donors from the bottom of his heart", while committee members were presented with a gold scarf pin, set with the club colours.

Come August, however, the crisis loomed large. Henry Lingham wrote,

> *   *   *   *
> The Northfleet club have been asked to take their team on tour to Spain for the Christmas holidays, but in view of the Continental trouble, it is not likely that the trip will be undertaken.
> *   *   *   *

"The serious crisis that has arisen owing to the outbreak of war and its effect on Kent football was discussed at some length and [we concluded] that the club programme be carried out as far as possible and that the position be placed before the players."

Numerous Kent League teams faced problems, with many players having already enlisted with the army, navy or territorials. Woolwich Arsenal, Sheppey United and the army teams were withdrawn but the League, briefly, gave the green light for football to continue for the rest.

But at an emergency meeting in September, KCFA representatives decided it was no longer possible to do so, despite the Football League and even the War Office – not to mention several Kent League clubs – wishing for things to continue as normal for a while longer.

There was a business side to the argument, too. Season-ticket sales had slumped and professional players who had not taken up arms were entitled to look for other work – some considered playing abroad in countries not yet drawn into the conflict. That in turn, it was felt, would leave clubs bereft of players should the authorities

> *   *   *   *
> A crowd estimated at 1,200 assembled on the Dartford ground, where the local team played off their postponed English Cup-tie with Northfleet. An even contest ensued, resulting in a win for Dartford by the odd goal in seven. Northfleet opened the scoring soon after the start, and held the lead until close on the interval, when Quinn, the ex-Woolwich man, suddenly came into the picture and scored twice for Dartford in double quick time. Northfleet, however, equalised through Beldham on the resumption, but again Quinn responded with another couple and placed the issue beyond doubt, though Beldham managed to reduce the gap before the final whistle went. The winners visit Chatham this Saturday in the fourth round.
> *   *   *   *

decide to reinstate competition further down the line.

As far as Northfleet were concerned, they were left with the aforementioned FA Cup games. Three matches with Sittingbourne in the competition gave the season a semblance of normality, but the Brickies took the opportunity to let their local territorial regiments in for free and the show of khaki behind the pitch ropes was a reminder of the country's situation. Moreover, Sittingbourne had drafted in a number of players from the military and had only four who remained as civilians among their ranks. Their team selection in the subsequent replay also depended upon whether their soldier footballers had been sent on active duty or not.

The Northfleet team that played in what would prove to be the last game for nearly five years, against Dartford, was Joel; Joy; Treadwell; Nash; Fincham; Tyler; Church; Arthur Seccombe; Beldham; Dunn; Henry Seccombe.

The only other game played during the season was a friendly with Gravesend United to raise money for the War Relief Fund and obtain volunteers for the armed forces. Despite a patriotic appeal by Colonel Griffith, President of the KCFA, and the offer of an additional half crown for every man accepting the King's shilling by Joe Lingham, only 11 of the 400 crowd stepped forward to volunteer and just eight pounds was collected for the war fund.

Soon after the Dartford defeat (*see left*), the Northfleet committee decided to disband the club for the duration of the war. The conflict was clearly not going to be "over by Christmas" and Joe Lingham said, "It was evident that the manhood of our country would be required for services against the enemy. It was generally felt that it was not the time to play games."

All the club's equipment was donated to the armed forces for the war effort. On 16th November, a financial check was made in order to pay all existing debts to tradesmen and it was "agreed that no further meetings be held except upon notification by the Hon Sec. until the end of the war."

Lingham was on record as being disappointed that the considerable outlay on ground improvements could not now be recouped and more so that a "first-rate team" – some of whom had offered to play for half wages or even free in the situation – would not get the chance to prove their mettle. For some of them, that would come instead on the battlefield.

Results 1914/15

Date		Opponent	Competition	Venue	Score	Scorers	Attendance
Sep	12	Gravesend United	Friendly	home	3-0		400
Oct	10	Cray Wanderers	FACPr	home	3-1		
	24	Sittingbourne	FAC1Q	away	2-2	Dunn 2	
	31	Sittingbourne	FAC1Q R	home	2-2	Stewart, Church	
Nov	07	Sittingbourne	FAC1Q 2R	away	2-1		
	14	Dartford	FAC2Q	away	3-4	Beldham 2, Seccombe	1,200

League Tables (West Kent League)

West Kent League 1903/04

FINAL TABLE	PL	W	D	L	F	A	Pts
Cray Wanderers	14	12	2	0	47	13	26
Eltham	14	8	2	4	31	15	18
Crayford Athletic	14	4	8	2	27	20	16
Dartford	14	5	3	6	17	28	13
Gravesend United	13	4	4	5	23	24	12
Bromley	12	3	4	5	24	28	10
Swanscombe	14	2	3	9	19	37	7
Northfleet United	**13**	**2**	**2**	**9**	**13**	**36**	**6**

* Two games not completed

● *The Dartford side of 1904/05 – in red and white stripes – that finished one place and one point behind Northfleet. The Fleet scored a double over the Darts during this season, 4-2 and 2-1, their first victories of the 20th century over the old enemy*

West Kent League 1904/05

FINAL TABLE	PL	W	D	L	F	A	Pts
Catford Southend	20	15	1	4	64	15	31
Eltham	20	13	5	2	53	16	31
Cray Wanderers	20	12	2	6	50	25	26
Gravesend United	20	11	3	6	39	27	25
Prices Athletic	20	7	4	9	30	46	18
Crayford Athletic	19	7	3	9	31	32	17
Swanscombe	19	7	3	9	26	31	17
Northfleet United	**20**	**7**	**3**	**10**	**37**	**50**	**17**
Dartford	20	6	4	10	39	59	16
Lewisham Montrose	20	5	2	13	34	56	12
Holmesdale	20	4	0	16	17	59	8

* One game not completed

West Kent League 1905/06

FINAL TABLE	PL	W	D	L	F	A	Pts
Eltham	14	14	0	0	55	12	28
Orpington	14	11	0	3	46	23	22
Cray Wanderers	14	8	2	4	40	17	18
Dartford	14	3	6	5	27	27	12
Northfleet United	**14**	**5**	**2**	**7**	**19**	**25**	**12**
Swanscombe	14	4	3	7	33	41	11
Crayford United	14	2	3	9	12	29	7
Prices Athletic	14	0	2	12	12	70	2

* Woolwich Argus had their record expunged

West Kent League 1906/07

FINAL TABLE	PL	W	D	L	F	A	Pts
Northfleet United	**19**	**15**	**2**	**2**	**69**	**21**	**32**
Metrogas	20	15	1	4	46	21	31
Dartford	19	13	1	5	53	34	27
Northumberland Oddfellows	20	11	1	8	47	38	23
Foots Cray	20	7	4	9	38	42	18
Callenders Athletic	20	6	4	10	34	35	16
Cray Wanderers	20	5	6	9	24	38	16
Eltham	18	6	3	9	34	40	15
Crayford	20	5	3	12	27	52	13
Swanscombe	20	6	1	13	30	63	13
Orpington	20	4	4	12	34	55	12

* Two games not completed

West Kent League 1907/08

FINAL TABLE	PL	W	D	L	F	A	Pts
Northfleet United	**20**	**16**	**2**	**2**	**83**	**29**	**34**
Gravesend United	20	16	0	4	58	22	32
Metrogas	20	10	3	7	35	31	23
North Woolwich	18	9	4	5	41	22	22
Dartford	18	9	2	7	46	33	20
Crayford	19	9	1	9	37	31	19
Orpington	20	7	5	8	40	42	19
Charlton Albion	20	6	2	12	37	47	14
Northumberland Oddfellows	19	4	6	9	30	59	14
Cray Wanderers	20	3	5	12	22	62	11
Foots Cray	20	2	2	16	19	53	6

* Three games not completed

League Tables (Kent League)

Kent League Division 1 1906/07

FINAL TABLE	PL	W	D	L	F	A	Pts
Sheppey United	14	11	1	2	34	13	23
Northfleet United	14	9	0	5	37	19	18
Gravesend United	14	7	1	6	39	27	15
Faversham	14	7	1	6	24	22	15
Royal Navy Depot	14	5	3	6	24	25	13
Dover	14	5	3	6	22	31	13
Cray Wanderers	14	4	1	9	20	31	9
Maidstone Church Inst.	14	3	2	9	21	38	8

• *1906/07 saw Fleet's first league meeting with Dover (above), a 6-0 win at Stonebridge Road the result for the Kent League runners-up*

Kent League Division 1 1907/08

FINAL TABLE	PL	W	D	L	F	A	Pts
Northfleet United	16	14	1	1	54	13	29
Royal Scots	16	9	6	1	24	11	24
Sheppey United	16	7	3	6	34	26	17
Faversham	16	8	1	7	26	26	17
Maidstone Church Inst.	16	6	2	8	23	34	14
Dover	16	4	6	6	24	40	14
Gravesend United	14	5	1	8	21	26	11
Royal Navy Depot	16	3	3	10	26	33	9
Royal West Kent Regt.	14	2	1	11	12	35	5

Kent League Division 1 1908/09

FINAL TABLE	PL	W	D	L	F	A	Pts
Northfleet United	16	13	1	2	52	22	27
Gravesend United	16	11	3	1	40	16	25
Tunbridge Wells Rangers	16	10	2	4	58	19	22
Royal West Kent Regt.	16	8	2	6	38	27	18
Royal Navy Depot	16	6	3	7	28	34	15
Sheppey United	16	5	3	8	33	32	13
Faversham	16	4	3	9	24	51	11
Maidstone Athletic	16	3	1	12	18	49	7
Dover	16	2	2	12	14	51	6

Kent League Division 1 1909/10

FINAL TABLE	PL	W	D	L	F	A	Pts
Northfleet United	22	17	2	3	74	31	36
Sittingbourne	22	15	3	4	55	23	33
Dartford	22	12	4	6	45	27	28
New Brompton Reserves	22	11	5	6	55	35	27
Chatham	22	10	7	5	38	28	27
Gravesend United	22	9	5	8	34	36	23
Royal Navy Depot	22	10	2	10	38	53	22
Sheppey United	22	9	2	11	38	34	20
Metrogas	22	5	6	11	33	46	16
Maidstone United	22	5	3	14	26	53	13
Rochester	22	4	2	16	22	56	10
Royal Engineers Depot Battalion	22	3	3	16	21	54	9

• *Rochester FC's first Kent League game against the Fleet arrived in 1910 – they lost it 5-1 against the eventual champions. The club didn't survive the war*

Kent League Division 1 1910/11

FINAL TABLE	PL	W	D	L	F	A	Pts
Millwall Reserves	26	20	2	4	72	24	42
Crystal Palace Reserves	26	20	2	4	86	36	42
New Brompton Reserves	26	17	4	5	59	28	38
Sittingbourne	26	12	7	7	58	46	31
Metrogas	26	12	6	8	69	53	30
Chatham	26	12	5	9	42	37	29
Gravesend United	26	8	6	12	37	53	22
Rochester	26	9	4	13	43	66	22
Maidstone United	26	9	3	14	51	56	21
2nd Royal Irish Rifles	26	9	3	14	45	60	21
Sheppey United	26	7	6	13	49	55	20
Dartford	26	7	5	14	35	52	19
Northfleet United	26	7	4	15	38	64	18
Orpington	26	3	5	18	42	83	11

Kent League Division 1 1911/12

FINAL TABLE	PL	W	D	L	F	A	Pts
Millwall Reserves	28	24	2	2	98	24	50
New Brompton Reserves	28	17	6	5	64	38	40
Crystal Palace Reserves	28	15	6	7	75	48	36
Chatham	28	14	6	8	56	41	34
Gravesend United	28	12	5	11	64	50	29
Bromley	28	12	5	11	70	68	29
Maidstone United	28	11	7	10	63	64	29
Northfleet United	**28**	**10**	**5**	**13**	**47**	**48**	**25**
Sittingbourne	28	10	4	14	59	59	24
Metrogas	28	9	5	14	60	69	23
Rochester	28	9	5	14	44	62	23
Sheppey United	28	9	4	15	60	62	22
Dartford	28	7	7	14	37	61	21
Cray Wanderers	28	8	4	16	44	69	20
2nd Royal Irish Rifles	28	5	5	18	36	92	15

Once again the Dublin Fusiliers were beaten by the narrow margin of a goal, Northfleet being the latest team to lower the Irishmen's flag. It was, however, Doyle's fine work in the soldiers' goal which kept the score at such narrow limits, for the civilians had the best of matters all through. Doyle's efforts to save his side, however, were negatived by one of his colleagues, Ryan, who had the misfortune to turn the ball into his own goal and this gave the Cementers the victory.

● *Regimental football sides were a common occurrence right up until the Second World War. The 2nd Royal Dublin Fusiliers (pictured) finished one off the bottom of the Kent League in the last season before the Great War erupted. In the summer of 1914, the 2nd Battalion of the regiment was stationed at Milton Barracks in Gravesend and when war broke out, initially stayed behind to defend England against a potential German landing. They embarked for France on 22nd August, 1914, and took part in the Battle of Mons, helping delay the German advance on Paris.*

Pictured left is the South Eastern Gazette cutting from the last meeting at Stonebridge Road between Northfleet and the army side, in March 1914

Kent League Division 1 1912/13

FINAL TABLE	PL	W	D	L	F	A	Pts
Millwall Reserves	28	20	5	3	79	21	45
Crystal Palace Reserves	28	19	4	5	91	35	42
Royal Navy Depot	28	13	7	8	52	34	33
Northfleet United	**28**	**14**	**5**	**9**	**58**	**55**	**33**
Dartford	28	14	3	11	66	35	31
Chatham	28	12	4	12	62	54	28
Metrogas	28	10	8	10	45	38	28
Sittingbourne	28	10	7	11	54	59	27
Gillingham Reserves	28	10	7	11	46	65	27
Maidstone United	28	9	8	11	48	55	26
Sheppey United	28	10	4	14	37	48	24
Gravesend United	28	7	7	14	34	52	21
Bromley	28	9	2	17	45	69	20
Rochester	28	8	2	18	42	81	18
Cray Wanderers	28	6	5	17	41	75	17

Kent League Division 1 1913/14

FINAL TABLE	PL	W	D	L	F	A	Pts
Crystal Palace Reserves	30	25	1	4	110	26	51
Millwall Reserves	30	18	5	7	79	35	41
Woolwich	30	18	3	9	76	42	39
Northfleet United	**30**	**17**	**5**	**8**	**63**	**49**	**37**
Maidstone United	30	17	2	11	64	58	36
Chatham	30	15	6	9	75	47	36
Tunbridge Wells Rangers	30	14	5	11	65	66	33
Southend Reserves	30	12	7	11	45	51	31
Dartford	30	13	3	14	57	57	29
Sittingbourne	30	12	3	15	41	64	27
Gravesend United	30	10	6	14	51	52	26
Sheppey United	30	11	3	16	55	62	25
Bromley	30	9	4	17	36	57	22
Royal Navy Depot	30	8	5	17	40	53	21
2nd Royal Dublin Fus.	30	8	4	18	36	57	20
Rochester	30	1	2	27	26	134	4

Chapter Three:
Remembrance

1914-1919

If there was some corner of a football field in England left untouched by the effects of the Great War, one would have been hard pressed to find it come Armistice Day, almost four years exactly since the disbandment of Northfleet United in November 1914.

The hordes of eager young men who downed tools, took up arms and marched off to war included thousands of professional and amateur footballers. Many enlisted in whichever regiment would take them on the spot. Others joined the famous Pals Battalions and still more made up the Footballers' Battalions that were specially formed from late 1914 onwards.

And with the Christmas Truce of that same year burned into the British psyche, football and conflict became inextricably linked, encompassing all the heroism, horror, romance and tragedy of the age.

Northfleet United was no different to any other club in the country. Disappointed at being unable to carry on – especially as for the first time they were financially solvent, had a setup to rival many a Southern and Football League club and were back on the road to success – they nevertheless did their patriotic duty, exhorting their players and supporters to join the greater fight.

And like many an institution and household, it didn't come without a cost as several men who had worn the club colours made the ultimate sacrifice.

In the following pages are the stories we know about, of the Northfleet players who died and those who survived. There were doubtless many, many more accounts that – like the men who were lost – went undocumented.

Six of the men who played in Northfleet red before 1914 returned five years later to do so again – but at least three of their number had fallen in battle in the intervening years, while many more had sacrificed years of their life and been wounded on foreign fields.

KENT MESSENGER, AUGUST 15, 1914.

THE WAR.

GREAT BATTLE IMMINENT.

Various Encounters go in Favour of the Belgians.

KENT ON THE ALERT.

News of the great battle, between two million troops over 200 or 300 miles of frontier

Sir Gilbert Parker stated that he would contribute to the local fund £100 in four instalments of £25 (applause).

A Collecting (Organising) Committee was formed of the Mayoress, Canon Gedge, Rev. G. W. Mennie, and the President of the Free Church Council with a view to adopting a suggestion by Mr. Baynes that the district should have a band of some 75 collectors for the fund.

The meeting was adjourned to enable Sir Gilbert Parker to make further inquiries at Northfleet as to its disposition to join Gravesend in regard to the fund, and also to make inquiries in London to the points raised by the discussion.

Gravesend's Position and Outlook

MAYORAL MANIFESTO TO THE RESIDENTS.

At a meeting of the Gravesend Town Council on Wednesday, the Mayor (Alderman A. E. Enfield) made an interesting statement as to Gravesend's position in regard to the war. "Since the outbreak of the war," he said, "I have been giving careful consideration to the measures which we non-combatants in Gravesend, as loyal and patriotic subjects of his Majesty King George, ought to take in

would be their duty to report to the committee periodically and hand over to the hon. treasurer the moneys collected.

News has reached me this week that Beldham, Northfleet's centre-forward, who used to play for Chatham, has joined the Norfolk Regiment. This is about the 13th member of the Northfleet Club to enlist since the war broke out.

● *Gravesend's Milton Barracks and home of the Royal Dublin Fusiliers who played in the Kent League in 1914*

> *Of the 13 teams in the Gravesend football league, 169 men enlisted in the first two months, while newspaper reports confirmed that 13 Northfleet United men had enlisted during the first phase of the war...*

As recreation and leisure slid down the list of priorities in the autumn of 1914, football was undergoing something of a soul-searching exercise.

Clearly a business and way of life to clubs, committee men and players alike, whilst still greatly enjoyed by the masses, its continuance at a time of unparalleled national crisis was a thorny subject.

When a German newspaper admonished the enemy, writing that "the young Britons prefer to exercise their long limbs on the football ground, rather than to expose them to any sort of risk in the service of their country", it merely fanned the flames.

Given the prevailing climate and the likelihood of dwindling attendances, Northfleet United was forced to send letters to its players offering them half wages or merely expenses and – if desired – transfers. "Without exception," wrote Joe Lingham, "they stood loyally by the club and are entitled to no small meed of praise for their action."

Lingham wanted to persevere with the season and pointed out that most of the club's players and much of its committee were already actively engaged in the war effort as government workers.

The *Kent Messenger* and *Gazette* unlike the *Gravesend Reporter*, were initially reluctant to back any ban on football. "Why should football be attacked with so much vigour", wrote the former as late as December 1914, "and horse racing (which has been supported lately by His Majesty the King) left alone? The footballers' business is just as serious to the professional footballer as is building to the bricklayer or carpenter. If a fellow is willing to enlist, football would not

stop him, and the average crowd are not all composed of young men, as some of the know-alls would have us believe."

Nonetheless, Northfleet had – three months into the war – finally succumbed to the inevitable and shut its gates. Around the town, there was little time for weekend football. The local cinema had volunteered its services as a recruitment station, riots in neighbouring Gravesend had targeted perceived German establishments and thousands thronged the streets to see the King and Queen pass through the two towns en route to London. Meanwhile, the wounded from many of the engagements in the early part of the war were being transported up the Thames by ship and onwards inland

COUNCILLOR LINGHAM, CHAIRMAN.

THE whole Council in Committee have this day unanimously formed themselves and their officers into a Committee to be called The Northfleet Subsidiary War Emergency Committee with the power and intention of largely adding to their number, for the pur-

Strong attacks are just now being made upon footballers and the crowd at a football match. But these attacks should be made with some discrimination. It must be remembered that some of those found on the football ground or behind the ropes are engaged in making armaments and ammunition; others are employed in numerous processes that lead up to the making of a uniform; and yet others have to do with keeping up the food supply. To say that these should all spend their leisure in lugubrious occupations is not the way in which to keep up the spirit of a nation. No doubt the professional footballer and some others as well could be much better employed in serving their country elsewhere; but the charge against all and sundry must not be of too sweeping a character.

via Gravesend and the stark realities of the conflict were brought home to all.

Seven hundred men from the local cement industry had joined up and of the 13 teams in the Gravesend football league, 169 men enlisted in the first two months, while newspapers reported that some 13 Northfleet United men had enlisted during the first phase of the war.

Joe Lingham was chairman (*see cutting, left*) of the Northfleet Urban District Council and, along with his construction business, was kept busy with all manner of civil matters including home defence, air-raid precautions and fire safety in the town.

There is little record of what use, if any, the football ground was put to. Many grounds around the country were commandeered by the military, while Gravesend's Pelham Road was used for Empire Day parades and such like.

Northfleet had previously rented their ground out in the summer to showmen and even contemplated letting the pitch out for grazing in 1914. Moreover, schools and amateur sides played on it from time to time and, like any large recreation ground during the war years, it was likely used to host such occasions as regimental and school sports events, military inspections and so on.

Football continued in the League and FA Cup for a time and guest players would turn out in the colours of big clubs around the country for morale reasons. Moreover, there were plenty of regimental matches amongst training battalions or units home on leave; indeed former Northfleet players like Beldham, Buchan, Goad, Gooda and others were regulars for their regiments throughout the war.

Lance Corporal William Kennedy, 1890–1915

William Kennedy, a star of the Northfleet United treble-winning side of 1909/10, lost his life at the Battle of Loos (*pictured right*) in October 1915, one of the countless 'unknown soldiers', his body never found in the carnage that resulted in 50,000 British casualties.

Born in Grays, Essex, in 1890 to John Kennedy and Jeanie McKenzie, the fourth of eight children, William was a schoolteacher and also proved to be adept on the football field. He played amateur football for his local side, Grays Athletic, and moved to Northfleet in 1909 alongside another signing, the then-unknown teenager Charles Buchan.

By the time he starred for the 'Cementers' in the 1910 Kent Senior Cup Final, he was in high regard. The *South Eastern Gazette* said of him, "To watch Kennedy is to follow one of the best features of Northfleet's play. Probably the Cementers' best catch of the season."

Kennedy scored Northfleet's opening goal in the 2-0 final defeat of Chatham, heading home a corner from one of the other casualties of the war, Edwin Myers (*see over page*).

He was instrumental, too, in Northfleet's third Kent League title in succession, scoring more than 50 goals in all competitions (which included the Thames & Medway Combination, also won by the Fleet) and was "considered by many to be the equal of Buchan", who remembered Kennedy as one of Northfleet's best players in his later autobiography.

He turned out for Southend in several guest appearances and it was no surprise that he was picked up by West Ham United, then managed by Syd King who had been Northfleet's skipper back in 1895.

Kennedy scored on his debut against Brighton & Hove Albion and earned four goals in 10 league games that season. He also did well the following year, scoring a hat-trick against Brentford on 21st October, 1911. Unfortunately he suffered a serious knee injury in an FA Cup tie against Middlesbrough on February 8 the following year and was unable to play professional football again.

On the outbreak of the First World War, Kennedy joined the British Army as a lance corporal. He volunteered for the London Scottish Regiment in deference to his roots (his father hailed from Lanarkshire and his mother from Ayrshire).

Depending how early on in the war he signed up, as part of 'A' Company 1/14th County of London Battalion, it is possible he saw action in some of the famous early engagements of the war including the Battle of the Marne, the retreat from Mons, Messines and Ypres.

One can only imagine what a terrible year 1915 was for the Kennedy family. On 12th September, William's elder brother John was killed at Gallipoli. He was Fourth Engineer Officer on the troop ship HMS *Minnetonka* and had previously taken part in the famous landings at Anzac Cove. He was buried on the Greek island of Lemnos.

Within a month, William would have met the same fate. Two weeks after his brother's death, his battalion was ordered to Loos as part of the largest British offensive of 1915.

The attack began on September 25 and by mid-October the objective, a fortified position known as the Hohenzollern Redoubt, had changed hands between the British and Germans several times. There were 20,000 casualties in the first two weeks and the British were back at their starting positions. On October 13, they made one final push.

At 1400 hours, Kennedy was part of the unit launching a new attack. The German defences and wire were untouched by the feeble artillery barrage and with German shells now landing heavily around the attacking troops, the outcome was doomed. With immediate heavy losses of officers and men (across the entire attack front, there were 3,643 casualties, mostly in the first 10 minutes), the survivors were left facing impenetrable wire with little cover and no way to get through. The men of Kennedy's 'A' Company were some of those who reached the furthest forwards.

Whilst this halt in the 'advance' was forced upon the men, and they did their best to seek cover, a call was made for volunteers to cross the shell-swept zone to the dressing station in order to obtain aid for wounded comrades. Lance Corporal Kennedy and two others volunteered to go and they were last seen crossing the area amid the falling shells. It was foggy at the time and for some considerable period afterwards there was hope that they had lost their way and become prisoners. The hope was futile, however, and it can only be presumed that Kennedy was killed in the shelling as no trace of him or his two fellow volunteers was ever found.

The official history of the battle suggested that, "The fighting on October 13-14 had not improved the general situation in any way and had brought nothing but useless slaughter of infantry."

Like so many others killed on the Western Front, Kennedy had no known grave and was commemorated on the nearest memorial to where he vanished, in this case the Loos Memorial where his name is joined by 21,000 others. He is also remembered on his local Grays war memorial alongside his brother (below), on his parents' headstone and

in his regiment's roll of honour at Edinburgh Castle.

Corporal Edwin Myers, 1888–1916

A longside teammate William Kennedy, Blackheath-born Edwin Bertram Myers tasted glory in Northfleet's first win in a Kent Senior Cup final, in 1910. Six years after that momentous event, he was killed at the Battle of Flers-Courcelette on the Somme.

Myers was born on 5th July, 1888, to his electrical engineer father (also Edwin) and mother Bertha, the eldest of seven children. He grew up in south-east London, the various census forms recording him as having lived in Greenwich, Charlton and Dartford.

He signed for the Fleet in 1908 and barely out of his teens, the left-winger got a taste of playing in front of big crowds, turning out for the Fleet in front of 4,000 supporters against Croydon Common in the Fourth Qualifying Round of the English (FA) Cup, only the club's second appearance in the competition.

'Micky' or 'Albert' as he was known to his teammates was a part of the 1909 side that reached the Kent Senior Cup final, which the Fleet lost 4-2 to Maidstone in front of a crowd of between 7,000–8,000. The following season he went one better, again reaching the final against Chatham, only this time the Fleet won it 2-0 in front of a 6,500 attendance.

In a curious tragedy, the first Fleet goal was scored from a Myers corner, headed home by William Kennedy – the very two players who died in the Great War that followed. That season he also helped win the club's third Kent League title in succession, as well as the Thames & Medway Combination.

After that success, Myers moved to Crystal Palace in 1910 but there is little evidence to suggest he actually turned out for the south London side. He was also an able cricketer, on the staff at The Oval, and it is believed he played professional cricket for Surrey between 1910 and 1914.

Myers returned to Northfleet in 1912 and again tasted Kent Senior Cup glory, playing in the 1913 final against Gravesend United. He was in the thick of the action "all afternoon and delivered a series of magnificent centres."

Still at the club in 1913/14, Myers was unfit for the last Kent Senior Cup final before the war when, in one more cruel irony, he was replaced by another soon-to-be casualty in Henry Seccombe.

Soon after the outbreak of hostilities in August 1914, Myers joined the Army, rising to the rank of corporal in the London Regiment (First Surrey Rifles), 21st Battalion.

After training in St Albans, he served on the Western Front from 1915 and on 10th September, 1916, was moved to the front line

● *The new wonder weapon – the tank – is deployed for the first time on 15th September, 1916, at Courcelette. Edwin Myers lost his life on the same day, in the same battle*

around High Wood, near the village of Miraumont. It had taken the British more than two months to reach the short distance of 6km following the first Somme offensive in July and the fighting in the area was variously described as "grim" and "hellish".

On the day he died, 15th September 15, Myers was part of the support wave of British (47th/London Division) and Canadian troops in what became known as the Battle of Flers-Courcelette – the third and final offensive of the Battle of the Somme – attacking along a wide front that involved the first use of tanks.

From his division's war diaries, we know that his battalion stood in reserve for an attack on High Wood. With almost 600 men, Myers was called into action to assist an assault in the early afternoon. By 5.30pm that evening, with the men advancing under heavy shell and machine-gun fire, they were brought to a halt just short of their objective. The battalion was all but annihilated. Of the 567 soldiers that had attacked High Wood four hours before, just two officers and 60 men survived. Corporal Edwin Myers was not one of them. Some time between noon and early evening, the "coltish" left winger, one of the stars of the pre-war Northfleet United team, was killed by German machine-gun fire. He was 28.

The overall battle, which lasted a week, did not meet its strategic objective but was deemed "tactically gainful". To be precise, the front line advanced all of 2,500 yards.

Edwin Myers is buried at Adanac Military Cemetery on the Somme and his name is inscribed on a war memorial by the Kennington Oval, where he played cricket.

● *The memorial outside the Oval (left) and Myers' burial place at Adanac (below)*

Rifleman Henry Seccombe, 1896–1917

> FOOTBALLER KILLED.—Enthusiasts of the old winter pastime will regret to know that Pte. Harry Seccombe, Rifle Brigade, has been killed in France. This youngster played at outside left for Northfleet several times, and was quite a favourite. His elder brother, Arthur, the old inside-right, is in the R.F.A.

Barely out of his teens, Henry 'Harry' George Seccombe was the younger brother of a Northfleet club legend – Arthur Seccombe, who went on to have a long career at Stonebridge Road after the war.

Henry wasn't so lucky. Born in Plumstead to labourer William and his wife Isabella, he turned up at Northfleet a year or two after his brother began to establish himself in the side.

At just 18, he played in the Kent Senior Cup final of 1914, replacing the injured Edwin Myers who died a year before him on the Western Front.

Full of promise and blessed with the same pace and eye for goal as his brother, Henry was expected to go on to greater things than

Kent League football but the war intervened.

He enlisted in the Rifle Brigade, part of the 16th Battalion, at Royal Arsenal Woolwich and was shipped out to France, landing in Le Havre in March 1916. His unit, of which he was in the line with at the time, saw action on the Somme and he was later wounded, in February 1917, receiving a gunshot in the upper leg.

Henry recovered and was sent back to the line in early summer around the Ypres area. Throughout spring, the British Army had been preparing for a massive offensive intended to be the breakthrough action of 1917 that would become known as 'Passchendaele', the Battle of Third Ypres. Half a million British soldiers poured into the sector.

Before that battle could begin, Henry met his end. He was in either 'A' or 'B' Company which, according to his unit's war diary, was billeted in Ypres and working on railway construction on 13th June. Two soldiers, one of them Henry Seccombe, were killed by shellfire and five others wounded.

He is buried at Vlamertinghe Military Cemetery in Belgium. His brother Arthur, of course, survived the war having also seen action on the Western Front, with the Royal Artillery.

Those who survived...

Lieutenant Charles Buchan

As if playing for Sunderland, Arsenal and England, winning a Football League title, twice appearing in an FA Cup final and then carving out a career as a broadcaster and writer wasn't enough, Charles Buchan was also a decorated war hero.

One of the stars of Fleet's 1909/10 side before he hit the big time, he had to see out the 1914/15 season until he could join up and then he enlisted immediately in the Grenadier Guards, seeing action in some of the war's biggest battles – on the Somme (where 380 men and 8 officers were killed from his battalion on his first day in battle), Ypres, at Cambrai where he won the Military Medal for bravery, and at Passchendaele. He started the war as a private but ended it as a lieutenant in the Sherwood Foresters.

One might think such an experience would have figured extensively in his later biography, *A Lifetime In Football*, but Buchan – like many men of his generation – barely mentioned his wartime experiences.

Where he did, it was usually in tandem with a mention of his beloved football, for he played in army and exhibition games throughout the conflict. One such recollection was, "Out in France… my first game was just behind the Somme front, just after the big push in July 1916, at our camp in Mariecourt a little north of Albert. From the playing field we could see the spire of Arras church.

"Legend had it that when the statue of the Virgin Mary hanging at right angles fell, the war would end. We devoutly wished it would fall right then and took a few potshots ourselves at it with a ball. No sooner had we started than the German shells began to drop perilously near the field. So we packed up and restarted on another pitch. The game had to go on!"

Buchan won his Military Medal in November 1917 at Cambrai when his unit was pinned down in battle. In an effort to save his men, he stormed a German lookout post with his troops close behind him. They took the lookout post but in doing so Buchan was bayoneted in the foot by a surviving German soldier. Luckily for Buchan (and more so given the career he wanted to rekindle after the war) the bayonet went straight through the gap between his toes.

He then, under enemy fire, ran back to the mess tent to get his men food as their rations had run out, his cause presumably helped by the fact he was something of a decent sprinter.

Buchan's Military Medal was publically announced on 12 December, 1917, and he was nominated for a Commission shortly after he won it.

After the war, Buchan supported the widows and orphans of those who did not return as best he could and also made sure that those of his colleagues who could not play professional football for whatever reason as a result of the war, had some form of job in the sport to keep them going.

Corporal Dick Goad

Something of a daredevil by all accounts, Albert 'Dick' Goad was a bus driver who had played for both Northfleet and Gravesend before the war.

His first two spells at Northfleet came either side of a season and a bit at Gravesend in 1911/12 and while not the most talented or an automatic choice in the side, he seems to have played semi-regularly in his time at the club.

Born in 1891 in Wandsworth, he moved to Kent as a youngster, living in Fiveash Road, Gravesend, and then Shepherd Street, Northfleet. He joined the motor transport arm of the Army Service Corps in 1915 and recounted his exploits to the *Kent Messenger* in August 1918, who reported them as follows:

"A well-known local footballer, Corpl. A.R. (Dick) Goad, is achieving athletic fame at his station 'somewhere in France'. Always a popular and interesting figure in the Gravesend and Northfleet team – he played outside left – Corpl. Goad had evidently been turning the training he received as a footballer to some account, if one can go by the number of prizes he obtained at his company's annual sports on August Bank Holiday. He won a handsome clock and vases as first prize in a 100 yards handicap and further accolades in the 200 yards flat handicap, another 100-yarder and finally the 440 yards. At the close the worthy Corporal was carried round the field shoulder high by his cheering mates.

"He is 27 years of age and has been in the Army three years having now spent two years in France, during which time he has naturally experienced some rather exciting adventures, especially in dispatch riding. On one occasion, a Hun airman – a prince – was coming down, owing to lack of petrol, close to Corpl. Goad and his colleague. They gave chase and his friend succeeded in "bagging" the prince, for which (having been born under a lucky star), he was granted a month's leave!

"Once Corpl. Goad was instrumental in saving several soldiers from injury. A number of them, including himself, were in a hut, and the footballer, having filled a Primus stove with petrol, had set light to it. Then he noticed there was a leak in the stove and the petrol was escaping. Knowing there would be an explosion, he picked the stove up, walked to the door of the hut and was in the act of throwing it out when it exploded in his face, burning him terribly.

"Prior to the war, Corpl. Goad had driven a motor bus for some years for the Gravesend and Northfleet Tramways Company. 'I am in the pink and am up to my old game – footer,' he cheerily says in his latest letter to his wife."

It would not be long before Goad was reunited with her and he was sent home on leave in the autumn; while there, the Armistice was signed and he survived the war. He remained local to the area, playing for the club once more in 1919/20, and died in 1961.

There were numerous others who fought in the war that remain undocumented. Since contemporary newspaper reports rarely printed first names of players, it is impossible to identify many of them and match them with military records, particularly where they have common surnames.

There may have been others in the Northfleet side who were killed in the four years of conflict, but with names like Smith, Williams, Lee or Hills, for example, it cannot be stated with any certainty.

● *This 1915 postcard of the Norfolk Regiment's football team shows Northfleet's Beldham in the side. Sadly, the caption does not feature the names in order, so it is unclear which one of them is the Northfleet man*

We know chairman Joe Lingham lost his brother-in-law on board the cruiser HMS *Cressy* in the first weeks of the war when the ship was torpedoed by a German U-boat. And Northfleet Invicta founder committee member and player William Ware lost his 19-year-old son,

"GASSED."—Pte. Fred Treadwell (formerly of High Street) is home on convalescent leave after being "gassed."

FOOTBALLER WOUNDED.—A private letter from a chum states that "Sonny" Goodhind, the well-known Dartford footballer, is among the wounded in France.

also William – tragically just one week from the end of the war.

Other Northfleet players who survived include **Arthur Seccombe** who came through service in the Royal Artillery only to lose his brother. Also in the Royal Artillery were his 1914 teammate **Fred Treadwell**, who was sent home after being gassed, as well as a member of the 1904/05 side, **Alfred Scollard**, who made it through the war and died in 1928. Former Crystal Palace and Dartford man **George 'Sonny' Goodhind**, who joined Northfleet in 1912, was another artilleryman on the wounded list.

Kent Senior Cup finalist **Gordon Hoare**, who had played for Great Britain in the 1912 Olympics (*pictured left*), served with the Army Service Corps, reaching the rank of lieutenant. Another who rose to the same heights was **John Grant**, the man who scored 11 goals in a game and played for Woolwich Arsenal and Genoa. He enlisted with the Inniskilling Fusiliers.

Lance Corporal **Alf Grieves**, a former trainer of the club, saw plenty of action with the Tank Corps, including one of their first en masse engagements at the Battle of Cambrai. He contracted dysentery and was sent to Liverpool to convalesce in 1918.

ON THE ROAD TO RECOVERY.—Pte. Wm. J. Gooda, of the Royal West Kents, only son of Mrs. Gooda, of Station Street, who was seriously wounded on July 15th, is now well on the road to recovery in a hospital at Devonport. He joined up in August, 1915, and went to France in May last.

Former goalkeeper and local boy Private **William Gooda** was another who was sent home. He enlisted at Gravesend in 1915 with the 10th Battalion of the Queen's Own (Royal West Kent) Regiment and was often mentioned in the newspapers playing in goal for the West Kents throughout his first year. He spent only a few months in France, from May to July 1916, until a rifle shot tore much of his right shoulder apart. Dangerously ill for a time, he recovered sufficiently to be posted to depot duty. His injuries were such, however, that he could not return to active duty and after a time in reserve, he was honourably discharged in September 1917.

Another who kept his football skills finely honed while in the army was **H Beldham**, a former Customs House, Gravesend and Chatham player, who secured a place at Northfleet United in 1914. Together with the Seccombe brothers and Fred Treadwell, he was part of the last ever pre-war Northfleet side that lost to Dartford in the FA Cup, Beldham scoring twice in that game.

Beldham joined the Norfolk Regiment and was a regular member of their football team. It is not known what happened to him after 1915 but he does not appear on any list of casualties.

1919 : Kent plans its football rebirth

With the Armistice having come into effect in November 1918, thoughts slowly turned to the peacetime recovery. But with plenty of men still waiting to be demobbed throughout 1919, civilian life only gradually returned to 'normal' – though 'normal' was far removed from the society that had existed pre-1914. Football was played in 1918/19, as it had been throughout the war, on a largely regional basis. In Kent, the county's football association had visions of staging a commemorative competition named the Victory Cup – but to get that off the ground it relied upon disbanded or defunct clubs getting back on their feet.

Colonel Frank Griffith, president of the KCFA before the war, had given thought to restarting after the war even before the association had halted football in 1914, saying, "Let Kent be first to close down, and let us to see to it that we are the first to start." Unfortunately for Griffth, he was not around to see the reconstruction, having been killed in January 1917 while serving with the Royal Artillery.

In December 1918, Horace Porter – chairman of the KCFA – wrote to local papers that the association "must carry out his [Griffith's] wishes. And further we owe it to the fighting men who will soon be returning to see to it that the winter sport is once more in full vigour."

For some clubs, that task was more difficult than for others. Gravesend United, for instance, were effectively homeless, their Pelham Road ground having been commandeered for the war effort by the armed forces. Northfleet were in potentially better shape, with their Stonebridge Road ground intact. But for all clubs there was the problem of locating former players who may or may not have survived the war and finding new players to make up the numbers. For individual leagues, referees, officials and others vital to the administration of the game had to be recruited or tempted back.

In Northfleet, a meeting was convened in January 1919 to discuss the merits of the KCFA's 'Victory Cup' invitation and the reconstruction scheme for football as a whole. "After giving the matter very careful consideration," Lingham wrote of the Victory Cup invitation, "it was decided that the time was not opportune for the club to restart, mainly on the ground of the great expenses it would necessarily incur." Instead, it was agreed that meetings were to be held in April and May with a view to restarting the club in time for the 1919/20 season.

At a packed May meeting at the Factory Club (see page 66), support for breathing new life into the club was considerable. Half of the £150 initially needed was collected at the meeting and season-tickets were put on sale.

Football was back in Kent and, more importantly for the Fleet, back in Northfleet. "In any way that the game can once more rise to the splendid traditions which Kent enjoyed in previous times," wrote the KCFA's Porter, "let us turn our best attention. If Colonel Griffth were now with us, his signal would now be 'Carry on'. And in his spirit, we go forward."

Chapter Four:
Kings of the county

● *Reconstituted after the Great War, Fleet line up in 1920 in front of their grand and newly opened main stand. From left – Tiny Joyce, McDermid, Morrison, Billy Swayne, Vincent, Day, Barnfather, Daisley, O'Conor, George Harber, Barnett, Gilbert Aldous*

1919-1929

The guns had finally fallen silent in November 1918 but it would be 10 months before football was back on its feet and operating in a semblance of normality.

The 1918/19 'season', such as it was, continued the wartime policy of regionalising informal leagues as the bigger clubs played ad hoc fixtures with guest players starring for them.

For the likes of Northfleet and countless other non-league clubs around the country, there was no continuity to fall back on as the three- or four-year hiatus imposed by the war had taken its toll. Players were dispersed, wounded or killed, football grounds (as in the case of Gravesend United) comandeered by the military and, quite apart from the healing process required after four years of conflict, there was a Spanish flu pandemic to contend with.

For all that, the football authorities swung into gear for the 1919/20 season – and Northfleet, spearheaded as usual by Joe Lingham, answered the call of the Kent League.

There was a sense of unfinished business, with a new stand at Stonebridge Road waiting to see action and players such as Arthur Seccombe still young enough to fulfil the promise they had shown before 1914.

The roaring Twenties was a decade where Northfleet excelled, winning a record five Kent Senior Cups in succession, finished as Kent League champions on two occasions and returned – albeit briefly – to the Southern League.

It was a period that saw an abundance of Football League alumni ply their trade in North Kent and it heralded the beginning of a relationship with Tottenham Hotspur that would benefit both clubs in the decade that followed – and in Spurs' case, far beyond.

And through it all, Joe Lingham remained as he had through the 1890s and beyond the First World War, guiding his club and maintaining a watchful eye over the constant financial pressures that continued to engulf the Fleet from time to time.

1919/20

● *Resurrected once more, with a little help from Joe Lingham (far right). Players line up as follows: Evans, Arthur Seccombe, Dick Goad, George Green, John Geggus, Bill Lawrence, Makepiece, George Harber. Front row: Daisley, Fred Jewhurst, W Tyler (captain).*

After five years of enforced inactivity for the greater good, Fleet were back with a bang, winning the Kent League title in fine style and finishing runners-up in the Kent Senior Cup. The entertainment-starved citizens of North Kent came pouring down Stonebridge and Galley Hill to watch their heroes, with crowds averaging 3,500.

The club had reformed from its slumbers at a meeting on 7th May, 1919, at the Factory Club, Northfleet, with a meeting chaired by Joe Lingham. As one of the founders of the club 29 years earlier he was well aware of the financial pitfalls and laid his cards on the table at the start of the meeting. He stated that at least £1,500 would be needed together with an average gate of 2,500 if the club was to survive and prosper. He reported the club's existing assets amounted to one guinea and if they were to enter senior football for the upcoming 1919/20 season, they would need a minimum of £150 within days to repair and maintain the ground, buy new equipment and pay entry fees.

Two former players, Ned Shotton and Percy Terry, donated two guineas each and by the end of the meeting £80 had been donated with much more promised. The meeting ended with the re-election of Joe Lingham as chairman, Percy Neame as secretary and councillor Tom Church as president.

Six pre-war players returned to the club including captain Tyler and ace marksman Arthur Seccombe who, tragically, was to lead the Northfleet line without his brother, killed at Ypres in 1917. George Harber,

brother of Ernest who played in 1914, also signed. Goalkeeper John Geggus alongside Makepiece were both plucked from Gravesend, with the Shrimpers unable to resume playing having lost their Pelham Road ground to the War Ministry. They were unable to find alternative facilities and although Northfleet offered them ground-sharing facilities at Stonebridge Road, this was declined – mainly because Gravesend had no players and next to no officials either.

Fourteen clubs competed for the Kent League, including ambitious newcomers Charlton Athletic and old rivals Chatham, Maidstone, Sheppey and Sittingbourne.

Fleet began strongly with four straight league wins, scoring 16 goals, and they also battled through three rounds of the FA Cup before losing out at home to Sheppey by the odd goal in seven. Once again games were fiercely contested and in one match, Fred Jewhurst left the field at the final whistle aided by a walking stick. In another game, in a precursor of Manchester United's famous "grey shirts excuse", goalkeeper Geggus had to play in a vest after the opposition complained that his jersey was the same colour as their shirts, causing them much apparent confusion.

With a firm grip on the Kent League, a strong challenge was made for the blue riband of Kent football – the Senior Cup.

Having hammered Royal Ordnance in the opening round there was fierce controversy and plenty of ill will when Royal Artillery, drawn at home, were forced to switch the game to Northfleet by the KCFA because they did not have an enclosed ground available.

The army side threatened to pull out but begrudgingly turned up – not, however, before their captain delivered a letter of protest to the referee at kick-off. With the uncertainty over whether the game would actually go ahead, it was surprising that 4,000 attended the game, which was comfortably won by the Fleet.

The semi-final against Sittingbourne was played at The Valley, with Arthur Seccombe once again coming up trumps to score the only goal in front of 5,000 supporters. Alas, Maidstone – with home ground advantage – won the final 2-1. George Harber had given Fleet the lead but their cause was not aided by the sending-off of skipper Tyler (though by then the Stones had taken what proved to be a winning lead).

Despite this disappointment it had been a great season and it finished with a declared profit of £41 11s 10d. The Southern League authorities were impressed enough to invite the Fleet to enter the competition for the 1920/21 season but the club declined the offer, sensibly recalling the financial problems of their previous spell at that level.

● Above: an evocative scene from April 1920, of a friendly when Clapton Orient, then in the Football League Division Two, were the visitors and won 6-0. Again, the similarity with the modern day is striking, with supporters queuing in the same place against more or less the same backdrop. The queue, snaking up Stonebridge Hill, would not perhaps be quite so long for a friendly these days!

Below: Fleet supporters once again turned up en masse at Maidstone United's Athletic Ground for a Kent Senior Cup final against their county-town rivals. Skipper Tyler was sent off for Northfleet, who scored first courtesy of George Harber, but the Stones struck twice to deny the visitors. Fleet's Kent Senior Cup campaign drew four-figure crowds in each round as the public, hungry for entertainment after four dark years of war, eagerly sought local football

For results, see over page ➜

Results 1919/20

Aug 30	Shoeburyness Garrison	Friendly	home	0-1		
Sep 06	Sittingbourne	KL	home	4-1	Harber, Daisley, Makepiece, Seccombe	
13	RN Depot	KL	home	5-0	Seccombe 2, Jewhurst, Lavery, Daisley	
20	Gillingham Reserves	KL	away	3-2	Seccombe (pen), Lawrence, OG	
Oct 04	Catford Southend	FAC Pr	home	4-2	Makepiece, Seccombe, Tyler, Daisley	
11	Margate	FAC1Q	home	7-2	Jewhurst 2, Seccombe 2 (1pen), Daisley, Makepiece, Lawrence	
15	Gillingham Reserves	KSS1	away	1-2		
18	Sheppey United	KL	away	4-3	Daisley, Denny, Lawrence, Seccombe	
25	Royal Ordnance	FAC2Q	away	3-1	Lawrence, Seccombe, OG	3,000
Nov 01	Tunbridge Wells Rangers	KL	home	1-1	Makepiece	
08	Sheppey United	FAC3Q	home	3-4	Harber 2, Tyler	
15	Chatham	KL	away	3-2	Harber 2, Seccombe	
22	Maidstone United	KL	away	1-2	Carter	
29	RN Depot	KL	away	2-1	Seccombe, Lawrence	
Dec 06	Vickers Crayford	KL	away	3-0		
13	Maidstone United	KL	home	1-0	Harber	
20	Chatham	KL	home	1-0	Seccombe	
25	New Brompton	KL	home	7-2		
26	Gravesend League	Friendly	home	3-3		
27	Royal Ordnance	KL	away	2-2		
Jan 03	Royal Engineers	Friendly	home	1-2	Makepiece	
10	Charlton Athletic	KL	away	1-1	Evans	
17	Royal Ordnance	KSC1	home	6-1	Seccombe 2 (1 pen), Harber, Evans, Lawrence, Makepiece	
24	Royal Ordnance	KL	away	1-0	Lawrence	
31	Sittingbourne	KL	away	1-0	Lawrence	
Feb 07	Gillingham Reserves	KL	home	3-1	Seccombe 2, Lawrence	
14	RASC	KSC2	home	4-1	Lawrence, Seccombe, Daisley, Harber	
21	Sheppey United	KL	home	3-0	Makepiece 2, Lawrence	
28	RASC	KL	away	4-1		
Mar 06	Vickers Crayford	KL	home	4-0	Lawrence, Evans, Daisley, OG	
13	Sittingbourne	KSC SF	at Charlton	1-0	Seccombe	
20	Margate	KL	home	6-2	Lawrence 2, Harber, Seccombe, Evans, Makepiece	
27	Tunbridge Wells Rangers	KL	away	5-1	Lawrence, Rawlinson, Harber, Seccombe, OG	
Apr 03	Clapton Orient	Friendly	home	0-6		
05	Maidstone United	KSC Final	at Maidstone	1-2	Harber	
10	New Brompton	KL	away	6-0	Evans, Seccombe, Rawlinson, Makepiece, Harber, Tyler	
24	Charlton Athletic	KL	home	1-2	Seccombe	
May 01	Margate	KL	away	2-0		

● *Rewarded for the form that helped Northfleet to the Kent League title in 1920, Jewhurst, Makepiece and Tyler all got the opportunity to play at a higher level with Charlton Athletic in the Southern League in the following season*

1920/21

Fleet were unable to hold on to the Kent League title despite being in a strong position for most of the season. A 2-1 victory over Charlton before 7,000 people at Stonebridge Road appeared to have swung the title Fleet's way but a stutter in mid-April saw them pick up just one point from three games, including a narrow defeat at Charlton which handed the title to the Addicks, as the ambitious south London club moved ever closer to attaining Football League status.

Consolation came with a fourth victory in the Kent Senior Cup as Ramsgate were beaten 1-0 in front of a 10,000 crowd at Maidstone, the irrepressible Arthur Seccombe scoring a fine individual goal after 25 minutes to secure victory.

The team had also reached the final of the Kent Senior Shield – an invitation competition in which the KCFA requested eight teams to contest a trophy donated by Gravesend MP Sir Gilbert Parker. Fleet lost out 2-0 to Margate in a game played at neutral Chatham.

● *Being so close to the action is something that has made Stonebridge Road special down the years. Here, the not-so 'Tiny' Joyce, Fleet's goalkeeper, poses for a photograph right in front of supporters before a friendly with West Ham in March 1921. This is taken at what is now the Swanscombe End, though in those days was the Black Eagle end, with the pub of the same name just visible above the heads of fans to the upper left of the picture*

There had been wholesale changes within the playing staff during the close season with Fred Jewhurst (who would score at the first ever professional match at The Valley), Makepiece and Tyler all leaving for Charlton. Two other key forwards Lawrence (Ramsgate) and Evans (Sittingbourne) also departed, Lawrence eventually turning up at Dartford, while Seccombe was tempted by Millwall but stayed loyal to the Fleet despite a highly generous £6 a week offer.

He certainly had competition as top scorer with Arthur Layton signing from Clapton Orient and scoring an avalanche of goals. Other useful signings were full backs O'Conor (Maidstone) and Barnfather from Grays, while England amateur international centre half Billy Swayne signed from Tufnell Park. New goalkeeper 'Tiny' Joyce, standing well over six feet, proved equally adept.

Off the field, the magnificent new stand on the north side of the ground, stretching 190ft and with a capacity of 1,216, was given a grand official opening on 4th December, 1920, by Mrs Fehr, wife of the KCFA President (though it had been open to the paying public for a couple of months beforehand).

Hundreds of subscribers had provided suitable funding for the stand, which was built by Joe Lingham's building company. Two further tea huts and improvements to the terraces were funded by the newly formed Supporters Association, an idea Lingham had mooted in committee meetings prior to the First World War.

With crowds again averaging 3,500, a profit was once more recorded.

For results, see over page ➜

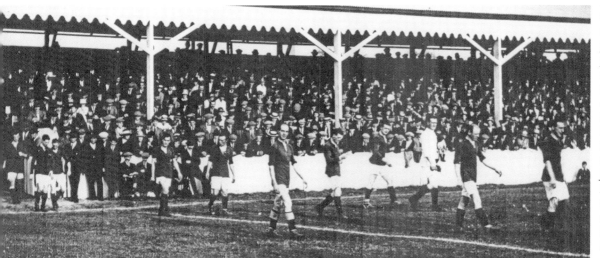

● *A scene repeated countless times over the past 100 years as the players emerge from the Stonebridge Road tunnel. This is from a 1920 game against Sheppey United. Players on show include Seccombe, Swayne, goalkeeper Joyce and Harber. Note the spectators at the rear of the stand, which went further back in those days and is now boarded off*

1920/21 (continued)

● Some never-before-published photographs of Northfleet at the beginning of the 1920s. The picture at the top shows a band entertaining the crowd, with the Northfleet End behind them. The Huggens College spire and The Plough are visible, in the days before terracing or cover of any sort was built there. Above is a similar scene in the corner, giving an unprecedented view of Stonebridge Hill and The Plough, from inside the ground. Nowadays this corner is the entrance from the turnstiles and the location of the toilet block. Both photos date from October 1920

Left: A rather murky photograph but it shows the first ever Fleet Supporters' Association, formed in 1920/21. The gentleman (presumably sitting) behind the shield appears oddly out of perspective with his colleagues!

Results 1920/21

Date		Opponent	Competition	Venue	Score	Scorers	Att
Aug 28		Shoeburyness Garrison	Friendly	home	**6-0**	Seccombe 3, Layton 2, Harber	
Sep 04		Folkestone	KL	away	**1-3**	Harber	
	11	Vickers Crayford	KL	home	**2-1**	Layton Seccombe	
	18	Folkestone	KL	home	**2-1**	Seccombe, Ing	
	25	Whitstable	FACPr	home	**6-2**	Seccombe 3, Layton 2, Harber	
	29	Maidstone United	KSS1	away	**1-0**	Harber	
Oct 02		Margate	KL	home	**4-1**	Barnett 3, Seccombe	
	09	Sheppey United	FAC1Q	home	**4-1**	Layton 2, Barnfather, Seccombe	4,290
	16	Bexleyheath Labour	KL	home	**7-0**	Layton 4, Seccombe, Barnett, Harber	
	23	Worthing	FAC2Q	away	**5-0**	Layton 3, Daisley (pen), Seccombe	
	27	Sheppey United	KSS SF	home	**3-1**		
	30	Tunbridge Wells Rangers	KL	away	**2-1**	Harber, Layton	
Nov 06		Maidstone United	FAC3Q	away	**0-5**		
	13	Sittingbourne	KL	home	**3-2**		
	20	Royal Marines	KL	away	**3-2**		
	27	Middlesex Regiment	KL	away	**5-0**		
Dec 04		Maidstone United	KL	home	**1-2**	Seccombe	3,000
	08	Margate	KSS Final	at Chatham	**0-2**		
	11	Maidstone United	KSC1	away	**1-0**	Barnfather	
	18	Chatham	KL	home	**1-1**	Layton	
	25	Royal Engineers Depot Battalion	KL	home	**10-0**	Layton 5, Morrison, Barnett, Daisley (pen), Harber, Seccombe	
	27	Gillingham Reserves	Friendly	home	**2-1**	Lewis, Rogers	
Jan 01		Sittingbourne	KL	away	**1-3**	Seccombe	
	08	Royal Marines	KL	home	**3-3**	Townrow, Seccombe, Layton	
	15	Middlesex Regiment	KL	home	**11-2**	Layton 5, Harber 3, Swayne, Miller, Ing	
	22	Margate	KSC2	away	**0-0**		
	26	Margate	KSC2 R	home	**3-2**	Daisley, Harber, Layton	2,591
	29	Royal Ordnance	KL	home	**3-0**	Barnett, Seccombe, Layton	
Feb 05		Chatham	KL	away	**1-2**	Daisley	
	12	Maidstone United	KL	away	**1-0**	Rogers	
	19	Sittingbourne	KSC SF	at Chatham	**2-0**	Barnett 2	5,693
	26	RN Depot	KL	away	**1-0**	Harber	
Mar 03		West Ham Reserves	Friendly	home	**4-3**	Day 2, McDermid, Harber	4,000
	09	Royal Engineers Depot Battalion	KL	away	**2-1**		
	12	Ashford Railway Works	KL	home	**2-0**	Barnett (pen), Vincent	
	19	Sheppey United	KL	away	**0-2**		
	25	Charlton Athletic	KL	home	**2-1**	Barnett, Layton	
	26	Vickers Crayford	KL	away	**5-1**	Aldous 2, Rogers, McDermid, Vincent	
	28	Ramsgate	KSC Final	at Maidstone	**1-0**	Seccombe	10,000
Apr 02		Ashford Railway Works	KL	away	**2-1**	Barnett, Day	
	09	Sheppey United	KL	home	**5-1**	Seccombe 4, Vincent	
	11	Royal Ordnance	KL	away	**2-0**	Day, Barnett	
	16	Bexleyheath Labour	KL	away	**1-0**	Barnett	
	23	Ramsgate	KL	away	**1-1**	Barnett	
	25	Charlton Athletic	KL	away	**0-2**		
	27	Ramsgate	KL	home	**1-2**	Daisley	
	30	Tunbridge Wells Rangers	KL	home	**2-1**	Seccombe, Barnett	
May 02		RN Depot	KL	home	**5-2**	Seccombe 2, Caller, Harber, Vincent	4,000
	07	Margate	KL	away	**0-1**		

1921/22

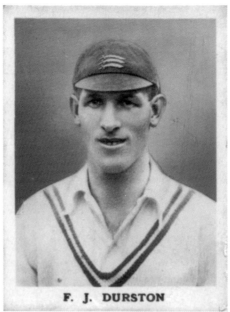

F. J. DURSTON

● *Newcomers in the 1921/22 season, above from left – Bert Goodman from Margate, who had previously played for Tottenham; giant goalkeeper Jack Durston, here in the garb of a Middlesex county cricketer; and another cricketer, Harry Howell (Warwickshire) – two of a number of Northfleet players who excelled at both sports*

Left: the 1921/22 team with more off-field staff than players! The names (players only) are... Middle row: W Hardy, L Gardner, P Keene Front row: E O'Connor, Fred Barnett, Arthur Seccombe, Arthur Layton, C Venables, Bill Channell, C Daisley, Billy Swayne

It was another solid season for the Fleet, though on this occasion minus the return of any silverware. The club finished as runners-up in both the Kent League and Kent Senior Shield, whilst also enjoying their longest ever run in the FA Cup, reaching the fifth and final qualifying round (a stage that was discontinued after a major revamp of the great competition in 1925).

The prospect of defending their Kent League title was never going to be easy once Maidstone United declared their intentions by signing up a string of Football League players and giving them 'jobs' in the local Sharps Toffee factory (where the owner also happened to be chairman of the club).

Fleet made several new signings, the most notable being goalkeeper Jack Durston who at 6ft 5in was even taller than the goalkeeper he replaced – 'Tiny' Joyce.

Durston was not only an outstanding goalkeeper, having previously played at Brentford and QPR, but an excellent cricketer who won the county championship

with Middlesex in both 1920 and 1921 and gained an England appearance as a fast bowler against Australia in 1921.

Other newcomers were Bert Goodman (Margate), Dilley (Reading) and Keene (Maidstone), while further enhancements were made to the ground courtesy of improved terracing behind the Northfleet End goal, extending the capacity there by a further 1,500.

Despite the new players, no-one was able to stop the Stones romping to the treble of Kent League, Kent Senior Cup and Kent Senior Shield with a wage bill far higher than their rivals.

The boom years after the end of the war were now over and crowds everywhere were down – not helped by the election of Charlton Athletic to the Football League. Of the Kent clubs, only Northfleet finished in the black thanks to the foresight of their management committee and they ended the season with a balance of £25 2s 6d.

One boost was the return of old rivals

Dartford who, having disbanded in 1914, were now back at a new ground at Watling Street and a point there in the final game of the season secured the Kent League runners-up spot for Fleet.

The roots of a relationship with Tottenham that would emerge in full the following season, were put in place in March 1922 when Northfleet attempted to recruit Spurs' reserve full back Jimmy Ross from White Hart Lane as manager.

Northfleet offered terms of £8 per week, suggesting that £1 of this might be paid by Spurs in return for their having first call on any Fleet players over a three-year period. The offer was rejected but, together with a game against Tottenham reserves in April, the two clubs were warming to one another.

For the second season in succession, Fleet finished as runners-up in the Kent Senior Shield, where an unfortunate own goal from Daisley proved vital in a narrow 2-1 defeat.

Results 1921/22

Date	Opponent	Comp	Venue	Score	Scorers	Att
Aug 27	Ramsgate	KL	home	2-2	Layton (pen), Seccombe	
Sep 03	Tunbridge Wells Rangers	KL	away	3-2	Dilley 2, Layton	
10	Chatham	KL	home	1-1	Howell	
17	Folkestone	KL	away	2-1	Seccombe, Howell	
24	Shoreham	FAC Pr	away	6-0	Seccombe 3, Howell, Barnett, Layton	700
28	Margate	KSS1	home	4-1	Barnett 2, Layton, Seccombe (pen)	2,500
Oct 01	Folkestone	KL	home	3-1	Howell 2, Seccombe	
08	Margate	FAC1Q	away	1-0	Keene	
15	Margate	KL	home	1-3	Dilley	
22	Folkestone	FAC2Q	home	4-2	Seccombe 2 pens, Howell 2	
26	Folkestone	KSS SF	home	3-1	Swayne, Keene, Layton	
29	Dartford	KL	home	3-0	Howell 2, Seccombe (pen)	
Nov 05	Chatham	FAC3Q	away	3-0	Barnett, Howell, Layton	4,900
12	RMLI	KL	home	4-0	Seccombe 2, Barnett 2	
19	Guildford United	FAC 4Q	home	1-0	Layton	5,000
26	Sittingbourne	KL	home	0-0		
Dec 03	Gillingham	FAC5Q	home	0-0		
07	Gillingham	FAC5Q R	away	1-3	Seccombe	6,000
10	Ashford RW	KSC1	away	2-3	Howell 2	
17	Bexleyheath	KL	away	3-0	Howell 2, Layton	
24	Maidstone United	KSS Final	away	1-2	Layton	
26	Dartford	Friendly	home	1-3	Gibbon	3000
27	Dartford	Friendly	away	0-0		
31	Maidstone United	KL	away	1-8	Layton	
Jan 07	RN Depot	KL	home	2-1	Venables, Seccombe (pen)	
14	RN Depot	KL	away	3-0	Layton 2, Howell	
21	Chatham	KL	away	1-1	Howell	
28	Crystal Palace Reserves	Friendly	home	1-2	Layton	
Feb 04	Ashford Railway Works	KL	home	5-1	Seccombe 3, Venables, Layton	
11	Sheppey United	KL	home	2-2	Layton, Seccombe	
18	Ramsgate	KL	away	2-1	Howell, OG	
25	Sheppey United	KL	away	2-1	Layton, Venables	
Mar 04	RMLI	KL	away	3-2	Venables 2, OG	
11	Ashford Railway Works	KL	away	1-1	Layton	
18	Bexleyheath	KL	home	7-1	Seccombe 3, Layton, Daisley, Barnett, Venables	3,000
25	West Norwood	Friendly	away	3-1	Swayne, Howell, Layton	
Apr 01	Maidstone United	KL	home	0-2		
05	Sittingbourne	KL	away	1-0	Layton	
08	Tottenham Hotspurs Reserves	Friendly	home	5-3	Seccombe 2, Layton, Howell, Barnett	
14	Custom House	Friendly	home	2-0	Howell 2	2,000
15	Tunbridge Wells Rangers	KL	home	4-0	Seccombe 2, Barnett, Evans	
17	Woolwich	KL	home	6-0	Channell 3, Layton 2, Seccombe	
22	Margate	KL	away	0-1		
29	Sittingbourne	KL	home	4-0	Channell, Barnett, Howell, Secombe	
30	Woolwich	KL	away	4-2	Layton 2, Seccombe 2	
May 06	Dartford	KL	away	2-2	Venables, Seccombe (pen)	

1922/23

When Joe Lingham stood up to address the AGM of the football club on 7th July, 1922, at the Factory Club, he had a surprise awaiting the 200-plus audience.

For the first time the club were to appoint a manager to run team matters rather than the committee which had been used throughout the club's history – which now stretched back 32 years.

The man appointed to bring more success to the club was Bert Lipsham, a former winger for Sheffield United with whom he won the 1902 FA Cup Final. He was also an ex-England international who had managed Millwall between 1911 and 1918.

The fact that Mr Lingham also announced a reduction in the wage bill of one third didn't seem to dampen the enthusiasm of the meeting. This harsh decision was necessitated by falling gates across the country since the immediate post-war years – times were tough, unemployment was rising, money was short and Joe Public was feeling the financial pinch.

Lipsham made a few new signings – the most notable were goalkeeper McKee who arrived from Grays, George Grant (from QPR, who had also played for Arsenal) at full back and forward Stan Sayer from Lipsham's old team Millwall. Former Olympic champion, Manchester City and Reading player Ted Hanney also finished his career at Stonebridge Road.

An excellent start was made with a 6-1 drubbing of Tunbridge Wells Rangers and by mid-October the team was undefeated. This ended at Botany Road, Sheerness, where old rivals Sheppey United lowered our colours 2-0 and this defeat was quickly followed by exits from the FA Cup and Kent Senior Shield as well.

Optimism soon began to wane and whispers began about Lipsham's managerial policy of picking his favourites. The mood was not helped by successive 1-0 defeats to the old enemy Dartford over Christmas, although it lightened with a 9-0 win over wooden spoonists Woolwich in the last game of 1922.

The New Year began poorly with two more cup exits in the Kent Senior Cup and Chatham Charity Cup. The big test came with the visit of league leaders Maidstone

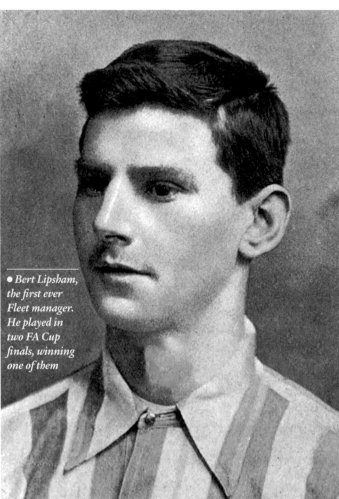

● *Bert Lipsham, the first ever Fleet manager. He played in two FA Cup finals, winning one of them*

● *Left: Tottenham manager Peter McWilliam who would bring through plenty of players from the Northfleet nursery, including Ted Ditchburn*

United who were once again dominating amid much disquiet from their rivals. As a result, some clubs proposed the maximum wage should be £2 a week and that all teams should field three amateurs – but the FA threw out the proposals.

Maidstone were still backed by Sharps Toffees, where Mr Henry Sharp was chairman of both the club and the company. At the end of the season the company withdrew their funding but it didn't stop Maidstone once more confirming their superiority with a 3-0 victory at Stonebridge Road.

Following another uninspiring performance in a 1-1 draw with the Royal Marines, Northfleet decided to terminate the manager's contract on 12th February, 1923,

● *Fred Barnett – the first main link between Northfleet and Tottenham in a relationship that would really blossom*

and return to the old way of a management committee running the club.

The first priority was the serious financial situation brought about by a lack of cup success, in turn reducing the crowds, and also the paying-off of Lipsham. It befell the usual benefactors – Messers Lingham, Gunn, Hardy and Sargeant – to provide a four-figure fee to keep the club going.

Then came an incident that would transform the entire club when Tottenham came in to sign Fleet winger Fred Barnett (he had impressed by scoring both goals in a victory over a Tottenham reserve team). The two clubs had always enjoyed a good relationship going right back to the time they were rivals in the Southern League and cordial discussions between Joe Lingham and Tottenham manager Peter McWilliam arrived at an agreement that would be mutually beneficial to both clubs.

It was agreed that Spurs would begin to send promising youngsters to Stonebridge Road to sharpen and toughen them up for the hurly burly of Kent League football (which was still one of the top non-league competitions in the country), while at the same time strengthening the Fleet squad.

In the meantime results gradually improved with the dressing room now seemingly more settled.

But silly points were still being dropped, none more so than in the 2-2 home draw with Margate in which Fleet managed to miss three penalties, all taken by different players. One missed the goal and the other two were saved by the Gate goalkeeper, though both were poorly taken according to contempary reports.

Fleet ended the Kent League season in fourth position and looked forward to the new season and their new connection with Tottenham Hotspur.

Results 1922/23

Aug 26	Shoeburyness Garrison	Friendly	home	**6-1**	Barnett 2, Weston 2, Sayer, Houston	
Sep 02	Tunbridge Wells Rangers	KL	home	**6-1**	Seccombe 2, Weston 2, Sayer, OG	
09	RN Depot	KL	away	**3-1**	Sayer, Weston, OG	
16	Grays Athletic	Friendly	home	**1-1**		
23	Folkestone	FACP	away	**3-3**	Weston 2, Sayer	
27	Folkestone	FACPr R	home	**4-1 (aet)**	Houston 2, Sayer, Weston	
30	RMLI	CCC1	home	**2-1**	Sayer, Weston	2,000
Oct 04	Maidstone United	KSS1	home	**1-1**	Houston	
07	Chatham	FAC 1Q	home	**0-0**		
11	Chatham	FAC 1QR	away	**3-1**	Weston 3 (1 pen)	
14	Sheppey United	KL	away	**0-2**		
21	Sittingbourne	FAC 2Q	away	**0-2**		
28	RMLI	KL	home	**5-1**	Sayer 2, Weston 2, Seccombe	
Nov 01	Maidstone United	KSS1 R	away	**0-1**		
04	Ramsgate	KL	away	**3-1**	Sayer, Weston, Hanney	
11	Sittingbourne	KL	away	**0-0**		
18	Bexleyheath	KL	away	**2-1**	Weston (pen), Sayer	
25	Tunbridge Wells Rangers	KSC1	away	**2-0**	Houston, Sayer	
Dec 02	Tunbridge Wells Rangers	KL	away	**1-2**	Sayer	
09	Folkestone	KL	home	**1-1***	* abandoned 45 minutes bad light	
16	Tottenham Hotspurs Reserves	Friendly	home	**2-0**	Barnett 2	
23	Chatham	KL	away	**2-2**		
25	Dartford	KL	home	**0-1**		
26	Dartford	KL	away	**0-1**		
30	Woolwich	KL	home	**9-0**	Houston 3, Hanney 2, Barnett 2 (1 pen), Crane, Sayer	
Jan 06	Ashford Railway Works	KL	home	**2-2**	Weston, Hall	2.000
13	Sittingbourne	KSC2	away	**1-2**	Houston	2,500
20	Chatham	CCC SF	home	**0-1**		
27	Sheppey United	KL	home	**3-1**	Barnett 3	
Feb 03	Maidstone United	KL	home	**0-3**		
10	RMLI	KL	away	**1-1**	King	
17	Arsenal Reserves	Friendly	home	**4-2**	King, Houston, Pilcher, OG	
24	Gillingham Reserves	KL	away	**1-3**		
Mar 03	Chatham	KL	home	**5-0**	Pilcher 2, McDonald, King (pen), Weston	
07	Folkestone	KL	home	**1-3**		
10	Maidstone United	KL	away	**1-2**	McDonald	
17	Bexleyheath	KL	home	**5-2**	Chipperfield 3, Houston, Bell (pen)	
21	Erith & Belvedere	KL	home	**4-0**	Bell 2, Houston, Pash	
24	Margate	KL	home	**2-2**	Bell, Houston	
30	Dartford	Friendly	home	**4-1**	Pilcher 2, Weston (pen), Seccombe	
31	RN Depot	KL	home	**9-0**	Weston 4, Bell 3, Chipperfield 2	
Apr 02	Dartford	KL	away	**2-2**	Bell, Chipperfield	
07	Gillingham Reserves	KL	home	**6-0**	Chipperfield 2, Seccombe 2, Houston 2	
11	Woolwich	KL	away	**5-1**	Houston 2, Seccombe, Weston, Bell	
14	Erith & Belvedere	KL	away	**1-0**	Chipperfield	
18	Sittingbourne	KL	home	**2-0**	Weston, Seccombe (pen)	
21	Tottenham Reserves	Friendly	home	**2-0**	Seccombe 2	
21	Ashford Railway Works	KL	away	**1-5**	McDonald (pen)	
23	Folkestone	KL	away	**0-1**		
28	Ramsgate	KL	home	**4-1**	Houston 3, Pilcher	
May 05	Margate	KL	away	**3-1**		

1923/24

Two trophies won and another shared gave evidence of a highly successful season on the cup front, while in the Kent League fourth place was attained.

Despite the new agreement with Tottenham, only one player was sent down for the start of the new season – centre half Harry Skitt. He proved to be an excellent signing; commanding in defence and also capable of scoring vital goals, it was no surprise when he was called back to White Hart Lane at the end of the season. He established himself in the Spurs first team the following season, playing the first of more than 200 games for Spurs. Other newcomers were local youngsters goalkeeper Joe Hill and forward Jimmy Bell, along with Folkestone centre forward Ted Goldsmith.

The Kent League season got off to a modest start, with Fleet losing three of the first four games and they were soon out of the FA Cup, too, losing surprisingly at Ramsgate. Charlton had returned to the Kent League with a strong reserve side and swiftly took an iron grip on the championship, leaving Northfleet to concentrate on their other cup commitments – a policy that would prove fruitful. Soon after the turn of the year, Fleet obtained a second Tottenham player in Bill Lane, a bustling centre forward who would quickly make his mark – and 40 years later would return to manage Gravesend & Northfleet.

In the Kent Senior Cup Chatham, Ashford and Sittingbourne were swept away and Dartford were beaten in the final thanks to a sixth-minute Goldsmith goal in front of an 8,000 crowd at Maidstone.

A week later Fleet were attempting to add the Kent Senior Shield against Gillingham, having already seen off RN Depot and Sittingbourne. And although Fleet lost 3-2 to Charlton in an ill-tempered game which featured a full-scale punch-up between players and spectators (after Fleet favourite Arthur Seccombe had been badly fouled by a Charlton defender), the Addicks were thrown out of the competition for fielding an ineligible player. Fleet won the toss for home advantage in the final but neither side managed a goal after 120 minutes and the teams agreed to share the Shield.

● *Above: Bill Lane represented Northfleet and Gravesend either side of a long Football League career. He was back at Stonebridge Road as manager in 1961 and guided Fleet to their best ever FA Cup run in 1963 Inset: Harry Skitt was the first in a long line of successful – albeit temporary – Tottenham exports*

H. Skitt

Fleet's third final of the season was again at Stonebridge Road in the inaugural Kent League Cup, with Dartford, RN Depot and Sittingbourne having been despatched along the way.

Fleet faced Ashford Railway Works and two Jimmy Bell goals proved enough. In each final Fleet had also had the luxury of missing penalties, Skitt being the culprit in this particular match.

Although Tottenham had sent only two players down to Northfleet, both Lane and Skitt had proved valuable signings. Sadly, neither would play in the red shirt again as both moved back to Tottenham to make their mark in the Football League.

Results 1923/24

Date	Opponent	Comp	Venue	Score	Scorers	Att
Aug 25	Erith & Belvedere	KL	away	**4-2**	Bell 2, Seccombe, Pilcher	
Sep 01	Charlton Reserves	KL	home	**0-1**		
08	Chatham	KL	away	**0-1**		
15	Sittingbourne	KL	home	**0-2**		
22	Sheppey United	FACPr	home	**2-2**	Pilcher, Bell	
26	Sheppey United	FACPr R	away	**4-3**	Skitt 2, Bell, Lohse	
29	Erith & Belvedere	KL	home	**1-0**	Lohse	
Oct 06	Ramsgate	FAC1Q	away	**2-4**		
13	Gillingham Reserves	KL	away	**3-2**	Houston 2, Pilcher	3,000
20	Gillingham Reserves	KL	home	**4-0**	Goldsmith, Skitt, Houston, Pilcher	2,800
27	Maidstone United	KL	home	**4-0**	Bell 2, Houston 2	3,000
Nov 03	Ashford Railway Works	KL	away	**2-2**	Bell, Skitt (pen)	
07	RN Depot	KSS1	home	**3-1**	Houston 2, Pilcher	
10	Tottenham Reserves	Friendly	home	**3-1**	Houston 2, Pilcher	
14	Chatham	CCC1	home	**0-0**		
17	Sheppey United	KL	home	**2-0**	Goldsmith 2	
24	Chatham	KSC1	home	**0-0**		
Dec 01	Chatham	KSC1 R	away	**5-1**	Goldsmith 2, Houston 2, Seccombe	
08	Tunbridge Wells Rangers	KL	away	**1-2**	Skitt	
15	Charlton Reserves	KSS2	home	**0-0**		
22	Tunbridge Wells Rangers	KL	home	**1-0**	Seccombe	
25	Dartford	Friendly	home	**1-1**	Bell	
26	Dartford	KLC1	away	**1-0**	OG	
29	Woolwich	KL	away	**0-1**		
Jan 05	Woolwich	KL	home	**4-0**	Lane, Seccombe, Skitt, Smith	
12	Ashford Railway Works	KSC2	home	**5-0**	Bell 2, Seccombe 2, Lane	
19	Bexleyheath Town	KL	away	**6-0**	Parsons 3, Seccombe 2, Goldsmith	
26	Charlton Reserves	KL	away	**1-1**	Parsons	
Feb 02	Ashford Railway Works	KL	home	**4-3**	Lane 2, Skitt (pen), Houston	
09	Sittingbourne	KL	away	**2-0**	Bell, Lane	
16	Sittingbourne	KSC SF	at Chatham	**2-2**	Lane, Bell	5,000
23	Chatham	CCC1 R	away	**1-3**	Garmonsway	
27	Sittingbourne	KSC SF R	at Chatham	**2-0**		
Mar 01	Chatham	KL	home	**3-3**	Lane, Smith, Skitt	
05	Charlton Reserves	KSS2 R	away	**2-3***	Pilcher, Lane *Charlton expelled, fielded ineligible player*	
08	Sheppey United	KL	away	**1-1**	Lane	
15	Ramsgate Athletic	KL	away	**1-2**	Bell	
22	Ramsgate Athletic	KL	home	**6-1**	Bell 2, Lane 2, Goldsmith, Pilcher	
26	RMLI	KL	away	**2-0**	Bell, Lane	
29	RN Depot	KL	home	**4-0**	Lane 2, Seccombe 2	
Apr 05	RMLI	KL	home	**2-0**	Bell, Lane	
09	Sittingbourne	KSS SF	home	**2-1**	Lane 2	
12	RN Depot	KLC2	home	**6-1**	Lane 4, Todd, Seccombe	
18	Dartford	KL	home	**0-2**		
19	Bexleyheath Town	KL	home	**1-2**	Lane	
21	Dartford	KSC Final	at Maidstone	**1-0**	Goldsmith	8,000
26	RN Depot	KL	away	**1-1**	Pilcher	
28	Gillingham	KSS Final	home	**0-0**		
May 01	Sittingbourne	KLC SF	home	**4-2**	Lane 2, Seccombe, Goldsmith	
02	Ashford Railway Works	KLC Final	home	**2-0**	Bell 2	
03	Dartford	KL	away	**0-4**		

1924/25

● *Northfleet assembled another impressive side for the 1924/25 season, which enjoyed a run of 30 wins in 31 matches. Back row, from left – W Treadwell, A Neame, L Gardner, W Watt, S Todd, S Sargeant (in bowler hat), J Richardson, G Pleasants, W Goodman, S Bailey, J Pye, G Grant, W Hardy, J Lingham. Front row – S Mulford, W Gray, W Pilcher, T Roe, A Sanders, B Houston, J Bell, A Seccombe*

Slate grey skies and pouring rain greeted the annual trial match between the reds and whites (as the two competing sides were traditionally known) which ended in a highly competitive 2-2 draw – and generated hopes that were far brighter than the gloomy weather.

As Harry Skitt and Bill Lane returned to White Hart Lane after successful seasons in Fleet colours, they were replaced by Jock Richardson and Tommy Roe who would prove to be equally productive. Two more excellent signings were goalkeeper George Pleasants from Charlton and Tommy Pye, a solid centre half from Fulham. Forwards Arthur Sanders from Fletton United and Sid Mulford from Brentford added firepower to the attack.

Arthur Seccombe, now in his 14th season at Stonebridge Road, was appointed captain and it was a memorable one for him. He made history by being the first player to score direct from a corner kick following the end of the FA rule that a goal could not

be awarded in such a manner. And later in the season he would score the club's 100th league goal as they went on to shatter the Kent League record of 102 goals by chalking up 114.

Fleet had started well with a 5-1 thrashing of a Maidstone side now shorn of their benefactors' cash but were unlucky to make an early FA Cup exit when coming up against the eventual Kent League champions Chatham. A further blow came with an early exit from the Kent League Cup after a disappointing home defeat by Sheppey. However, this heralded the start of a remarkable run from the middle of November as the team really began to click, winning eight successive games including crushing victories over Dartford at Christmas, before the festive season ended with a reverse once again at the hands of Chatham (the third game in as many days).

As before, this defeat heralded another fantastic run, this time of 22 successive league and cup victories. This run would

bring victory in both the Kent Senior Cup and Kent Senior Shield but despite a fantastic 30 wins in 31 matches, it wasn't enough to overcome Chatham for the Kent League title and Fleet had to settle for second place.

One particular highlight was the Kent Senior Cup semi-final against Grays Thurrock in February which was filmed and shown in the Gem Cinema in Gravesend for the whole of the following week. The 6-0 win earned Northfleet yet another final.

And the final victory over Sittingbourne in April in front of 12,000 people at Maidstone was very impressive. With the half-time score at a stalemate of 2-2, Fleet powered to an 8-2 victory after a stunning second-half display. They then completed a silverware double when overcoming the formidable Chatham side in the Shield final at Dartford, winning 1-0 thanks to a 72nd minute Jimmy Bell goal.

Once again the team had given their supporters a season to remember.

Results 1924/25

Date	Opponent	Competition	Venue	Score	Scorers	Attendance
Aug 30	Maidstone United	KL	home	5-1	Mulford 2, Bell, Pilcher, Roe (pen)	
Sep 06	Ashford Railway Works	FAC Pr	away	3-1	Roe 3	
13	Sittingbourne	KL	away	1-3	Roe	
20	Chatham	FAC1Q	away	2-3	Bell, OG	
27	Sittingbourne	KL	home	1-0	Seccombe	
Oct 04	Gillingham Reserves	KL	away	2-0	Seccombe, Bell	
11	Margate	KL	home	8-2	Roe 4, Bell 3, Mulford	
18	Sheppey United	KL	home	1-2	Pilcher	
25	Catford Southend	KL	home	3-2	Roe 2, Pilcher	
Nov 01	Arsenal Reserves	Friendly	home	0-1		
08	Sheppey United	KLC1	home	1-3	Bell	
15	Maidstone United	KL	away	2-0	Pilcher, Bell	
22	Grays Thurrock United	KL	home	4-1	Pilcher 2, Sanders, Seccombe	
29	Chatham	KL	home	3-0	Pilcher 2, Sanders	
Dec 06	Cray Wanderers	KSC1	away	5-0	Sanders 2, Pilcher 2, Mulford	
13	Grays Thurrock United	KL	away	4-0	Pilcher 2, Roe, Bell	
20	RN Depot	KL	home	2-1		
25	Dartford	KL	home	5-0	Roe 3 (2 pens), Sanders, Pilcher	6,000
26	Dartford	KL	away	4-1	Sanders 2, Seccombe, Pilcher	7,500
27	Chatham	KL	away	1-3	Bell	
Jan 03	Woolwich	KL	home	6-0	Roe 3, Sanders 2, Bell	
10	Ashford Railway Works	KL	away	5-2	Bell 3, Roe, Sanders	
17	Royal Marines	KL	home	7-0	Roe 3, Bell 2, Sanders, Pilcher	
24	Sheppey United	KSC2	home	2-1	Seccombe, Bell	
31	Bexleyheath Town	KL	home	4-0	Roe 2, Sanders, Bell	
Feb 07	Erith & Belvedere	KL	away	2-1	Roe, Bell	
14	Charlton Reserves	KSS SF	home	2-1	Pilcher 2	
21	Grays Thurrock United	KSC SF	at Dartford	6-0	Sanders 2, Roe 2, Bell, OG	6,000
28	Tunbridge Wells Rangers	KL	home	4-0	Sanders 2 (1 pen), Houston, Seccombe	
Mar 07	Woolwich	KL	away	5-0	Roe 3, Sanders 2	
11	Tunbridge Wells Rangers	KL	away	5-0	Bell 3, Sanders 2	
14	Erith & Belvedere	KL	home	5-0	Bell 2, Pilcher, Roe, Seccombe	
19	Catford Southend	KL	away	3-0	Pye, Bell, Roe	
21	RN Depot	KL	away	3-1	Sanders 3	
28	Gillingham Reserves	KL	home	3-1	Bell 2, Pye	
Apr 04	Sheppey United	KL	away	3-0	Bell, Seccombe, Sanders	
10	Grays Athletic	KL	home	2-0	Bell 2	
11	Bexleyheath Town	KL	away	3-0	Sanders 2, Bell	
13	Sittingbourne	KSC Final	at Maidstone	8-2	Bell 3, Roe 2 (1 pen), Sanders 2, Pye	12,000
18	Royal Marines	KL	away	2-0	Mulford, Sanders	
22	Chatham	KSS Final	at Dartford	1-0	Bell	
25	Ashford Railway Works	KL	home	3-0	Bell 3	
29	Grays Athletic	KL	away	1-2	Pilcher	
May 02	Margate	KL	away	2-2	Sanders, Roe	

● *Spurs' youngsters Tommy Roe and Jock Richardson slotted into the gaps left by Bill Lane and Harry Skitt on their return to White Hart Lane*

1925/26

● Newcomers in 1925 – two more from Spurs in Arthur Rowe (left), a future Tottenham manager, and Eugene 'Taffy' O'Callaghan (centre), who would win caps for Wales. Charlie Alton (right), Brentford's former skipper, was also lured to Stonebridge Road

This was a stunning season in which the Fleet scored an incredible 217 goals in 50 matches, including friendlies. The team won the Kent League, Kent Senior Cup and were finalists in the Kent Senior Shield – the final to be held over into the 1926/27 season.

The season began once again under grey skies and pouring rain for the traditional reds versus whites trial game which ended in a thrilling 4-4 draw in which the quality of play greatly impressed the locals.

Tottenham had recalled both defender Jock Richardson and impressive frontman Tommy Roe and sent down two more raw recruits in Arthur Rowe, a right half, and Eugene "Taffy" O'Callaghan, a twinkle-toed inside forward who would go on to play international football for Wales. Rowe, meanwhile, would become a White Hart Lane legend a quarter of a century later by managing the team that were Football League champions for the first time in their history – something repeated by another Fleet and Spurs legend, Bill Nicholson, 10 years later.

Another useful signing was full back Charlie Alton, who had been Brentford's captain the previous season.

The Kent League season began in sensational style with a crushing 16-1 victory over Royal Navy Depot – one of three double-figure victories, although the navy boys gained a measure of revenge by inflicting one of only four league defeats on Fleet later in the season. The five forwards all got on target in the navy game and a forward line-up of Pilcher, O'Callaghan, Sanders, Bell and Seccombe brought fear to any defence. By the end of the season they had amassed 182 goals in all games between them.

A new ruling on the offside law certainly helped the goal glut, reducing from three to two the number of defenders needed in front

of a forward to render him offside.

The fact the Fleet were given exemption into the First Round proper of the FA Cup for the first time helped the club take a firm grip on the league. As their rivals battled through the early qualifying rounds of the competition, the Fleet were able to get league games played and points under their belt.

Meanwhile, progress was made in other cup competitions with Charlton beaten in the Kent Senior Shield, despite fielding nine of the team that had played in their last Football League game. The Fleet also moved remorselessly towards a third successive Kent Senior Cup with victories over Grays Thurrock, Sheppey and Chatham, before victory in the final over Folkestone where, fittingly, Arthur Seccombe scored the only goal.

Despite giving them two hard games, Fleet were unable to get the better of QPR in the FA Cup but continued to carry all before them in the league, bringing up a century of goals in only the 19th league game on their way to breaking their own goal record with 172.

As the goals continued to hit the back of the net, Ashford Railway Works decided on a tactic used by many before and since – intimidation. A series of brutal tackles forced O'Callaghan, Pilcher and Sanders off the field at various times which left the Stonebridge Road faithful furious. Sadly for Taffy O'Callaghan it was the end of his road as a Fleet player after he suffered a dislocated shoulder in the 3-1 victory... but not before he scored his 46th goal of the season prior to returning to White Hart Lane. That strike rate just pipped Bell on 41, while Sanders scored 36, Pilcher 32 and Seccombe 27. Cook on nine was the next highest.

Despite the success, Fleet were unable to shake off the determined challenge of old rivals Chatham until the penultimate game at Erith, where a 2-1 victory put the title beyond the reach of their rivals.

It was appropriate that the final game of the season was at Margate and their venue at the Dreamland ground because it had indeed been a season of dreams for the club

● Margate's home at Dreamland, with their pitch to the right of this photograph

Results 1925/26

Aug 29	Shoeburyness Garrison	Friendly	home	4-3	Bell, Pilcher, Sanders, Houston	
Sep 05	RN Depot	KL	home	16-1	O'Callaghan 4, Bell 4, Seccombe 3, Pilcher 2, Sanders, Pye, OG	
12	Woolwich	KL	home	4-0	Sanders 2, Bell, O'Callaghan	
19	Peterborough & Fletton United	Friendly	home	4-0	Houston, Pilcher, Bell, Seccombe	
26	Dartford	Friendly	away	2-1	Sanders, Pilcher (pen)	
Oct 03	Erith & Belvedere	KL	home	4-1	Todd 4	
10	Sittingbourne	KL	away	0-3		
17	Sittingbourne	KL	home	2-1	Pilcher 2	
24	Woolwich	KL	away	9-2	Seccombe 3, Bell 2, O'Callaghan 2, Houston, Sanders	
31	Bexleyheath Town	KL	home	5-2	O'Callaghan 2, Pilcher 2, Seccombe	
Nov 02	Charlton Athletic	KSS1	away	2-1	O'Callaghan, Bell	
07	Ashford Railway Works	KL	away	10-4	Seccombe 3, Pilcher 2, Bell 2, O'Callaghan 2, Sanders	
12	Catford Southend	KLC1	home	2-1	Pilcher 2	
14	Margate	KL	home	1-0	Sanders	
21	Sheppey United	KL	away	8-1	Pilcher 2, Bell 2, Seccombe 2, Sanders , OG	
28	Queens Park Rangers	FAC1	home	2-2	Pilcher 2	
Dec 03	Queens Park Rangers	FAC1 R	away	0-2		7,000
05	Grays Thurrock United	KSC1	home	6-2	O'Callaghan 2, Pilcher 2, Seccombe, Sanders	
12	Gillingham Reserves	KL	home	3-1	O'Callaghan 2 Sanders	
19	Grays Athletic	KL	home	4-2	Bell, Alton (pen), O'Callaghan, Sanders	
25	Dartford	KL	home	6-1	Sanders 3, O'Callaghan 2, Seccombe	
26	Dartford	KL	away	2-2	Bell, Houston	
28	Maidstone United	KL	away	6-0	Seccombe 2, Rowe, O'Callaghan, Bell, Sanders	
Jan 02	Gillingham Reserves	KL	away	7-1	Seccombe 2, Sanders 2, Bell 2, O'Callaghan	
06	Folkestone	KSS2	home	4-2	Pilcher 2, Sanders 2	
09	Sheppey United	KL	home	1-1	Bell	
16	Catford Southend	KL	away	4-3	Bell 2, Sanders 2	
23	Sheppey United	KSC2	home	7-1	Sanders 2, O'Callaghan 2, Bell, Pilcher, Seccombe	
30	Grays Thurrock United	KL	home	8-1	Sanders 3, Seccombe, Alton (pen), Bell, Pilcher, O'Callaghan	
Feb 06	Maidstone United	KL	home	9-0	O'Callaghan 4, Clark 3, Bell, Houston	
13	RN Depot	KL	away	1-2	Sanders	
20	Chatham	KSC SF	home	4-1	Bell 2, Sanders 2	6,000
24	Dartford	KLC2	home	1-2	O'Callaghan	
27	Tunbridge Wells Rangers	KL	away	7-3	O'Callaghan 3, Bell 2, Sanders, Rowe	
Mar 06	Tunbridge Wells Rangers	KL	home	10-1	O'Callaghan 5, Pilcher 3 (1 pen), Sanders, Houston	
13	Chatham	KL	away	0-0		
20	Chatham	KL	home	3-2	O'Callaghan 2, Pilcher	
22	Grays Thurrock United	KL	away	2-1	Bell 2	
27	Royal Lancashire Regiment	Friendly	home	8-5	O'Callaghan 4, Bell 2, Cook 2	
Apr 02	1st Royal Warwicks	KL	home	7-2	O'Callaghan 3, Sanders 2, Seccombe, Bell	
03	Bexleyheath Town	KL	away	2-0	Sanders, Bell	
05	Folkestone	KSC Final	at Maidstone	1-0	Seccombe	11,500
10	Ashford Railway Works	KL	home	3-1	O'Callaghan, Alton (pen), Sanders	
14	Royal Marines	KL	away	1-2	Cook	
17	Royal Marines	KL	home	8-1	Bell 3, Cook 2, Pilcher 2, Mason	
22	Catford Southend	KL	home	8-0	Cook 3, Bell 2, Pilcher, Quanton	
24	1st Royal Warwicks	KL	away	2-0	Quanton, Cook	
29	Grays Athletic	KL	away	4-1	Quanton 2, Cook, Seccombe	
30	Erith & Belvedere	KL	away	2-1	Bell 2	
May 01	Margate	KL	away	3-4	Cook, Mason, Houston	

1926/27

> *For Arthur Seccombe [left] it was the end of the road – after 450 appearances, 250 goals and 16 winners' medals in all competitions for the club – a proud record indeed....*

Two more cups were added to the trophy cabinet with the held-over Kent Senior Shield and a fourth successive Kent Senior Cup providing success.

Despite these triumphs, the bread and butter of the Kent League provided only disappointment, Fleet finishing a moderate fifth. What was even more surprising was that, for most of the season, the front line consisted of four of the five forwards who had wreaked havoc on the opposition the previous season. Only Taffy O'Callaghan who – understandably – had been called back by Tottenham was missing, leaving Wally Pilcher, Arthur Sanders, Jimmy Bell and captain Arthur Seccombe in his 15th and final season to carry on where they had left off.

Taffy had one more appearance for the club in the unlikely surrounds of The Bat & Ball ground for a cricket challenge between Gravesend Cricket Club and Northfleet United. Fleet, with the help of some Kent cricketers, managed 91, with Taffy scoring a duck and Arthur Seccombe recording just two runs to prove cricket was not their game. Gravesend in reply were skittled out for 74.

Newcomers brought in were the Fulham pair Alec Chaplin, a full back, and Harry Bagge, an experienced half back. Later in the season, Albert Evans was sent down from Tottenham to add more dash to the forward line.

The club only had to wait until 9th October for their first trophy with a high-scoring 7-5 victory over Gillingham (despite the concession of ground advantage to the Gills) to carry off the Kent Senior Shield. But Fleet's defence of the Shield, only two weeks later, ran into problems after they failed to arrange a date for the replay of the Chatham tie and resigned from the competition (*see left*).

At the end of the month Fleet suffered

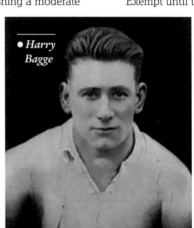

● *Harry Bagge*

a blow when goalkeeper Moody was carried off early in the game at Sittingbourne with a shoulder injury and the 10 men suffered a heavy 7-1 defeat. A week later they also fell to Sheppey, leaving the club's defence of the Kent League title fast slipping away.

Exempt until the First Round proper of the FA Cup, Fleet overcame Sittingbourne by 3-1 with an Arthur Sanders hat-trick. The reward was a trip to Luton Town where Jimmy Bell scored both the first and last goals of the game; alas the Hatters scored six in between to record a rather flattering 6-2 victory.

The new year saw the team determined to hold on to the Senior Cup and Royal Marines, Dartford and Chatham were defeated as the club reached its fourth succesive final. Sheppey United awaited them and, in a highly entertaining game, Albert Evans scored the vital goal in the 37th minute.

Arthur Sanders had been snapped up by Tottenham in mid-season, a rare case of a player going from Northfleet to Tottenham rather than the other way round. But he was released to play in the final and finished up as top scorer with 29 goals. For Arthur Seccombe it was the end of the road – after 450 appearances, 250 goals and 16 winners' medals in all competitions for the club – a proud record indeed.

Off the field, Percy Neame resigned as secretary after a 13-year stint and finances were of concern, with crowd receipts down £500 and wages up by £300.

A new shilling fund was promoted to raise money with Joe Lingham adding sixpence for every shilling collected. This helped the club to once more take the plunge into Southern League football after a near 30-year absence, especially with several Kent League rivals doing likewise. The result made the county competiton distinctly unattractive for ambitious clubs.

Having failed to arrange a date for the Kent Senior Shield re-play with Chatham, Northfleet United tendered their resignation from the Competition for this season. The Cup Competition Committee of the K.C.F.A., in accepting the resignation, have fined Northfleet £5 for their failure to comply with the original order.

Results 1926/27

Date	Opponent	Competition	Venue	Score	Scorers	Attendance
Aug 28	Erith & Belvedere	KL	home	**0-1**		
Sep 04	Gillingham Reserves	KL	away	**4-3**	Bell 3, Sanders	
11	Gillingham Reserves	KL	home	**3-3**	Bell 2, Sanders	
18	RN Depot	KL	away	**2-1**	Sanders, Bell	
25	Grays Thurrock United	Friendly	home	**0-2**		
Oct 02	Charlton Reserves	Friendly	away	**4-2**	Bell, Cooke, Sanders, Rae	
09	Gillingham	KSS Final	away	**7-5**	Sanders 2, Bell 2, Cooke 2, Pilcher	
16	Sittingbourne	KL	home	**1-2**	Pilcher	
20	Chatham	KSS1	home	**1-1***	Seccombe *Fleet resigned from competition*	
23	Sheppey United	KL	away	**2-3**	Sanders, Cooke	
30	Sittingbourne	KL	away	**1-7**	Seccombe	
Nov 06	Bexleyheath Town	KL	home	**4-0**	Rowe, Pilcher (pen), Sanders, Bell	
13	Tunbridge Wells Rangers	KL	away	**3-6**	Anderson 2, Bell	
20	Margate	KL	home	**3-2**	Sanders 3	
27	Sittingbourne	FAC1	away	**3-1**	Sanders 3	
Dec 04	Sheppey United	KL	home	**3-3**	Sanders 2, Anderson	
11	Luton Town	FAC2	away	**2-6**	Bell 2	9,000
18	Loyal Regiment	KLC1	away	**2-2**	Bell 2	
25	Dartford	Friendly	home	**2-1**	Sanders, Anderson	3,000
27	Dartford	Friendly	away	**2-0**	Sanders, Bell	
29	Loyal Regiment	KLC1 R	home	**5-0**	Anderson 2, Sanders, Cooke, OG	
Jan 01	Maidstone United	KL	away	**8-2**	Pilcher 2, Seccombe, Sanders, Pye, Alton (pen), Cooke, Bell	
08	Royal Marines	KL	away	**5-1**	Sanders 3, Pilcher, Seccombe	
15	Maidstone United	KL	home	**5-2**	Bell 2, Pye, Cooke, Sanders	
22	Royal Marines	KSC1	home	**8-0**	Sanders 3, Bell, Seccombe, Rowe, Pilcher, Cooke	
Feb 05	Erith & Belvedere	KL	away	**5-3**	Bell 2, Sanders 2, Cooke	
12	Dartford	KSC2	home	**4-2**	Seccombe, Bell, Pilcher, Cooke	
19	Tunbridge Wells Rangers	KL	home	**4-1**	Bell 2, Rowe (pen), Bagge	
23	Margate	KLC SF	home	**2-1**	A.Evans, Pilcher	
26	Ashford Railway Works	KL	home	**4-0**	A.Evans 2, Cooke, Pilcher	
Mar 05	RN Depot	KLC Final	home	**2-3**	Bell, Rae	
12	Chatham	KSC SF	at Maidstone	**2-0**	Sanders, A.Evans	
19	Chatham	KL	away	**1-3**	A.Evans	
26	Chatham	KL	home	**4-0**	A.Evans 3, Bell	
Apr 02	Ashford Railway Works	KL	away	**1-2**	Pilcher	
09	RN Depot	KL	home	**4-3**	Pilcher, Radford, Bell, OG	
15	Loyal Regiment	KL	home	**3-0**	A.Evans 2, Pilcher	
16	Bexleyheath Town	KL	away	**3-0**	Bell 2, A.Evans	
18	Sheppey United	KSC Final	at Maidstone	**1-0**	A.Evans	
24	Loyal Regiment	KL	away	**1-2**	A.Evans 2, Pilcher	
30	Royal Marines	KL	home	**4-0**	T.Evans, Cooke, Radford, Pilcher	
May 07	Margate	KL	away	**1-1**	A.Evans	1,450

1927/28

The challenge of Southern League football was successfully achieved, with Fleet finishing an impressive third – far better than anything achieved in the Victorian era of their previous residence in the competition. That said, the league of the 1920s was far weaker than in those long ago halcyon days when Tottenham, Southampton, Bristol City and the like provided the opposition.

It was also peculiar to have a season kick-off without the legendary Arthur Seccombe who, at the ripe old age of 34, had finally ended his record-breaking Fleet career.

To fill the huge vacuum left by his retirement, two experienced forwards were signed: Joe North from Arsenal and George Edmonds, who had appeared in the FA Cup Final for Wolves six years earlier.

Frank Alford moved south from Scunthorpe with a good reputation as a tricky winger. Tottenham sent down half-back Jack Illingworth and later in the season Alf Day, while Jack Mackesy – another half-back – came from West Ham. Other additions were goalkeeper Cummings from Middlesex local football and Henry Garbutt, late of Castleford.

After a disappointing defeat in the opening game at Gillingham, the team quickly adapted to the new division and were soon just behind the leaders. Less favourably, there were two disappointing cup defeats by a single goal, firstly at Sheppey in the Kent Senior Shield and then much more disappointingly at home to amateurs London Caledonians in the FA Cup in front of 4,500.

This left just the Kent Senior Cup and, having won it for four years in succession, the club were determined to keep their stranglehold on the trophy. Victories over Chatham, Margate and RN Depot once more saw a red invasion to Maidstone on Easter Monday, this time against Sittingbourne who had also joined the Southern League.

Both sides had won their home games against each other so predictions for the final were tricky. True to previous finals form, Fleet once more rose to the occasion, winning the trophy for an incredible fifth successive season by a 3-1 margin with

● Six of the best in Northfleet's first Southern League season for 28 years. Top: Frank Alford, Jimmy Bell who won his fifth Kent Senior Cup in succession and Jack Mackesy, who played for West Ham during the First World War. Above and left: Kent Senior Cup final goalscorers George Edmonds, Joe North and (left) Tottenham's Alf Day

goals from Alf Day, George Edmonds and Joe North.

Two players, Wally Pilcher and Jimmy Bell, had played in all five victorious finals and once more there were scenes of joy when the players arrived back at Northfleet station to be greeted by delighted fans.

Five days later Fleet visited Rockingham Road as Kettering bid to win the Southern League championship and, despite putting

in a decent shift, the Poppies clinched the title with a 3-2 victory. During the season the main stand had the roof extended to cover the enclosure at the front – always a popular place for supporters to stand.

New baths were installed in the dressing rooms after the wooden vat previously used for the purpose had rotted away, with the bottom falling out after over-vigorous scrubbing following one game!

With more than 2,000 miles covered during the season and wages amounting to £1,949 18s 6d, the club was grateful for the shilling fund and a generous donation from Tottenham for balancing the books. There was a small deficit of £20 18s to show for another excellent season that saw crowds average 3,500.

> *New baths were installed after the wooden vat previously used for the purpose had rotted way, with the bottom falling out after over-vigorous scrubbing following one game!*

Results 1927/28

Date	Opponent	Comp	Venue	Score	Scorers	Att
Aug 27	Gillingham Reserves	SL	away	2-4	Garbutt, Alford	3,500
Sep 03	Sheppey United	Friendly	home	1-1	North	
10	Folkestone	SL	home	4-1	North 2, Radford 2	
14	Dartford	Friendly	home	5-1	Pilcher 2, Pye, Featherby, North	
17	Gillingham Reserves	SL	home	3-1	Featherby 2, Walker	
24	Tottenham Hotspur Reserves	Friendly	home	3-2	Radford, Alford, Bell	3,000
Oct 01	Boscombe Reserves	SL	away	1-0	Chaplin	
08	Chatham	SL	home	2-2	Radford, Walker	
15	Sittingbourne	SL	away	4-5	North 2, Bell, Taylor	
19	Sheppey United	KSS1	away	0-1		
22	Grays Thurrock United	SL	home	0-2		
29	Sittingbourne	SL	home	4-2	North, Walker, Edmonds, OG	800
Nov 02	Brighton Reserves	SL	away	1-3	Edmonds	
05	Poole	SL	home	7-1	**North 4, Alford, Bell, Pilcher**	
12	Grays Thurrock United	SL	away	3-1	Walker, Pilcher, Alford	
19	Aldershot	SL	home	4-1	Edmonds 2 (1 pen), Bell, Pilcher	
26	London Caledonians	FAC1	home	0-1		4,500
Dec 03	Loyal Regiment	Friendly	home	2-3	Pilcher, Edmonds	
17	Chatham	SL	away	1-1	Edmonds	
24	Poole	SL	away	1-1	Walker	
25	Dartford	SL	home	*0-0	*Abandoned due to snow, 55 mins	
31	Peterborough & Fletton United	SL	away	0-3		
Jan 07	Boscombe Reserves	SL	home	3-1	Pilcher, Knott, North	
14	Southampton Reserves	SL	away	2-2	Edmonds, Alford	
21	Guildford City	SL	home	9-2	North 3, Edmonds 2, Bell 2 Pilcher, OG	
28	Chatham	KSC1	away	7-1	Edmonds 2, North 2 (1 pen), Alford, Knott, Pilcher	
Feb 04	Norwich City Reserves	SL	home	6-3	Pilcher 3, Rowe, North, Edmonds	
11	Sheppey United	SL	away	1-2	Pilcher	
18	Margate	KSC2	away	3-2	North 3 (1 pen)	
25	Kettering	SL	home	1-0	North	
Mar 03	Norwich City Reserves	SL	away	0-1		
07	Brighton Reserves	SL	home	4-0	Edmonds 2, Radford, Bell	
10	RN Depot	KSC SF	at Dartford	4-1	Edmonds 3, Pilcher	2,300
14	Peterborough & Fletton United	SL	home	3-0	Bell 2, North (pen)	
17	London Universities	Friendly	home	10-4	North 3, Bell 2, Pilcher 2, Radford 2, Rowe	
24	Millwall Reserves	SL	home	1-1	North	
28	Dartford	SL	away	0-1		
31	Folkestone	SL	home	5-1	North 2, Bell 2, Edmonds	
Apr 06	Sheppey United	SL	home	2-1	North, Bell	
09	Sittingbourne	KSC Final	at Maidstone	3-1	North, Day, Edmonds	
14	Kettering Town	SL	away	2-3	Bell 2	2,651
18	Southampton Reserves	SL	home	1-1	Alford	
21	Guildford City	SL	away	2-2	North, Bell	
25	Dartford	SL	home	2-1	Edmonds, Pilcher	
28	Millwall Reserves	SL	away	1-0	Bell	
May 05	Aldershot	SL	away	1-4	Alford	

1928/29

● *Ins and outs: Arthur Sanders (1) returned from White Hart Lane and was a key player, scoring 20 goals, while former England schoolboy Les Howe (4) was sent off the Tottenham production line with Jack Illingworth (inset).*

Going in the other direction were goalkeeper Bill Moody (2) as well as Wally Pilcher (3) who was a vital player in Northfleet's five consecutive Kent Senior Cup victories – and he played in every final. In 1924/25, he scored 19 times, including a brace in the Kent Senior Cup semi-final. He scored 32 times in 1925/26

> " *The season began with Alec Chaplin missing games through 'thickening of his muscles' – the modern translation of that being unknown!* "

Just one trophy was added to the cabinet in a quieter season that saw Fleet drop to ninth of 19 clubs in the Southern League.

Several players moved to Tottenham, notably Arthur Rowe along with Fleet's own discoveries Bill Moody and Wally Pilcher. Arthur Sanders was returned to Northfleet after a handful of games for Spurs and, with Jimmy Bell's and George Edmonds' signatures secured for another season, there was plenty of firepower up front which was supplemented by newcomers Bill Jones, Len Thomas and Joe Johnson.

Captain Alec Chaplin was again key to the defence while the young Spurs duo Les Howe and Jack Illingworth were again to the fore.

The season began with Chaplin missing games through 'thickening of his muscles' – the modern translation of that being unknown!

The team made a solid start and produced the performance of the season by dishing out a 5-0 drubbing to eventual champions Kettering on their own ground.

Progress was also made in the FA Cup, with Northfleet eventually losing out 5-1 at home to Charlton Athletic in the Second Round proper before a bumper crowd of 8,000 – a new record for the club.

With the team in mid-table, concentration was now focused on the two county cups. Dartford and Sittingbourne were seen off in the Senior Shield, allowing efforts to be given over to an attempted sixth successive Senior Cup. Erith were quickly disposed of by 7-1 and a home quarter-final with Sheppey United should have provided further progress but a lacklustre performance allowed the Islanders to sneak home 1-0 and Fleet's stranglehold on the competition was at last ended.

At least Fleet were able to record revenge in a Kent Senior Shield victory over Sheppey to gain some consolation for conceding a league double and the Senior Cup. Jimmy Bell (2), Les Howe, Arthur Sanders and Len Thomas scored in a 5-2 victory.

The season did prove troubling to the administrators as crowds generally dropped and, in a hard-hitting statement, chairman Joe Lingham warned local people that if they were not prepared to support Southern League football the committee would not be undertaking the arduous task of attempting to gain admission to the Football League that had been mooted during the season.

A loss of £574 for 1928/29 was also a big disappointment, especially after record receipts had been achieved in the Charlton FA Cup game.

Results 1928/29

Date	Opponent	Competition	Venue	Score	Scorers	Attendance
Aug 25	Charlton Athletic Reserves	Friendly	home	**3-1**	Edmonds 2, Bell	
Sep 01	Bournemouth Reserves	SL	away	**0-2**		
08	Gillingham Reserves	SL	home	**8-4**	Johnson 4, Jones 3, Edmonds	
15	Chatham	SL	away	**1-1**	Edmonds	
19	Dartford	KSS1	away	**1-1**	Thomas	2,500
22	Dartford	SL	home	**7-2**	Thomas 3, Edmonds 2 (1 pen), Sanders, Johnson	
29	Kettering Town	SL	home	**1-2**	Sanders	
Oct 06	Grays Thurrock United	SL	away	**2-0**	Houston, Sanders	
13	Bournemouth Reserves	SL	home	**2-1**	Edmonds 2	
20	Kettering Town	SL	away	**5-0**	Alford 2, Sanders 2, Johnson	
27	Norwich City Reserves	SL	home	**5-0**	Jones 3, Johnson 2	
31	Southampton Reserves	SL	home	**1-2**	Thomas	
Nov 03	Aldershot	SL	away	**1-0**	Alford	
10	Thames Association	SL	away	**2-1**	Bell, Johnson	
17	London Universities	Friendly	home	**7-1**	Webb 3, Johnson 2, Bell 2	
24	Ilford	FAC1	home	**5-2**	Bell 2, Johnson 2, Sanders	
28	Southampton Reserves	SL	away	**2-4**	Johnson, Bell	
Dec 01	Guildford City	SL	home	**3-1**	Sanders, Johnson (pen), Alford	
08	Charlton Athletic	FAC2	home	**1-5**	Johnson	8,000
15	Aldershot	SL	home	**4-1**	Bell 4	
22	Sheppey United	SL	away	**1-4**	Thomas	
25	Dartford	KSS1 R	home	**3-1**	Johnson 2, Bell	
26	Dartford	SL	away	**6-1**	Bell 4, Edmonds 2	
29	Peterborough & Fletton United	SL	home	**1-4**	Thomas	
Jan 02	Brighton Reserves	SL	away	**2-2**	Bell 2	
05	Poole	SL	home	**3-1**	Johnson, Edmonds, Houston	
09	Brighton Reserves	SL	home	**2-2**	Bell 2	
12	Millwall Reserves	SL	home	**1-1**	Johnson	
19	Gillingham Reserves	SL	away	**1-6**	Edmonds	
26	Erith & Belvedere	KSC1	home	**7-1**	Bell 2, Alford, Rowe, Johnson, Thomas, Sanders	
Feb 02	Sittingbourne	SL	away	**0-1**		
09	Guildford City	SL	away	**3-6**	Sanders, Bell, Edmonds	
16	Sheppey United	KSC2	home	**0-1**		2,014
23	Thames Association	SL	home	**5-3**	Bell 2, Howe, Sanders, Johnson	
Mar 02	Sittingbourne	SL	home	**3-0**	Howe (pen), Houston, Bell	
09	Peterborough & Fletton United	SL	away	**0-2**		
13	Sittingbourne	KSS SF	home	**6-2**	Bell 3, Thomas, Webb, Howe	
16	Chatham	SL	home	**5-0**	Sanders 3, Howe (pen), OG	
23	Poole	SL	away	**1-2**	Sanders	
29	Sheppey United	SL	home	**0-1**		
30	Folkestone	SL	home	**2-3**	Sanders, Jones	2,500
Apr 01	Grays Thurrock United	SL	home	**3-0**	Sanders 2, Houston	
06	Norwich Reserves	SL	away	**0-1**		
13	Sheppey United	KSS Final	home	**5-2**	Bell 2, Howe, Sanders, Thomas	2,000
15	Millwall Reserves	SL	away	**3-0**	Bell, Jones, Thomas	
20	Tottenham Reserves	Friendly	home	**3-5**	Sanders, Houston, Johnson	
May 04	Folkestone	SL	away	**1-4**	Sanders	

1929/30

It was anything but third time lucky in the Southern League as previous seasons' finishes of third and then ninth became a lowly 16th of 18. And, more troubling still, the financial situation seriously deteriorated. A combination of disappointing results and the bleak industrial situation nationwide had seen thousands more local people join the ever-lengthening dole queues and, as a result, vacate the Stonebridge Road terraces.

Everything had begun so optimistically with the key signing of Tottenham veteran and England international Tommy Clay, a hero of Spurs' 1921 FA Cup success. This deal had nothing to do with the usual practice of Spurs sending down promising youngsters but the good relations between the clubs had nevertheless helped the transfer.

Both Jack Illingworth and Arthur Rowe returned to their parent club; Rowe had been called back the previous year but returned to help the Fleet in mid-season – but this time he was gone for good on his way to gaining legendary status at the Lane over the next two decades.

For the first time a trial match for the club was played at White Hart Lane where a specially selected team of promising youngsters featured against the Fleet. Several played again a few days later in the traditional Reds v Whites trial game but were generally found to lack the necessary attributes that the tough standard of the Southern League demanded. Other signings were goalkeeper Bill Yates, formerly at Watford; Matthew Hopper, a winger from Coventry; Tom McGovern, a forward with experience at Millwall and Bristol City; and Herbert Batten, who Everton had paid Plymouth Argyle the then-astronomical fee of £1,500 just a couple of seasons prior.

After a promising start with a 5-0 demolition of Gillingham in a friendly, the league season began in the way it would continue – disappointingly. Fleet lost at home to Guildford with a shot-shy performance and it wasn't until the seventh league game of the season that victory was attained, with a 2-1 win over Sittingbourne. The ever-reliable Jimmy Bell scored both goals.

An advertisement in the sporting papers sought new players to come on trial and 150 men of varying abilities responded, with two experienced Football League players Peter Mooney (Hull and Newcastle) and Bert Chandler (Derby and Newcastle) coming in.

The following week came the daunting trip to champions Kettering. A meeting at St Pancras was arranged for half an hour before the departure of the 11.00 Kettering train

● *December 1929 saw Northfleet take on Clapton Orient at the Homerton Ground. Pictured are the respective captains Arthur Grimsdell (Clapton Orient, left) and Tommy Clay (Northfleet, right) shaking hands, the curious thing about that being they had both won the FA Cup with Spurs in 1921 and together been part of the Tottenham side the previous season*

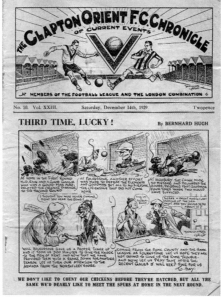

● *Clapton Orient's cartoon on the programme cover hopes Northfleet will not prove troublesome in the FA Cup – but is already looking forward to the possibilities of Round Three!*

and the party, consisting of 20 players and officials, were shocked to see centre forward Bill Jones (a notoriously bad timekeeper) arrive in plenty of time only for him to sheepishly admit his wife had tricked him by putting the clock on an hour to ensure he arrived in good time!

On reaching their destination, a meal had been arranged at The George Hotel where the players had to make do with boiled mutton and potatoes followed by toast and tea, while the rest of the party had something

even more substantial! A short stroll to the Rockingham Road ground followed and the pre-match feast seemed to have done the trick as Fleet battled to a 3-3 draw. It gave momentum to their FA Cup campaign with victories over Sittingbourne and Wimbledon before bowing out to Clapton (now Leyton) Orient 2-0.

The bid to defend the Kent Senior Shield ended with a replay defeat to Dartford, leaving only the Kent Senior Cup. Bromley and Tunbridge Wells Rangers were beaten in that and now only Sittingbourne stood in the way of a sixth appearance in seven years in the major final of Kent football. However, in a close encounter at Maidstone the Brickies triumphed by the only goal of the game.

By the end of the season, with gate receipts down a massive £761, the overall deficit was just over £500. As such, it was a relatively easy decision to resign from the Southern League and return to the Kent League, a disappointing but wholly understandable decision that ended the rather optimistic hopes of a Football League future for Northfleet for good.

Results 1929/30

Date	Opponent	Comp	Venue	Score	Scorers	Att
Aug 31	Gillingham Reserves	Friendly	home	5-0	Johnson 2, McGovern, Batten, Sherman	
Sep 07	Guildford City	SL	home	0-1		
14	Thames Association	SL	away	1-3	Johnson	
21	Thames Association	SL	home	1-2	Bell	
28	Aldershot	SL	away	2-2	Howe, Houston	3,000
Oct 05	Northampton Reserves	SL	away	1-4	Jones	
12	Folkestone	SL	away	0-4		
19	Sittingbourne	SL	home	2-1	Bell 2	
26	Kettering Town	SL	away	3-3	Jones 2, Radford	
Nov 02	Poole	SL	home	1-0	Mooney	
09	Norwich City Reserves	SL	away	0-3		
16	Sittingbourne	FAC4Q	away	4-2		
23	Grays Thurrock United	SL	home	4-0	Bell 2, Alford, Jones	
30	Wimbledon	FAC1	away	4-1	**Bell 2, Hopper, Howe**	10,250
Dec 04	Dartford	KSS1	away	2-2	Bell 2	
07	Poole	SL	away	1-3	Bell	200
14	Clapton Orient	FAC2	away	0-2		
21	Folkestone	SL	home	7-2	Havelock 6, Radford	
25	Dartford	SL	home	1-3	Davis	
26	Dartford	SL	away	0-3		
28	Peterborough & Fletton United	SL	home	1-4	Howe (pen)	
Jan 02	Millwall Reserves	SL	home	2-2	Bell ,Davis	
04	Dartford	KSS1 R	home	0-2		
11	Sittingbourne	SL	away	0-2		
15	Southampton Reserves	SL	home	0-1		
18	Aldershot	SL	home	1-3	Hopper	
25	Bromley	KSC1	away	6-2	Bell 2, Jones 2, Alford, Howe (pen)	
Feb 01	Sheppey United	SL	home	2-3	Davis, Howe (pen)	
08	Bournemouth Reserves	SL	home	2-2	Davis 2	
12	Southampton Reserves	SL	away	2-2	Davis, Alford	2,000
15	Bournemouth Reserves	SL	away	2-2	Hopper, Davis	1,500
22	Tunbridge Wells Rangers	KSC2	home	1-1	Brown	
26	Tunbridge Wells Rangers	KSC2 R	away	5-1	Bell 2, Lutterlock, Davis, Radford	
Mar 01	Sheppey United	SL	away	1-3	Davis	
08	Peterborough & Fletton United	SL	away	0-3		
15	Norwich City Reserves	SL	home	3-0	Bell, Radford, Day	
22	Sittingbourne	KSC SF	at Maidstone	0-1		4,000
24	Millwall Reserves	SL	away	2-4	Radford 2	
29	Northampton Reserves	SL	home	1-1	Davis	
Apr 05	Metropolitan Police	Friendly	home	1-2	Hopper	
09	Brighton Reserves	SL	away	0-2		
12	Kettering Town	SL	home	6-3	Radford 2, Davis 2, Havelock, Lutterlock	
18	Brighton Reserves	SL	home	3-1	Havelock, Radford, Davis	
19	Gillingham Reserves	Friendly	away	3-2	Havelock 2, Davis	
22	Grays Thurrock United	SL	away	2-6	Davis, Radford	
26	Guildford City	SL	away	1-2	Davis	

League Tables (Kent League)

Kent League Division 1 1919/20

FINAL TABLE	PL	W	D	L	F	A	Pts
Northfleet United	**24**	**19**	**3**	**2**	**70**	**22**	**41**
Maidstone United	24	16	1	7	50	31	33
Sheppey United	24	14	2	8	63	30	30
Charlton Athletic	24	12	5	7	45	28	29
Chatham	24	13	2	9	46	32	28
Gillingham Reserves	24	11	6	7	54	36	28
Margate	24	8	6	10	48	51	22
Royal Ordnance Factories	24	10	2	12	41	45	22
Royal Navy Depot	24	7	5	12	28	42	19
Tunbridge Wells Rangers	24	8	2	14	41	52	18
Vickers Crayford	24	8	2	14	38	59	18
Sittingbourne	24	7	4	13	34	52	18
New Brompton	24	2	3	19	18	87	6

Kent League Division 1 1920/21

FINAL TABLE	PL	W	D	L	F	A	Pts
Charlton Ath. Reserves	32	21	7	4	75	29	49
Maidstone United	32	20	7	5	82	27	47
Northfleet United	**32**	**21**	**3**	**8**	**76**	**40**	**45**
Ramsgate Athletic	31	17	9	5	71	35	43
Folkestone	31	16	7	8	73	38	39
Sittingbourne	32	15	7	10	69	49	37
Sheppey United	32	14	8	10	53	50	36
Margate	32	14	7	11	41	41	35
Tunbridge Wells	32	12	9	11	60	47	33
Ashford Railway Works	31	13	6	12	50	42	32
Chatham Reserves	32	13	5	14	54	47	31
Royal Ordnance Factories	32	9	7	16	35	68	25
Royal Navy Depot	32	9	6	17	37	57	24
Royal Marines	32	7	9	16	44	82	23
Bexleyheath Labour	32	6	8	18	36	82	20
Vickers Crayford	32	3	8	21	22	71	14
Royal Engineers	29	1	3	25	23	108	5

* Three games not completed

Kent League Division 1 1921/22

FINAL TABLE	PL	W	D	L	F	A	Pts
Maidstone United	28	24	3	1	92	12	51
Northfleet United	**28**	**18**	**6**	**4**	**78**	**36**	**42**
Folkestone	28	17	6	5	59	30	40
Ramsgate Athletic	28	13	7	8	52	36	33
Dartford	28	13	7	8	50	40	33
Sheppey United	28	14	3	11	50	27	31
Margate	28	11	8	9	43	36	30
Ashford Railway Works	28	9	11	8	42	40	29
Royal Navy Depot	28	11	5	12	44	48	27
Chatham Town	28	9	8	11	36	34	26
Sittingbourne	28	7	6	15	40	54	20
Royal Marines	28	5	7	16	31	61	17
Bexleyheath Town	28	7	3	18	26	86	17
Tunbridge Wells	28	5	6	17	33	58	16
Woolwich	28	2	4	22	16	88	8

● *Left: Margate were league opponents for the first time in 1919/20 – champions Northfleet defeated them twice and again in the FA Cup, scoring 15 times against the seasiders in just three matches that season*

Kent League Division 1 1922/23

FINAL TABLE	PL	W	D	L	F	A	Pts
Maidstone United	32	26	4	2	96	10	56
Sittingbourne	32	24	4	4	102	20	52
Dartford	32	17	9	6	41	22	43
Northfleet United	**32**	**17**	**5**	**10**	**88**	**41**	**39**
Folkestone	32	16	7	9	65	42	39
Ashford Railway Works	32	13	8	11	63	50	34
Royal Navy Depot	32	13	8	11	54	60	34
Sheppey United	32	13	7	12	53	43	33
Gillingham Reserves	32	11	9	12	58	56	31
Chatham	32	12	6	14	60	55	30
Royal Marines	32	12	3	17	43	71	27
Erith & Belvedere	32	10	6	16	39	63	26
Ramsgate Athletic	32	9	8	15	40	69	26
Tunbridge Wells	32	10	3	19	51	79	23
Bexleyheath Town	32	7	7	18	43	77	21
Margate	32	7	6	19	36	72	20
Woolwich	32	3	4	25	25	127	10

Kent League Division 1 1923/24

FINAL TABLE	PL	W	D	L	F	A	Pts
Charlton Athletic 'A'	30	25	3	2	79	19	53
Chatham	30	20	4	6	76	36	44
Sittingbourne	30	17	5	8	66	30	39
Northfleet United	30	15	5	10	61	35	35
Maidstone United	30	15	5	10	52	48	35
Sheppey United	30	15	4	11	70	50	34
Ashford Railway Works	30	13	7	10	61	48	33
Dartford	30	14	5	11	60	53	33
Gillingham Reserves	30	13	4	13	56	49	30
Tunbridge Wells	30	15	0	15	72	72	30
Erith & Belvedere	30	11	4	15	51	69	26
Royal Marines	30	9	6	15	39	55	24
Royal Navy Depot	30	9	5	16	48	63	23
Woolwich	30	7	4	19	31	77	18
Bexleyheath Town	30	5	3	22	32	88	13
Ramsgate Athletic	30	3	4	23	34	96	10

Kent League Division 1 1924/25

FINAL TABLE	PL	W	D	L	F	A	Pts
Chatham Town	34	31	1	2	111	24	63
Northfleet United	34	29	1	4	114	25	59
Dartford	34	21	6	7	77	42	48
Sittingbourne	34	18	7	9	69	40	43
Gillingham Reserves	34	17	6	11	77	52	40
Grays Thurrock United	34	16	8	10	65	46	40
Sheppey United	34	15	9	10	83	62	39
Tunbridge Wells	34	15	8	11	51	53	38
Catford Southend	34	17	2	15	72	54	36
Grays Athletic	34	11	8	15	55	57	30
Ashford Railway Works	34	12	6	16	56	67	30
Royal Marines	34	9	7	18	48	80	25
Erith & Belvedere	34	8	8	18	64	78	24
Margate	34	9	5	20	50	92	23
Bexleyheath Town	34	10	2	22	40	68	22
Royal Navy Depot	34	9	3	22	46	93	21
Maidstone United	34	7	4	23	39	92	18
Woolwich	34	5	3	26	33	125	13

Kent League Division 1 1925/26

FINAL TABLE	PL	W	D	L	F	A	Pts
Northfleet United	36	29	3	4	172	48	61
Chatham	36	27	5	4	125	31	59
Sittingbourne	36	23	7	6	122	46	53
Dartford	36	20	5	11	89	55	45
Gillingham Reserves	36	20	3	13	88	60	43
Ashford Railway Works	36	17	7	12	81	76	41
Margate	36	15	8	13	81	60	38
Grays Thurrock United	36	17	3	16	85	72	37
1st Royal Warks. Regt.	36	14	8	13	84	76	36
Catford South End	36	12	9	14	83	67	33
Royal Navy Depot	36	13	6	17	71	95	32
Maidstone United	36	13	4	19	59	119	30
Sheppey United	36	12	4	20	53	104	28
Bexleyheath Town	36	10	7	19	63	92	27
Grays Athletic	36	9	8	19	64	93	26
Erith & Belvedere	36	9	8	19	52	81	26
Tunbridge Wells Rangers	36	10	5	21	68	121	25
Woolwich	36	9	5	21	55	135	24
Royal Marines	36	8	2	26	60	126	18

Kent League Division 1 1926/27

FINAL TABLE	PL	W	D	L	F	A	Pts
Chatham	26	20	2	4	70	25	42
Sittingbourne	26	20	0	6	84	36	40
Margate	26	18	4	4	70	33	40
Sheppey United	26	15	4	7	64	34	34
Northfleet United	26	15	3	8	76	51	31
Gillingham	26	13	5	8	57	44	31
Tunbridge Wells Rangers	26	8	6	12	58	66	22
Maidstone United	26	7	8	11	66	82	22
Erith & Belvedere	26	7	6	13	47	62	20
Royal Navy Depot	26	8	4	14	47	63	20
Loyal Regiment	26	8	4	14	44	68	20
Ashford Railway Works	26	8	3	15	36	58	19
Bexleyheath & Welling	26	4	7	15	50	80	15
Royal Marines	26	2	2	22	34	105	6

League Tables (Southern League)

Southern League - Eastern 1927/28

FINAL TABLE	PL	W	D	L	F	A	Pts
Kettering Town	34	23	6	5	90	39	52
Peterborough & Fletton United	34	21	3	10	73	43	45
Northfleet United	**34**	**17**	**7**	**10**	**83**	**54**	**41**
Brighton & Hove Albion Reserves	34	20	0	14	90	63	40
Norwich City Reserves	34	17	6	11	69	69	40
Southampton Reserves	34	16	7	11	92	70	39
Aldershot Town	34	17	5	12	85	66	39
Sittingbourne	34	16	5	13	64	70	37
Millwall Reserves	34	15	6	13	66	59	36
Poole	34	15	5	14	39	84	35
Folkestone	34	12	6	16	71	91	30
Guildford City	34	12	5	17	65	89	29
Dartford	34	12	4	18	46	49	28
Gillingham Reserves	34	10	7	17	72	84	27
Sheppey United	34	11	3	20	57	87	25
Chatham	34	10	4	20	49	70	24
Grays Thurrock United	34	10	3	21	48	88	23
Bournemouth Reserves	34	9	4	21	48	62	22

Southern League - Eastern 1928/29

FINAL TABLE	PL	W	D	L	F	A	Pts
Kettering Town	36	24	4	8	96	46	52
Peterboro. & Fletton Utd	36	21	5	10	86	44	47
Brighton & HA Res.	36	19	9	8	91	56	47
Millwall Reserves	36	21	4	11	60	67	46
Bournemouth Reserves	36	20	5	11	82	58	45
Aldershot Town	36	18	5	13	68	52	41
Sheppey United	36	17	7	12	58	58	41
Folkestone	36	17	6	13	83	80	40
Northfleet United	**36**	**17**	**4**	**15**	**87**	**65**	**38**
Gillingham Reserves	36	15	8	13	68	70	38
Guildford City	36	13	11	12	85	78	37
Southampton Reserves	36	14	6	16	86	79	34
Poole	36	13	8	15	62	66	34
Thames Association	36	13	5	18	67	74	31
Dartford	36	10	6	20	56	106	26
Chatham	36	8	8	20	47	81	24
Sittingbourne	36	11	1	24	59	98	23
Norwich City Reserves	36	8	6	22	48	96	22
Grays Thurrock United	36	6	6	24	47	91	18

Southern League - Eastern 1929/30

FINAL TABLE	PL	W	D	L	F	A	Pts
Aldershot Town	32	21	6	5	84	39	48
Millwall Reserves	32	21	3	8	75	56	45
Thames Association	32	17	6	9	80	60	40
Peterboro. & Fletton Utd	32	18	3	11	66	39	39
Northampton Town Res.	32	17	4	11	86	60	38
Southampton Reserves	32	14	7	11	73	62	35
Sheppey United	32	15	5	12	76	69	35
Kettering Town	32	13	7	12	70	69	33
Dartford	32	14	5	13	57	59	33
Norwich City Reserves	32	14	3	15	69	69	31
Guildford City	32	13	2	17	65	97	28
Bournemouth Reserves	32	10	7	15	59	63	27
Brighton & HA Reserves	32	12	2	18	56	79	26
Folkestone	32	13	0	19	56	82	26
Sittingbourne	32	10	5	17	55	59	25
Northfleet United	**32**	**6**	**7**	**19**	**53**	**77**	**19**
Grays Thurrock United	32	7	2	23	54	101	16

● *Pictured opposite: while the 1920s prepared the groundwork for a Tottenham nursery at Northfleet, the 1930s would cement the relationship. This newspaper feature, from the Weekly Illustrated, 29th August 1936, shows trainer George Hardy putting young Tottenham hopefuls and numerous Northfleet players through their paces. "On the lookout for a budding international," says the newspaper "is better than paying £10,000 for one" – which was certainly the case as the Northfleet breeding ground turned out some great Spurs players during the following decade, as we shall see.*

"If you want to play in the Spurs first team," says Trainer George Hardy, "do as I tell you." George Hunt, International, is on Hardy's right.

—This Man Makes Footballers

Now that you've seen how a football is made, here is a glimpse at the method adopted to produce the right type of man to kick and head that football in the best possible way. Most first class clubs have nurseries for training and developing those men who have talent. These ambitious fellows belong to the Northfleet club which is the nursery for Tottenham Hotspur.

Physical fitness and alertness are essential to a footballer and these youngsters are given a variety of training to develop mind and muscle as you see in the pictures on the left.

Wherever these young footballers are the trainer is sure to be—see him in the background here keeping his eye on those trainees. He is on the look-out, for a budding International—which is better than paying £10,000 for one.

Chapter Five:
Earning their Spurs

● *The unmistakable backdrop of Stonebridge Road's main stand in the final season of Northfleet United Football Club. This is from a clash in April 1939 against Dartford (stripes) with two Northfleet players, partially obscured, on the attack. Fittingly, perhaps, it was Dartford who would provide the opposition in the last game Northfleet ever played – just as they had on the two previous occasions the Fleet had gone into hibernation, in 1898 and 1914*

1930-1946

Having rebuilt, consolidated, carried all before them in Kent and regained a Southern League place in the 10 years following the trauma of the First World War, no-one could have foreseen that by the end of the forthcoming decade, the club would be finished by another conflict.

But all that seemed a long way off as Northfleet entered the Thirties, their relationship with Tottenham Hotspur growing stronger with each passing season. Back in the Kent League after a brief flirtation with Southern League football, it didn't dampen the enthusiasm of supporters who were to enjoy another decade of rewarding football performed by many players who would go on to have glittering careers.

Fleet added five more Kent League titles to their haul and never finished lower than fourth as the Thirties yielded as much silverware as the decade that preceded it. Four Kent League Cup wins and one more Kent Senior Cup were also collected to enhance the club's roll of honour while there wasn't a single season in which Northfleet didn't score at least a century of goals.

Structural changes took place, too, with Tottenham coaches having much more involvement in the running of the playing side – and the quality of players that came through the Fleet's 'nursery' ranks was quite outstanding.

Northfleet provided a superb environment for future internationals and Football League champions to cut their teeth and the conveyor belt of talent included 100-goal-a-season George Ludford along with household names such as Bill Nicholson, Ron Burgess, Freddie Cox, Ted Ditchburn, Vic Buckingham and Les Bennett.

While Tottenham of course profited, with half of their 1951 title-winning squad being Northfleet old boys, the process wasn't all one-way. Spurs helped finance ground improvements and Stonebridge Road maintained its position as one of the jewels in Kent's crown. It may not have saved Northfleet in the post-war environment, but it gave the fledgling Gravesend & Northfleet the tools on which to build.

1930/31

The season began with this description of the first game courtesy of a local hack: "Supporters were walking around the ground in Panama hats, men wore open shirts and went jacketless while ladies were in their summer dresses under a piping hot sun". It did not sound like Stonebridge Road and indeed it was not. The panoramic scene was Eridge Road, where Tunbridge Wells got the better of Fleet in a friendly.

Now back in the Kent League, the slight drop in standard suited the Fleet – who did not lose a competitive match until their ninth of the season.

The key signing was Tommy Cook, a former England international centre forward from Brighton who had to miss the opening games as he was contracted to Sussex County Cricket Club where he was more than useful with a bat as much as he was a ball.

Les Howe returned to Tottenham after rapidly improving at Stonebridge Road and in his place Bert Smith and Fred Channell were sent down from White Hart Lane. Other new signings were George Johnson, a full back from Darlington, and Chesham school teacher Ray Tompkins, a centre forward.

Dover were early visitors – for the first time in 20 years – and were crushed 9-0 in torrential rain. At half-time Fleet changed their soaking wet shirts and came out for the second-half in pale pink shirts, which created plenty of caustic comments on the terraces. Their neighbours Folkestone fared little better the following week, losing 8-0 to the in-form Fleet. Dartford were next up, knocked out of the FA Cup before Fleet lost their own way at home to Exeter City in the First Round proper.

In the Kent Senior Shield, Northfleet were beaten by Margate in a semi-final on the new Hartsdown Park ground, Gate having vacated their old Dreamland Park venue. Dartford, meanwhile, were comfortable 5-2 victors in the Kent League Cup opening round. This left only the Kent Senior Cup where Fleet had a great tradition but they succumbed to Chatham in a first round replay.

Although Fleet continued to produce good league results, conceding a quickfire double in March to eventual champions Tunbridge Wells Rangers ended their title hopes and saw them finish fourth (but with an impressive 125 goals in the bag).

The financial side of the club was again a headache and although admission was reduced to 6d for adults to encourage

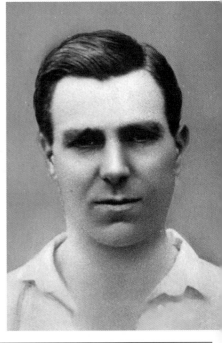

● Two views of Tommy Cook, the signing from Brighton in the summer of 1930. He won an England cap in 1925 and totted up 460 first-class games for Sussex in cricket, scoring more than 20,000 runs. He fought in both world wars, first as a 17-year-old in the Great War and then with the South African Air Force in the Second World War

● Tottenham's contribution in 1930/31 include Fred Channell (left) and Bert Smith (right). Channell – whose brother Bill had played for Northfleet in 1922 – was 20 years old when he arrived at Stonebridge Road, having had only non-league experience before that. He would go on to play at White Hart Lane from 1933–36. Higham-born Smith was at the other end of his career, having played for Huddersfield before the First World War and won the FA Cup with Spurs in 1921. He also gained two England caps, against Scotland and Wales, around the same time.

supporters into Stonebridge Road, gate receipts were down by £580. It began to look as though the club might need to follow the trend set by Bromley and Maidstone and go down an entirely amateur route, but not for the first time chairman Joe Lingham was able to use his powers of persuasion to obtain funds from various local supporters to clear the debts and begin the 1931/32 season with a clean slate.

Results 1930/31

Aug 30	Tunbridge Wells Rangers	Friendly	away	1-4	Tutt
Sep 03	Royal Marines	KL	home	3-1	Lutterlock, Harrison, Nicholls
06	Tilbury	KL	away	1-1	Brown
13	Dover	KL	home	9-0	Alford 4 (2 pens), Tompkins 3, Griffiths
17	Sheppey United	KSS1	home	3-0	
20	Folkestone	KL	home	8-0	Radford 3, Brown 2, Smith, Tompkins, Alford
27	RN Depot	KL	home	3-1	Radford, Brown, Houston
Oct 04	Sittingbourne	KL	home	3-1	Radford, Houston, Griffiths
11	Ashford Town	KL	away	1-1	Alford
18	Margate	KL	home	0-3	
25	Sittingbourne	KL	away	1-2	Channell
Nov 01	Ashford Town	KL	home	6-1	Channell 3, Radford, Bell, Alford
08	Margate	KL	away	1-3	Cook (pen)
15	Dartford	FAC4Q	home	1-0	Radford
22	Dartford	KL	home	3-4	Radford, Cook, Alford
29	Exeter City	FAC1	home	0-3	
Dec 06	RN Depot	KL	away	6-0	A.Smith 2, Radford 2, Day, Griffiths
13	Sheppey United	KL	home	7-0	Cook 5, Channell, Day (pen)
20	Canterbury Waverley	KL	away	0-2	
25	Gillingham Reserves	KL	home	4-1	Cook 2, Channell, Griffiths
26	Gillingham Reserves	KL	away	3-5	Radford 2, Alford
27	Bexleyheath & Welling	KL	home	7-1	A.Smith 2, Griffiths 2, Cook 2, Day (pen)
Jan 03	Maidstone United	KL	home	6-0	A.Smith 2, Brown 2, Channell, Griffiths
08	Margate	KSS SF	away	0-2	
14	Dartford	KLC1	away	2-5	Phillips, A.Smith
17	Maidstone United	KL	away	2-2	Cook 2
24	Chatham	KSC1	away	1-1	Radford
28	Chatham	KSC1 R	home	1-3	Channell
31	Canterbury Waverley	KL	home	6-4	Brown 2, Higden 2, Griffiths, Wright
Feb 07	Dartford	KL	away	2-4	Brown, Day
14	Tottenham Hotspur Reserves	Friendly	home	3-2	Cook, Channell, Day
21	Tilbury	KL	home	5-0	Levene 2, Griffiths, Houston, Cook
28	Sheppey United Reserves	KL	away	0-0*	*Abandoned snow 15 minutes
Mar 04	Royal Marines	KL	away	1-0	Day (pen)
07	Tunbridge Wells Rangers	KL	home	0-2	
14	Tunbridge Wells Rangers	KL	away	1-4	Brown
21	Dover	KL	away	5-2	Brown 2, Cook 2, OG
28	Sittingbourne Paper Mills	KL	home	4-0	Goldsmith 2, Cook, Day
Apr 03	Chatham	KL	home	5-2	Channell 3, Cook 2
04	Bexleyheath & Welling	KL	away	4-2	Griffiths 2, Day (pen), Goldsmith
06	Chatham	KL	away	1-4	Cook
11	Grays Thurrock United	KL	home	5-2	Hawkins 2, Alford, Cook, Griffiths
18	Grays Thurrock United	KL	away	1-2	Griffiths
25	Sittingbourne Paper Mills	KL	away	6-0	Goldsmith 2, Cook 2, Taylor 2
27	Sheppey United	KL	away	1-0	Goldsmith
May 02	Folkestone	KL	away	5-1	Goldsmith 2, Channell, Hawkins, Taylor

1931/32

The Tottenham influence became even stronger with the London club's experienced trainer Jimmy Anderson now taking over the running of Northfleet and bringing with him some more promising youngsters in Jack Acquroff and Tommy Ison. They added firepower to the attack while also drafted in was stylish young full-back Bill Whatley, destined to become a Welsh international and much further in the future a Gravesend & Northfleet manager.

Jack Illingworth and Les Howe also returned from White Hart Lane, not yet having made the breakthrough to first-team status, while the experienced Billy Houston (now in his ninth season, pictured above) was appointed captain. He was by this time the last link with the great side of the mid-1920s following the retirement of the stalwart Jimmy Bell (known as the "India Rubber Man" because of his amazing flexibility in reaching balls that appeared way out of reach). Bell took up the position of trainer with Dagenham upon hanging up his boots.

Reviewing the prospects for the new season, chairman Joe Lingham announced this would be the club's youngest ever team – and in his belief one of its best – and his confidence was well-founded. An opening-day nine-goal blast against Grays Thurrock started the ball rolling and though the next game proved something of a shock, with a 2-1 defeat to Royal Marines, it was to be one of only two league defeats all season.

The team were well supported home and away with hundreds taking advantage of the 9s 1d return to Folkestone to spend a day at the seaside, only to see Fleet slip out of the Kent Senior Shield in the opening round.

Progress was made in the FA Cup with a fourth qualifying round hammering of Chatham and large numbers of goals were being scored, with Acquroff particularly prolific and Cecil Sparks providing ample ammunition with his clever play. A trip to Bournemouth for the First Round proper provided a great opportunity for a giant-killing and had it not been for a superlative

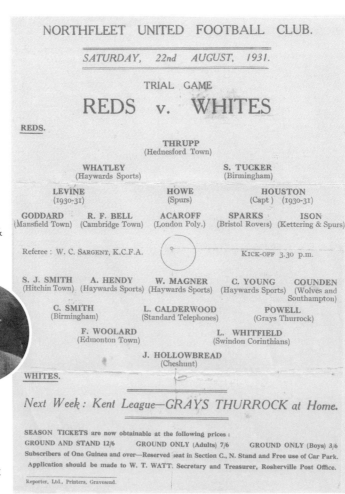

NORTHFLEET UNITED FOOTBALL CLUB.

SATURDAY, 22nd AUGUST, 1931.

TRIAL GAME

REDS v. WHITES

REDS.

THRUPP
(Hednesford Town)

WHATLEY   S. TUCKER
(Haywards Sports)   (Birmingham)

LEVINE   HOWE   HOUSTON
(1930-31)   (Spurs)   (Capt) (1930-31)

GODDARD   R. F. BELL   ACAROFF   SPARKS   ISON
(Mansfield Town) (Cambridge Town) (London Poly.) (Bristol Rovers) (Kettering & Spurs)

Referee : W. C. SARGENT, K.C.F.A.   KICK-OFF 3.30 p.m.

S. J. SMITH   A. HENDY   W. MAGNER   C. YOUNG   COUNDEN
(Hitchin Town) (Haywards Sports) (Haywards Sports) (Haywards Sports) (Wolves and
Southampton)

C. SMITH   L. CALDERWOOD   POWELL
(Birmingham)   (Standard Telephones)   (Grays Thurrock)

F. WOOLARD   L. WHITFIELD
(Edmonton Town)   (Swindon Corinthians)

J. HOLLOWBREAD
(Cheshunt)

WHITES.

Next Week : Kent League—GRAYS THURROCK at Home.

SEASON TICKETS are now obtainable at the following prices :
GROUND AND STAND 12/6   GROUND ONLY (Adults) 7/6   GROUND ONLY (Boys) 3/6
Subscribers of One Guinea and over—Reserved seat in Section C., N. Stand and Free use of Car Park.
Application should be made to W. T. WATT, Secretary and Treasurer, Rosherville Post Office.

Reporter, Ltd., Printers, Gravesend.

• Left: hopeful players take part in the annual Northfleet United Reds v Whites trial match.
Above: the Daily Express reports on Northfleet's near miss in the FA Cup at home to Bournemouth

PENALTY PAID BY NORTHFLEET.

FAILURE TO ACCEPT CHANCES AGAINST BOSCOMBE.

EARLY SHOCK.

Northfleet Utd. 0, Bournemouth and B. 1.

CLUBS who fail to take their chances seldom go far in the English Cup competition. Northfleet United paid the penalty for their lapses in this direction yesterday, when in their replay with Bournemouth and Boscombe, at Northfleet, they were beaten 1—0.

Northfleet had nearly all the play in the second half of this strenuously contested tie, but they had not a man who could steer the ball in the net, even when just a touch would have been sufficient.

Allowance, of course, must be made for the fact that McSevich saved superbly when Northfleet made a last desperate rally. It is scarcely true, however, to say that good goalkeeping pulled Boscombe through. McSevich would have experienced a lot more trouble but for the sterling work of Hayward, who returned to the defence.

Hayward played both with his head and his feet—which stood him in good stead against the swift raiders of Northfleet, who relied mainly on their feet.

Boscombe were undoubtedly the better team in the opening half. They were a goal up inside five minutes, Webb shooting through after White had hit the cross-bar, and Hollowbread had parried a shot from Beswick.

It took Northfleet some time to recover from this early blow, but gradually they found their feet. Their halves got a grip on the Boscombe forwards, mastered them and also found time to help in taking the fight to their opponents' end.

    Webb.

[caption under photo:] Webb.

• Bill Whatley arrived in 1930, some 24 years before he became Gravesend & Northfleet manager

---

display by the Cherries custodian Peter McSevich, Fleet would have triumphed rather than gaining a replay.

With home advantage, Northfleet fancied their chances but McSevich produced a repeat performance after Willie Webb had scored a sixth minute goal for Bournemouth and, despite dominating both games, Fleet were out of the cup for another year.

The Kent Senior Cup looked a good bet especially after a 1-0 opening round victory at Margate had eliminated one of the main challengers. Despite 500 Fleet fans travelling to Sheppey for the next round, however, their side suffered a shock 2-1 defeat.

At the end of 1931 the team travelled to White Hart Lane for a fixture with a strong Tottenham reserve side. A 3,000 crowd watched as Fleet took a 7-2 hammering though the scoreline didn't seem to do much damage to morale. Fleet powered on in the Kent League, losing only once more – at Margate in early April. The title was clinched in fine style, with four games to spare, after a 6-1 victory over Lloyds.

Further silverware was added with a hard-fought Kent League Cup victory over Folkestone at Stonebridge Road following a draw at Cheriton Road. The hero of the hour was another Spurs youngster with a decent future – Johnny Morrison with the 87th minute winner and the only goal of the game

Results 1931/32

Date		Opponent	Competition	Venue	Score	Scorers	Attendance
Aug	29	Grays Thurrock United	KL	home	**9-0**	Sparks 3, Ison 2, Bell, Acquroff, Howe (pen), Goddard	
Sep	05	Tottenham Hotspur Reserves	Friendly	home	**4-3**	Bell, Levene, Acquroff, Sparks	
	09	Royal Marines	KL	away	**1-2**	Ison	
	12	Folkestone	KSS1	away	**1-3**	Ison	
	19	Dartford	KL	away	**3-0**	Levene 3	
	26	Dartford	KL	home	**2-1**	Acquroff, Goddard	2,858
Oct	03	Dover	KL	home	**4-0**	Acquroff 2, Howe, Bell	
	10	Folkestone	KL	away	**3-2**	Levene, Bell, Sparks	
	17	Royal Marines	KL	home	**5-1**	Levene, Ison, Acquroff, Phillips, Sparks	
	24	Margate	KL	home	**3-1**	Phillips 2, Sparks	3,488
	31	Sheppey United	KL	away	**4-0**	Acquroff 2, Phillips, Sparks	
Nov	07	Maidstone United	KL	away	**4-1**	Sparks, Howe (pen), Acquroff, Goddard	
	14	Chatham	FAC4Q	away	**4-1**	Acquroff, Sparks, Ison, Phillips	
	21	Sheppey United	KL	home	**4-0**	Phillips, Sparks, Howe (pen), Acquroff	
	28	Bournemouth & Boscombe Athletic	FAC1	away	**1-1**	Sparks	
Dec	02	Bournemouth & Boscombe Athletic	FAC1 R	home	**0-1**		4,000
	05	Sittingbourne	KL	home	**8-0**	Sparks 2, Goddard 2, Phillips, Acquroff, Levene, Ison	
	12	RN Depot	KL	away	**7-0**	Acquroff 5, Sparks, Phillips	
	19	Bexleyheath & Welling	KL	home	**3-0**	McCarthy, Phillips, Goddard (pen)	
	25	Gillingham Reserves	KL	home	**3-0**	Goddard 2, Phillips	
	26	Gillingham Reserves	KL	away	**5-0**	Ison 3, Acquroff, Sparks	
	28	Tottenham Hotspur Reserves	Friendly	away	**2-7**	Acquroff 2	3,000
Jan	02	Folkestone	KL	home	**4-1**	Goddard 2, Acquroff, Phillips	2,480
	09	Canterbury Waverley	KL	away	**4-1**	Acquroff 3, Ison	
	13	Gillingham Reserves	KLC1	away	**6-0**	Phillips 4, Acquroff, Sparks	
	16	RN Depot	KL	home	**8-1**	Goddard 3, Phillips 2, Acquroff, Ison, OG	
	23	Margate	KSC1	away	**1-0**	Phillips	
	30	Ashford Town	KL	away	**1-0**	Phillip	
Feb	06	Tunbridge Wells Rangers	KL	home	**2-2**	Goddard (pen), Acquroff	5,000
	13	Maidstone United	KL	home	**12-1**	Acquroff 7, Goddard 3, Phillips 2	
	20	Sheppey United	KSC2	away	**1-2**	Phillips	
	27	Lloyds Sittingbourne	KL	away	**4-0**	Phillips 2, Goddard, Acquroff	
Mar	02	RN Depot	KLC2	away	**2-0**	Acquroff 2	
	05	Sittingbourne	KL	away	**2-1**	Goddard (pen), Ison	
	12	Folkestone	Friendly	away	**0-4**		
	19	Tunbridge Wells Rangers	KL	away	**1-0**	Houston	
	25	Chatham	KL	home	**2-2**	Morrison, Houston	3,580
	26	Bexleyheath & Welling	KL	away	**3-0**	Sparks, Morrison, OG	
	28	Chatham	KL	away	**1-0**	Morrison	
Apr	02	Margate	KL	away	**0-2**		
	06	Canterbury Waverley	KL	home	**2-0**	Levene, Acquroff	
	09	Ashford Town	KL	home	**2-0**	Goddard, Ison	
	13	Erith & Belvedere	KL	home	**8-0**	Acquroff 3, Morris 2, Goddard, Howe, Ison	
	18	Dartford	KLC SF	away	**3-2**	Morrison 2, Acquroff	
	23	Lloyds Sittingbourne	KL	home	**6-1**	Acquroff 2, Goddard 2, Morris, Howe	
	27	Folkestone	KLC Final	away	**1-1**	Goddard	
	30	Dover	KL	away	**3-1**	Acquroff 3	
May	02	Folkestone	KLC Final R	home	**1-0**	Morrison	4,000
	05	Erith & Belvedere	KL	away	**3-0**	Acquroff, Morris, Morrison	
	07	Grays Thurrock United	KL	away	**2-1**	Acquroff, Sparks	

1932/33

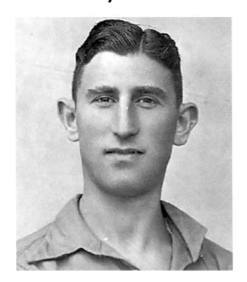

The ins and outs of 1932. Dave Levene (far left) was called back to Tottenham, while new players included Reg Bungay (above) and Bob Iverson (left, pictured as an Aston Villa player) Jack Aquroff (above, centre) was in his second season at the Fleet and continued to get amongst the goals until he, too, impressed enough to warrant a callback to White Hart Lane in the autumn

The margin between success and failure was clearly shown as going into the Easter holiday games Northfleet were hot favourites to retain the Kent League. They had also reached the Kent League Cup final, where Tunbridge Wells awaited them at their Down Farm ground.

Alas a disastrous trio of Easter games with a win, draw and defeat enabled Margate to take advantage and leap to the top of the table. After that setback, Fleet performed manfully to redress the situation but, despite scoring 19 goals in the last four league games, and taking maximum points, the damage had been done and the title was lost on goal average to the seasiders.

A strangely inept performance in the League Cup final saw Fleet tumble to a 5-1 defeat, only marginally better than the 6-0 defeat suffered at Tunbridge Wells in the league in January. It meant no silverware after a generally impressive season.

The strong influence of Tottenham Hotspur was further shown when, with the blessing of Fleet chairman Joe Lingham, it was Spurs manager Percy Smith (right) who made the announcement of Fleet's newcomers for the season.

They included a mix of several players returning from White Hart Lane having failed to make the grade and some new prospects for the future. Those players were Doug Hunt, Harry Sherman, Bob Iverson and Reg Bungay. Another impressive newcomer was Joe Allen, secured from Mansfield, while Les Howe, Dave Levene and Cyril Sparks departed Stonebridge Road having been given their opportunity with Tottenham in the Football League.

Jack Acquroff continued to be a goalscoring menace but after demolishing Tottenham Reserves 13-1 in a friendly, he along with Allen and Illingworth were on

> " *The strong influence of Tottenham Hotspur was further shown when, with the blessing of Fleet chairman Joe Lingham, it was Spurs manager Percy Smith who made the announcement of Fleet's newcomers for the season* "

their way back to White Hart Lane in the autumn, leaving a gap in the Northfleet team that was never completely filled.

Cup competitions provided plenty of disappointment as Dartford were delighted to knock Fleet out of both the FA Cup and Kent Senior Shield. There was also an early exit from the Kent Senior Cup at Margate.

Meetings were arranged to discuss a new Home Counties League featuring clubs including Chelmsford and Epsom but the Fleet, like all the other Kent clubs, were

worried by a drop in crowds and decided to stay loyal to the Kent League.

With the Southern League also experiencing problems due to declining membership (a poor economic situation in the country wasn't helping) it was felt the introduction of a new league at this time was something of a non-starter.

Just how poor the financial situation had become was highlighted by gate receipts some 30% down on the previous season and a loss recorded of £123 0s 2d on 1931/32.

Results 1932/33

Date	Opponent	Comp	Venue	Score	Scorers	Att
Aug 27	Lloyds Sittingbourne	KL	home	**7-1**	Acquroff 3, Allen 3, Sherman	
Sep 03	Dartford	KSS1	away	**3-3**	Allen, King, Sherman	
10	Erith & Belvedere	KL	home	**2-0**	Acquroff, Sherman	
17	Folkestone	KL	away	**1-2**	Acquroff	
24	Tottenham Reserves	Friendly	home	**13-1**		
Oct 01	Dartford	KL	home	**3-1**	Acquroff 2, Smy	
08	Sittingbourne	KL	home	**7-1**	Acquroff 2, Allen 2, Smy 2, Houston	
15	Royal Marines	KL	home	**14-0**	Acquroff 3, Smy 3, Allen 2, Sherman 2, Houston 2, Hendy, OG	
22	Canterbury Waverley	KL	away	**3-2**	Tutt 2, Allen	
29	Dartford	KSS1 R	home	**1-3**		4,700
Nov 05	Royal Marines	KL	away	**3-1**	Allen 2, Houston	
12	Dartford	FAC4Q	away	**0-2**		4,962
19	Bexleyheath & Welling	KL	home	**6-0**	Acquroff 3, Houston, Smy, Sherman	
26	Sheppey United	KL	away	**5-2**	Allen 3, Iverson 2	
Dec 03	Folkestone	KL	home	**3-1**	Veness, Allen, Iverson	
10	Dartford	KL	away	**1-0**	Palmer	
17	Gillingham Reserves	KL	home	**2-3**	Palmer, Sherman	
24	Gillingham Reserves	KL	away	**5-1**	Bungay 3, Iverson 2	
26	Margate	KL	away	**1-2**	Vernon	
27	Margate	KL	home	**4-2**	Bungay 3, Sherman	
31	Tunbridge Wells Rangers	KL	home	**5-3**	Bungay 3, Veness, Iverson	
Jan 03	Canterbury Waverley	KLC1	home	**5-1**	Bungay 2, Sherman 2, Iverson	
07	Maidstone United	KL	away	**6-3**	Sherman 3, Iverson 2, Veness	
14	Tunbridge Wells Rangers	KL	away	**0-6**		
21	Margate	KSC1	away	**1-3**	Smy	2,300
28	Lloyds Sittingbourne	KL	away	**1-0**	Iverson	
Feb 04	Sheppey United	KL	home	**3-1**	Powell, Bungay, Iverson	
11	Ashford Town	KL	away	**1-0**	Hendy	
25	Sittingbourne	KL	away	**1-0**	OG	
Mar 04	Tottenham Reserves	Friendly	away	**5-3**	Iverson 3, Hunt, Houston	4,002
09	Margate	KLC SF	away	**2-0**	Bungay, Iverson	3,500
11	RN Depot	KL	home	**4-0**	Bungay 2, Hunt, Smy	
18	RN Depot	KL	away	**7-1**	Hunt 3, Smy, Channell, Jones, Iverson	
25	Aylesford Paper Mills	KL	away	**2-1**	Hendy, OG	
Apr 01	Maidstone United	KL	home	**3-1**	Hunt, Iverson, Bungay	
08	Erith & Belvedere	KL	away	**4-3**	Hunt 2, Iverson, Smy	
14	Chatham	KL	home	**2-3**	Smy, Hunt	
15	Bexleyheath & Welling	KL	away	**1-1**	Iverson	
17	Chatham	KL	away	**2-1**	Palmer 2	
22	Ashford Town	KL	home	**6-2**	Palmer 3, Iverson, Smy, Bungay	
26	Tunbridge Wells Rangers	KLC Final	away	**1-5**	Hunt	3,000
29	Canterbury Waverley	KL	home	**6-3**	Iverson 2, Drinkwater, Bungay, Hunt, Palmer	
May 06	Aylesford Paper Mills	KL	home	**5-2**	Hunt 2, Iverson, Veness, OG	

1933/34

The Tottenham influence grew ever larger with the pre-season trial games taking place at White Hart Lane rather than Stonebridge Road and the public being excluded for the first time.

Tottenham took goalkeeper Page and full backs Illingworth and Cope back and despite the efforts of replacements Albert Webster, Vic Potts and Charlie Holmes, the defence was weaker as a result.

A disappointing opening-day home defeat to Canterbury confirmed this but the next six games were all won as Doug Hunt showed himself to be a great talent for the future with a glut of goals, well supported by Cliff Ferguson and Tommy Tebb. The latter was a Geordie who had played for Nelson in Third Division North and scored their last ever goal in the Football League, prior to joining Tottenham.

The Fleet were further boosted when Spurs allowed the free-scoring Jack Acquroff to return to Stonebridge Road and he would go on to score 22 goals while Hunt (despite returning to White Hart Lane in early March) topped the scoring charts with 35. An emerging young talent was sent down in Hunt's place and George Ludford was soon to become a Fleet legend. His amazing century of goals in a single season (1935/36) was remarkable but this was two years away and, in the meantime, he would score a modest six goals in 13 games through the tail end of 1933/34.

Although Fleet started their FA Cup campaign with a bang, reaching double figures against the outclassed Camberley & Yorktown, disappointment was just round the corner with a 2-0 home defeat by Dartford. The old enemy then dished out a further blow to Fleet's pride with a 3-0 Kent Senior Shield semi-final triumph. Further cup misery came with a home League Cup defeat to Tunbridge Wells Rangers.

Nonetheless, hopes were high in the Kent Senior Cup where Folkestone barred the way to the final, Fleet already having beaten them 9-0 and 2-0 in the Kent League. But Northfleet were in for a very nasty surprise, saving up their worst performance of the season for their most important game and losing 7-0. (Folkestone, along with Dartford and Margate, entered teams in both the

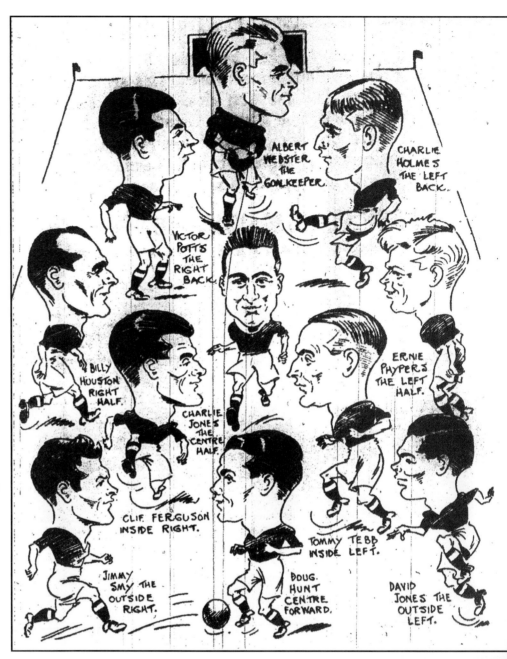

● *Above: the Northfleet side that defeated Aylesford Paper Mills 6-0 as depicted by cartoonist Syd Jordan. It included centre forward Doug Hunt (right), who top-scored in 1933/34 despite being called back by Tottenham. His career disrupted by the Second World War, he played for Sheffield Wednesday either side of a spell in the army*

Kent and Southern Leagues, enabling them to field stronger sides than the opposition expected in certain games – and this was one occasion.)

Now out of everything and with the Kent League title already out of reach, the team at least finished strongly, winning eight of the last 11 games to finish in fourth place and they scored 122 league goals – the most by any team that season.

Results 1933/34

Date		Opponent	Comp	Venue	Score	Scorers
Aug	26	Canterbury Waverley	KL	home	1-2	Ferguson
Sep	02	Bexleyheath & Welling	KL	home	6-0	
	16	Folkestone	KL	home	9-0	Hunt 4, Ferguson 2, Smy 2, D.Jones
	20	Charlton Athletic Reserves	KSS1	home	2-0	Tebb, Ferguson
	23	Aylesford Paper Mills	KL	away	6-0	Tebb 2, Hunt 2, Ferguson, C.Jones
	30	Royal Marines	KL	away	5-1	Ferguson 2, Cox, Tebb, Smy
Oct	07	Erith & Belvedere	KL	home	3-0	Tebb, D.Jones, Ferguson
	14	Dartford	KL	away	0-1	
	21	Ramsgate Press Wanderers	KL	home	1-3	Smy
	28	Margate	KL	home	1-3	Hunt
Nov	04	Ashford Town	KL	away	3-1	Acquroff 2, Ferguson
	11	Camberley & Yorktown	FAC4Q	home	11-1	Hunt 5, Ferguson 3, Tebb 2, D.Jones
	18	Lloyds Sittingbourne	KL	home	3-0	Smy, Acquroff, Hunt
	25	Dartford	FAC1	home	0-2	
	29	Dartford	KSS SF	away	2-2	Smy, Acquroff
Dec	02	Royal Marines	KL	home	7-0	Hunt 4, Acquroff, D.Jones, C.Jones
	09	RN Depot	KL	away	2-1	Acquroff 2
	16	Dartford	KL	home	3-0	Ferguson, Acquroff, Palmer
	23	Lloyds Sittingbourne	KL	away	5-0	Acquroff 2, Duffield, Holmes, OG
	25	Gillingham Reserves	KL	away	3-4	Smy, Acquroff, Jones (pen)
	26	Gillingham Reserves	KL	home	3-5	Acquroff, Duffield, Jones (pen)
	30	Folkestone	KL	away	2-0	
Jan	06	Canterbury Waverley	KL	away	3-3	Ferguson 2, Duffield
	10	Gillingham Reserves	KLC1	away	2-1	Acquroff, Hunt
	13	Aylesford Paper Mills	KL	home	1-0	Palmer
	20	Sheppey United	KSC1	away	4-2	Hunt 3, OG
	27	Margate	KL	away	1-3	
Feb	03	Ashford Town	KL	home	10-0	Smy 4, Hunt 2, C.Jones 2 (1 pen), Palmer 2
	10	Tunbridge Wells Rangers	KLC2	home	2-3	Palmer, Ferguson
	17	London Paper Mills	KSC2	home	3-0	Acquroff 2, Ludford
	24	Tunbridge Wells Rangers	KL	home	0-2	
	28	Dartford	KSS SF R	home	0-3	
Mar	03	Sittingbourne	KL	away	3-0	Ferguson 2, Hunt
	10	Folkestone	KSC SF	at Maidstone	0-7	
	14	London Paper Mills	KL	home	2-3	Hunt, Acquroff
	17	RN Depot	KL	home	4-3	Acquroff 2, Smy, Duffield
	21	Maidstone United	KL	away	5-1	Hunt 3, Ludford, Smy
	24	Sittingbourne	KL	home	6-1	Acquroff 2, Ludford 2, Duffield, Ferguson
	30	Sheppey United	KL	away	1-0	Ludford
	31	Bexleyheath & Welling	KL	away	3-1	Tebb 2, Duffield
Apr	02	Sheppey United	KL	home	7-0	Cook 5, Channell, Day (pen)
	07	Ramsgate Press Wanderers	KL	away	0-1	
	17	London Paper Mills	KL	away	0-2	
	19	Erith & Belvedere	KL	away	5-1	Ludford 2, Smy, Jones (pen), Ferguson
	21	Tunbridge Wells Rangers	KL	away	4-4	Ferguson 2, Smy, Palmer
May	05	Maidstone United	KL	home	4-1	Kerwood 3, Jones (pen)

1934/35

● *All change for the Fleet with a new-look team that lined up as: Back row – C Abbot, Jimmy Anderson, Joe Lingham, L Thomas, J Hibbert, Eric Sibley, Charlie Covington, Bert Ringrose, Vic Buckingham, WJ Treadwell, WH Hardy. Front row – G Jobson, George Bond, George Ludford, Jack Coxford, L Phillips, Bill Edrich, S Levett (secretary)*

A new-look Northfleet team playing attractive, attacking football gave supporters plenty to cheer about as they set about finishing as champions of the Kent League, winners of the Kent League Cup and runners-up in the Kent Senior Shield. As a result, crowds increased to an average of 2,000 and the season yielded a profit of £150.

During the close season, volunteers had carried out further improvements to the ground, painting the stands red and white, concreting further terracing at each end, extending the car park and putting high corrugated iron fencing along the Stonebridge Road side of the ground.

President Joe Lingham was elected on to the finance and general committee of the Football Association, adding further to his reputation, while Tottenham boss Percy Smith was also appointed club manager of Northfleet United, with Jimmy Anderson retained as team manager.

One familiar face missing from the club was Billy Houston who, after 11 highly successful seasons, decided to hang up his boots after the recurrence of a serious knee injury. Despite this blow a whole crop of promising youngsters arrived – from Spurs came Bert Ringrose, Vic Buckingham and Eric Sibley to strengthen the defence, while Fred Sargeant and 18-year-old Bill Edrich boosted the attack. Edrich would soon make his name as a Middlesex and England cricketer and have the honour of a stand named after him at Lord's. He was also a

● *Plenty of manpower makes Stonebridge Road ready for action in the summer of 1935, with major work carried out on the pitch following structural improvements the year before*

SOCCER PERSONALITIES AT NORTHFLEET

● *A 1934 cartoon depicting (clockwise from top left) Fred Sargeant, Joe Lingham, Thompson, Thomas, Bill Edrich, Eric Sibley, Vic Buckingham, Jack Coxford and Hibbert*

bomber pilot during the war, winning the Distinguished Flying Cross.

George Bond was signed from Millwall and was soon in fine goalscoring form while the experienced Jack Coxford arrived from Bournemouth. With key defenders

Coxford and Ringrose absent, the season started with a surprise home defeat to Lloyds Sittingbourne. But the team soon settled down and with 13 wins and three draws from their next 16 games to the end of 1934, they were soon top of the table.

And that was where they stayed.

The only disappointment was a shock exit from the FA Cup at home to Ashford but the consolation was victory in the Kent League Cup with an emphatic 3-0 win over Gillingham and an appearance in the Kent Senior Shield final where Dartford, with ground advantage, won 3-1 at Watling Street.

Results 1934/35

Aug 25	Lloyds Sittingbourne	KL	home	2-3	Bond, Ludford (pen)	
Sep 05	Bexleyheath & Welling	KL	home	3-2	Bond, Ludford, OG	
08	Canterbury Waverly	KL	away	3-1	Bond 3	
15	Folkestone	KL	home	4-1	Ludford, Kearns, Bond, OG	
22	Tilbury	Friendly	home	5-1	Bond 3, Ludford, Phillips	
29	Gillingham Reserves	KL	away	1-1	Ludford	
Oct 03	Ramsgate	KSS1	home	4-0	Coxford, Bond, Phillips, OG	
06	Tunbridge Wells Rangers	KL	away	4-0	Ludford 2, Brown, Bond	
13	Dartford	KL	home	5-0	Ludford 3, Hibbert, Phillips	2,500
20	Margate	KL	home	1-0	Bond	
27	Dartford	KL	away	2-2	Sibley, Ludford (pen)	
Nov 03	Aylesford Paper Mills	KL	home	0-0		
10	Ashford Town	FAC 4Q	home	2-3	Bond, Duffield	
17	Gillingham Reserves	KL	home	7-1	Bond 3, Sibley 2 (2 pens), Phillips, Thompson	
24	Erith & Belvedere	KL	home	1-0	Thompson	
Dec 01	Tottenham Reserves	Friendly	home	5-8	Woodhouse 2, Edrich, Phillips, OG	
08	Tunbridge Wells Rangers	KL	home	5-0	**Thompson 2, Edrich 2, Coxford**	
12	Ashford Town	KLC1	away	5-1		
15	Sheppey United	KL	away	5-0	Bond 3, Coxford, Buckingham	
22	Maidstone United	KL	away	5-2	Bond 3, Ludford, Edrich	
25	London Paper Mills	KL	home	5-1	Edrich 2, Thompson, Coxford, Sargeant	
26	London Paper Mills	KL	away	1-1	Thompson	1,500
29	Sheppey United	KL	home	9-2	Edrich 4, Thompson 2, Ludford 2, Hibbert	
Jan 05	Canterbury Waverley	KL	home	0-1		
12	Aylesford Paper Mills	KL	away	3-0	Bond, Sargeant, Ludford	
19	Maidstone United	KL	home	4-0	Bond 3, Thompson	
26	Sheppey United	KSC1	away	2-1	Sargeant, Edrich	
30	Gillingham Reserves	KSS SF	home	3-3		
Feb 02	Ashford Town	KL	home	1-1	Bond	
09	Folkestone	KL	away	1-0	Edrich	
16	Cray Wanderers	KL	home	3-1	Fallon, Edrich, Thompson	
23	London Paper Mills	KSC2	away	2-1	Sargeant, Bond	
Mar 06	Tunbridge Wells Rangers	KLC SF	away	3-0	Bond, Edrich, Ludford	
09	Ashford Town	KL	away	3-1	Sargeant, Coxford, Edrich	
16	RN Depot	KL	home	9-2	Bond 4, Sargeant 3, Thompson, Ludford	
23	Folkestone	KSC SF	at Ashford	1-3	Bond	
30	Margate	KL	away	0-3		
Apr 06	Lloyds Sittingbourne	KL	away	2-0	Thompson, Walker	
11	Cray Wanderers	KL	away	2-0		
13	Gillingham	KSS SF R	away	4-2		
19	Ramsgate Athletic	KL	home	5-0	Sargeant 2, Bond 2, Ludford	
20	Bexleyheath & Welling	KL	away	3-1	Ludford, Buckingham, OG	
22	Ramsgate Athletic	KL	away	1-1	Coxford	
25	Erith & Belvedere	KL	away	5-1		
27	Sittingbourne	KL	home	2-0	Thompson, Edrich	
May 01	RN Depot	KL	away	2-0		
02	Gillingham	KLC Final	home	3-0	Edrich 2, Bond	2,000
04	Sittingbourne	KL	away	1-1		
07	Dartford	KSS Final	away	1-3	Ludford	

1935/36

● *Kent League champions once more. Back row: WJ Treadwell, C Abbott, WH Hardy, Thompson, Jack Coxford, Arthur Hitchins, George Ephgrave, Vic Potts, Walter O'Dell, Bert Ringrose, Joe Lingham, Jimmy Anderson, S Levett.*
Front row: Arthur Attwood, George Ludford, Briggs, Stan Trigg

● *Spurs additions Bert Hall and Arthur Hitchin[s]*

O ne man dominated the Kentish football season and he was Fleet's centre forward George Ludford who scored an incredible 101 competitive goals – and it would have been 104 but three were ruled out in abandoned games.

Not surprisingly, under that weight of goals, Fleet retained the Kent League title with 158 scored (and 181 in all competitive games).

Several key players moved back to White Hart Lane – Buckingham, Edrich and Sibley were on their way while Bond tried his luck with Gillingham. Among those replacing them were Arthur Attwood (Brighton), Dave Walker (Golders Green), Stan Trigg (Hertford) and several more Tottenham youngsters such as Bert Hall, Arthur Hitchins, Walter O'Dell and, for a second spell, Vic Potts.

During the close season, major work was done on the pitch over a nine-week period. The Stonebridge Road pitch sloped by two feet from one corner of the Plough End to the other and had been a bone of contention for years so, in a major operation, 2,500 yards of soil were removed, with 1,200 yards of bedding soil replacing it. The whole area was regrassed using 32,700 turves from Cliffe Marshes, with the total cost coming to £1,000. Half of that was paid by Tottenham and Joe Lingham personally provided the other half.

The first three league games were all played away to allow the pitch to settle and the pre-season trial games once again took place at White Hart Lane. This partly explained a

CENTURY OF GOALS

George Ludford, Northfleet's centre-forward, who has scored 101 goals this season, is expected to sign for Tottenham Hotspur.

Ludford has twice netted six goals in a match, and has also scored eight 5's and four hat-tricks.

And this is his first season as a centre-forward!

"Hat-Trick George"

T HEY call him Hat-trick George at Tottenham—and are looking forward to the day when he signs on as a White Hart-lane professional.

His real name is George Ludford and; so far, his only connection with Tottenham is that he leads the attack of Northfleet, the Spurs' nursery club, and has twice turned out for Tottenham in London Combination games as an amateur.

* * *

In twenty-one matches for Northfleet this season, Ludford has scored sixty-two goals. Nearly three a match!

He has done the hat-trick no fewer than ten times.

slow start, with just one point gained from the opening two games – not to mention a 5-0 home hammering by Folkestone at the end of September, leaving Fleet in mid-table. After this the team settled down, scoring double figures in four games and only losing one more league game all season.

Goalkeeper Charlie Covington decided on a change of career in October after winning the Kent League three years in succession (first with London Paper Mills and twice with Fleet) and he joined the Surrey Police. He was replaced by a promising 17-year-old from Guernsey, George Ephgrave.

Success continued in the Kent League but Folkestone (FA Cup) and Margate (Kent Senior Shield) ensured the cups brought disappointment. And Margate inflicted more

misery with a single-goal victory in the Kent Senior Cup semi-final at Canterbury.

Despite these blows the team continued to reel off win after win in the league programme but couldn't shake off Folkestone, with both teams going into the last game level on points. But with Ludford's goals flowing, they gave Fleet a much superior goal average.

Ludford went into that final game against basement dwellers RN Depot on 99 goals. His aggression, powerful heading ability and fierce shot with either foot made him difficult to stop, particularly when things were going his way. During the season he twice scored six in a game, seven times scored five, four times scored four and on si[x] occasions scored a hat-trick.

The Royal Navy side was determined to make it hard for him to complete his century and while there was no doubt Fleet would get the victory required to win the title, the RN's close marking kept Ludford quiet. Fleet nevertheless stormed into a 5-0 lead with every other forward getting on to the scoresheet. With time running out, Ludford was the very picture of frustration but two late goals saw him pass his century in a mos[t] memorable season. It was hardly surprising that he was called back to White Hart Lane a[t] the end of a stunning season which had see[n] fans get full value for their 6d admission.

Results 1935/36

Date	Opposition	Comp	Venue	Score	Scorers
Aug 31	Gillingham Reserves	KL	away	1-1	Ludford
Sep 07	Erith & Belvedere	KL	away	1-2	Ludford
14	Lloyds Sittingbourne	KL	away	2-1	Trigg, Ludford
21	Tunbridge Wells Rangers	KL	home	7-1	Ludford 4, Coxford, Duffield, Thompson
26	Cray Wanderers	KL	away	6-3*	* match void - short time played
28	Folkestone	KL	home	0-5	
Oct 05	Cray Wanderers	KL	home	10-2	Ludford 5, Duffield 2, Macdonald 2, Thompson
09	Margate	KSS1	home	3-3	Walker, Potts, Attwood
12	Sittingbourne	KL	home	6-1	Ludford 4, Thompson, Potts (pen)
19	Folkestone	KL	away	1-1	Pritchard
Nov 02	Bexleyheath & Welling	KL	home	10-1	Ludford 5, Duffield 2, Macdonald 2, Thompson
09	Tunbridge Wells Rangers	KL	away	5-2	Ludford 5
16	Folkestone	FAC4Q	home	1-2	Duffield
23	Margate	KL	home	4-1	Ludford 3, Briggs
30	Maidstone United	KL	away	4-2	**Thompson 2, Potts, Ludford**
Dec 05	Margate	KSS1 R	away	1-2	
07	Erith & Belvedere	KL	home	5-1	Ludford 4, Trigg
14	Sittingbourne	KL	away	2-1	Trigg, Ludford
21	Aylesford Paper Mills	KL	home	13-0	Ludford 5, Thompson 3, Attwood 2, Briggs 2, Trigg
25	London Paper Mills	KL	home	4-0	Ludford 3, Attwood
26	London Paper Mills	KL	away	5-0	Ludford 5, OG
29	Gillingham Reserves	KL	home	2-1	Ludford 2
Jan 04	Canterbury Waverley	KL	away	1-0	Attwood
11	Ashford Town	KL	home	6-0	Ludford 3, Briggs, Thompson, Trigg
18	Aylesford Paper Mills	KL	away	3-1	Ludford 2, Walker
25	Canterbury Waverley	KSC1	away	2-1	Ludford 2
Feb 01	Dartford	KL	home	5-2	Ludford 5
08	Folkestone	KLC1	away	1-1	Edrich
15	Canterbury Waverley	KL	home	2-0*	* Abandoned 50 minutes - Fog
22	Lloyds Sittingbourne	KSC2	away	8-0	Ludford 5, Walker 2, OG
29	Canterbury Waverley	KL	home	1-1	
Mar 04	Maidstone United	KL	home	11-0	Ludford 6, Trigg 2, Attwood 2, Thompson
07	Margate	KL	away	1-5	Darling
14	RN Depot	KL	home	9-0	Ludford 5, Thompson 2, O'Dell, Coxford
21	Margate	KSC SF	at Cant'bury	0-1	
23	Folkestone	KLC1 R	home	4-2	Ludford 2 (1 pen), Attwood, Briggs
28	Ashford Town	KL	away	2-1	Ludford 2
Apr 10	Ramsgate Athletic	KL	home	7-0	Attwood 2, Briggs 2, Trigg 2, Ludford
11	Bexleyheath & Welling	KL	away	3-4	Briggs 2, Trigg
13	Ramsgate Athletic	KL	away	1-1	Hitchins
15	Sheppey United	KL	home	4-0	
18	Lloyds Sittingbourne	KL	home	0-0	
20	Dartford	KLC SF	away	3-3	
22	Sheppey United	KL	away	5-0	
25	Cray Wanderers	KL	away	2-3	Hinsby 2
27	Dartford	KL	away	4-0	Ludford 2, Briggs 2
29	Dartford	KLC SF R	home	0-1	
May 02	RN Depot	KL	away	8-0	

1936/37

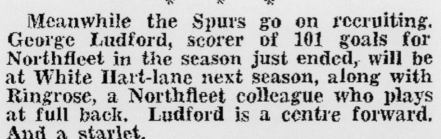

> Meanwhile the Spurs go on recruiting. George Ludford, scorer of 101 goals for Northfleet in the season just ended, will be at White Hart-lane next season, along with Ringrose, a Northfleet colleague who plays at full back. Ludford is a centre forward. And a starlet.

● *The close-season announcement in the Daily Express of the departure of George Ludford and Bert Ringrose (left) was tempered by the arrival of three players who would become giants of the game – Ron Burgess, Freddie Cox and Bill Nicholson. Although the three unblooded youngsters didn't make a major impact until the following season, their recruitment in 1936/37 helped Northfleet to a third successive Kent League title*

Northfleet United completed a hat-trick of Kent League titles – their 10th in all – and once again it was a close-run thing with goal average proving decisive for a second successive season. This time it was Margate who suffered the same fate as Folkestone in the previous season, losing out by the skin of their teeth.

The decisive factor once again was the sheer weight of goals scored by the Fleet, who netted 128 in 32 league games. They recorded 11 goals in three different league games and a further 11 in a Kent Senior Cup tie against minnows Bostall Heath.

All these goals were scored despite the predictable callback to Tottenham for goal centurion George Ludford who Spurs' manager Jack Tresadern quickly earmarked for success. Accomplished full-back Bert Ringrose also returned to headquarters (as he would once again in 1946 to play for the new Gravesend & Northfleet).

Tresadern and assistant Ben Ives selected the squad after private trials at White Hart Lane and among those arriving at Stonebridge Road were three highly notable players in Bill Nicholson, Ron Burgess and Freddie Cox (although none of them would play more than a handful of games in their debut season). Full-back Eric Sibley also returned as he was deemed not quite ready for Tottenham's first team.

● *Eric Sibley returned from Tottenham*

Ron Morgan signed from Wolves and was the man with the unenviable job of succeeding Ludford – and he did a good enough job without reaching even half of Ludford's incredible tally.

Cyril Trailor and Dave Fowler were snapped up from local football and quickly adapted to the step up in grade whilst Charlie Revell made his presence felt after signing from Callenders Athletic.

Unlike the previous season Fleet were quickly into top form, dropping just one point from their first seven league games. They progressed comfortably through the early qualifying rounds of the FA Cup and

also recorded a notable Kent Senior Shield win over a strong Charlton Athletic side.

All this led to a crunch FA Cup First Round home tie with Dartford in front of a 5,000 crowd. Fleet's great start to the season took a rapid turn for the worse as the Darts provided something of a footballing lesson to the tune of a 5-0 thrashing.

This defeat badly dented the Fleet's confidence and three of the next eight league fixtures up to the end of the year were lost. The new year did not begin well either, with one point from the first three games of 1937, and an exit from the Kent Senior Shield to boot.

Then came two successive 11-1 wins and the confidence was back. Those fine victories were followed by 13 successive Kent League wins that allowed Northfleet to wrestle the title from Margate, who until that point had looked likely winners after Fleet's mid-season stutter.

Margate did gain revenge by knocking Fleet out of the Kent Senior Cup at the semi-final stage with a 2-0 win at Gillingham while the team also renewed acquaintance with George Ludford in a friendly at White Hart Lane which saw Fleet win 4-3 despite two Spurs goals from Ludford.

Though it was a successful season, crowds were again down, with the campaign finishing to the tune of a £311 deficit.

Results 1936/37

Date	Opponent	Competition	Venue	Score	Scorers
Aug 29	Lloyds Sittingbourne	KL	home	2-1	Pidgeon, Morgan
Sep 05	Dartford	KL	away	3-3	Morgan 3
12	Erith & Belvedere	KL	away	4-2	Batty, Thomas, Fowler, Morgan
19	Whitstable	FACPr	away	3-0	Morgan 2, Fowler
23	Charlton Athletic Reserves	KSS1	home	1-0	Parr
26	Dartford	KL	home	2-0	Knight, Fowler
Oct 03	London Paper Mills	FAC1Q	home	1-0	Thompson
10	Tunbridge Wells Rangers	KL	home	4-0	Fairchild, Fowler, Morgan, Coxford (pen)
17	Chatham	FAC2Q	home	4-0	Morgan 3, Fowler
24	Cray Wanderers	KL	home	11-0	Morgan 4, Davey 3, Fowler 2, Knight 2
31	Callenders Athletic	FAC3Q	home	3-2	Morgan 2, Coxford
Nov 07	Canterbury Waverley	KL	home	2-0	Bates, Morgan
14	Dartford	FAC4Q	home	0-5	
21	Sittingbourne	KL	home	4-0	Fowler 3, Trailor
25	Tunbridge Wells Rangers	KL	away	1-2	Batty
28	Ashford Town	KL	away	1-0	Morgan
Dec 02	Tunbridge Wells Rangers	KLC1	home	3-0	Cox 2, Nicholson
05	Maidstone United	KL	away	4-0	Morgan 2, Cox, Nicholson
12	Margate	KL	away	0-3	
19	London Paper Mills	KL	home	4-0	Nicholson 2, Coxford 2 (2 pens)
25	Gillingham Reserves	KL	home	3-1	Revell 2, Coxford
26	Gillingham Reserves	KL	away	0-2	
Jan 02	Folkestone	KL	away	2-3	Fairchild 2
09	Canterbury Waverley	KL	away	1-1	Coxford
13	Folkestone	KSS SF	away	1-3	
16	Margate	KL	home	1-4	Trailor
23	Bostall Heath	KSC1	home	11-1	Trailor 5, Thompson 2, Cox 2, Knight, Kerwood
30	Folkestone	KL	home	11-1	Trailor 5, Cox, Kerwood, Thompson, Revell, Bates
Feb 06	Tottenham Reserves	Friendly	away	4-3	Trailor 2, Coxford (pen), Morgan
13	Aylesford Paper Mills	KL	away	1-0	Trailor
20	Canterbury Waverley	KSC2	away	2-2	
24	Canterbury Waverley	KSC2 R	home	3-1	
27	Ashford Town	KL	home	8-1	Trailor 3, Revell 3, Lambert, Morgan
Mar 13	Margate	KSC SF	at Cant'bury	0-2	
20	Sheppey United	KL	home	6-0	Trailor 3, Thompson, Cox, Coxford
26	Aylesford Paper Mills	KL	home	11-0	
27	Bexleyheath & Welling	KL	away	2-1	
Apr 03	Sittingbourne	KL	away	4-0	Cox 2, Trailor 2
10	Erith & Belvedere	KL	home	3-0	Fairchild 2, Trailor
14	Sheppey United	KL	away	4-0	
17	Lloyds Sittingbourne	KL	away	7-0	Revell 3, Morgan 2, Cox 2
20	London Paper Mills	KL	away	2-1	Morgan 2
21	Maidstone United	KLC SF	neutral	4-0	Knight 2, Dorling, Twocock
24	Maidstone United	KL	home	9-1	Cox 3, Morgan 2, Revell 2, Fairchild, Thompson
29	Cray Wanderers	KL	away	6-1	
May 01	Bexleyheath & Welling	KL	home	5-0	

1937/38

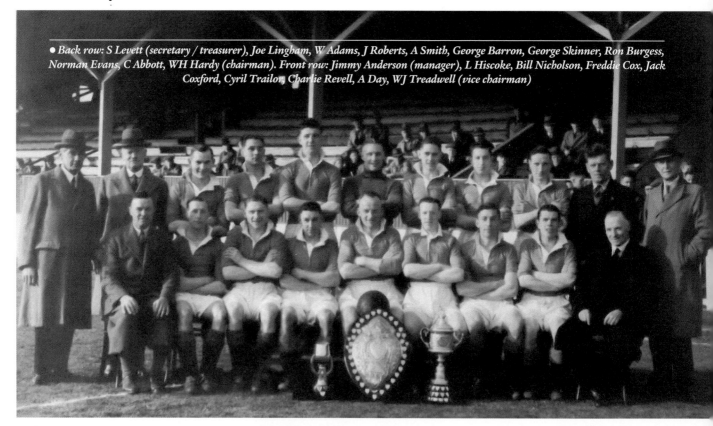

● Back row: S Levett (secretary / treasurer), Joe Lingham, W Adams, J Roberts, A Smith, George Barron, George Skinner, Ron Burgess, Norman Evans, C Abbott, WH Hardy (chairman). Front row: Jimmy Anderson (manager), L Hiscoke, Bill Nicholson, Freddie Cox, Jack Coxford, Cyril Trailor, Charlie Revell, A Day, WJ Treadwell (vice chairman)

For the third successive season the Kent League was decided on goal average. In the two previous campaigns Fleet had pipped Folkestone and Margate respectively but this time round it was a three-way tustle with Margate and surprise package Aylesford Paper Mills.

The crunch came in April with home games against both rivals but while Aylesford were dispatched 4-0, Margate grabbed a single-goal victory which proved enough for them to squeeze out Aylesford on goal difference, with Fleet just a point behind.

Despite this disappointment there was plenty of cup success. The Kent Senior Cup was won after a 10-year gap with a 2-1 victory over Dover where goals by Charlie Revell and A Day (not to be confused with the Alf Day of the early Thirties) – with almost the last kick of the game – secured a hard-earned victory. The team also qualified for the Kent League Cup final, to be played at the start of the following season.

A fortnight into the season the first silverware was placed in the trophy cabinet when the delayed 1936/37 League Cup final with Folkestone saw Northfleet triumph 2-0 with goals from George Skinner and Day.

A big blow was the controversial decision by the Football Association to bring in a rule preventing nursery clubs entering the FA Cup, even though several other clubs of a similar status were still allowed in. Despite

● A familiar backdrop at Park View Road, Welling, as Northfleet see a corner cleared in this 1938 meeting against Bexleyheath & Welling

this at least one influential member of staff made the cup final itself when Joe Lingham, through his position within the FA, led the teams out at the 1938 showpiece, with King George VI in attendance (where Preston North End defeated Huddersfield Town).

The club also represented Tottenham Hotspur in name at the Hastings Carnival by playing the local club as a thank you for them providing Spurs with training facilities when the First Division club visited the coast as a lead-up to cup ties.

Northfleet quickly settled, with two

future internationals – Ron Burgess and Bill Nicholson – proving to be outstanding players. In goal was the dependable George Barron (father of future Arsenal, Crystal Palace and QPR goalkeeper Paul Barron) while other newcomers were Freddie Cox and Les Medley from Tottenham, the free-scoring Charlie Revell from Callenders Athletic plus local Greenhithe youngster Reg 'Buster' Weston.

Despite another season of success, the trend of falling gates continued and the club finished once again with a deficit.

Results 1937/38

Date	Opponent	Competition	Venue	Score	Scorers	
Aug 28	Canterbury Waverley	KL	home	**4-1**	Trailor 2, Cox, Day	
Sep 04	Hastings & St Leonards	Friendly	away	**1-3**	Day	
11	Folkestone	KLC Final	home	**2-0**	Skinner, Day	**1936/37 Final*
18	Erith & Belvedere	KL	away	**1-0**	Trailor	
25	London Paper Mills	KL	home	**0-1**		
29	Tunbridge Wells Rangers	KSS1	home	**7-0**	Trailor 4, Skinner 2, Revell	
Oct 02	Sheppey United	KL	home	**5-3**	Trailor 2, Coulston, Coxford, Revell	
09	Lloyds Sittingbourne	KL	home	**6-0**	Coulston 2, Cox 2, Trailor, Skinner	
16	Bexleyheath & Welling	KL	home	**5-2**	Revell, Cox, Trailor, Coxford (pen), OG	
23	Maidstone United	KL	home	**1-1**	Coxford (pen)	
30	Folkestone	KL	home	**8-0**	Day 3, Trailor 2, Coulston, Coxford (pen), Cox	
Nov 03	Ipswich Town Reserves	Friendly	away	**5-2**		
06	Sittingbourne	KL	away	**1-1**	Skinner	
13	Aylesford Paper Mills	KL	away	**2-2**	Coxford (pen), Revell	
20	Ashford Town	KL	home	**8-0**	Revell 4, Coulston 2, Adams 2	
27	Dartford	KL	home	**10-1**	Adams 4, Trailor 4, Coulston, Revell	
Dec 04	Sheppey United	KL	away	**8-0**	Trailor 2, Tompkins 2, Revell 2, Coulston, Skinner	
11	Margate	KL	away	**0-0**		
18	Bexleyheath & Welling	KL	home	**3-2**	Coulston, Revell, Adams	
25	Gillingham Reserves	KL	home	**3-0**	Revell 2, Trailor	
27	Gillingham Reserves	KL	away	**1-2**	Trailor	
28	Dartford	KLC1	home	**4-1**	Trailor 2, Adams, Skinner	
Jan 08	Dartford	KL	away	**5-2**	Adams 2, Revell 2, Trailor	
15	London Paper Mills	KL	away	**3-1**	Trailor 2, Skinner	
22	Margate	KSS SF	away	**0-2**		
29	Sittingbourne	KL	home	**3-1**	Revell, Trailor, Adams	
Feb 05	Folkestone	KL	away	**2-1**	Adams, OG	
12	Ashford Town	KSC1	away	**3-0**	Trailor 2, Skinner	
19	Maidstone United	KL	away	**3-1**	Trailor 3	
23	Tunbridge Wells Rangers	KLC SF	away	**3-1**	Cox 2, Lewis	
26	Ashford Town	KL	away	**4-1**	Skinner, Coxford (pen), Hiscoke, Trailor	
Mar 12	Erith & Belvedere	KSC2	away	**2-1***	Coulston, Revell	*after extra time
19	Margate	KSC SF	at Maidstone	**1-0**	Skinner	
Apr 02	Lloyds Sittingbourne	KL	away	**1-2**	Cox	
09	Canterbury Waverley	KL	away	**1-1**	Adams	
15	Tunbridge Wells Rangers	KL	home	**7-0**	Day 4, Adams, Revell, Coulston	
16	Tunbridge Wells Rangers	KL	away	**2-1**	Day, Revell	
18	Dover	KSC Final	at Maidstone	**2-1**	Day, Revell	9,168
23	Cray Wanderers	KL	home	**4-0**	Trailor 3, Day	
30	Margate	KL	home	**0-1**		
May 04	Aylesford Paper Mills	KL	home	**4-0**	Day 2, Trailor, Weston	
06	Erith & Belvedere	KL	home	**8-0**		
07	Cray Wanderers	KL	away	**3-1**	Day, Evans, Cox	

● *The Factory Club, to the right of this 1937 picture of Northfleet High Street, remained the venue in which to convene for Northfleet United meetings and, in 1946, it gave birth to Gravesend & Northfleet as the members of what was left of the post-war Gravesend United and Northfleet United clubs met to agree terms on a combined future*

1938/39

● *The last days: Northfleet's final team photo, appropriately with Joe Lingham (now sporting a walking stick) who was also present in their first such photograph way back in 1891/92). Back row: S Harris (vice chairman), Gilbert Piper, W Adams, Sid Lown, R McLean, Ted Ditchburn, P Codd, E Duffield, J Roberts, R Smith (assistant secretary), Jack Coxford). Front row: S Levett (secretary and treasurer), WJ Treadwell (chairman), Norman Evans, L Hiscoke, Charlie Revell, Les Bennett, Reg Weston, Jimmy Anderson (manager), Joe Lingham (president). This photograph was taken behind the main stand, where the club offices are now*

● *A local youngster who would go on to have a huge future in the game, Ted Ditchburn is pictured here playing for Northfleet in 1938/39. He won six England caps and a Football League winner's medal in 1951*

A fourth Kent League title in five years proved the icing on the cake for the Fleet who finished two points clear of Gillingham Reserves. This came despite losing many key players of the likes of Bill Nicholson, Ron Burgess, Freddie Cox and George Barron who all moved back to Tottenham. And within a couple of months of the season kicking off, George Skinner and Cyril Trailor had followed.

Once again the ability to replenish the talent pool soon became evident as more future Spurs stars quickly showed their ability. Three of them would play a key role a decade later in Spurs becoming champions of England by winning the Football League.

Northfleet gained forwards Les Bennett and Les Medley along with goalkeeper Ted Ditchburn, a local lad residing in West Kent Avenue, who all proved their worth. And alongside veteran Jack Coxford at centre half, promising local youngsters Gilbert Piper, Sidney Lown and Jimmy Sperrin, the combination proved to be very effective under team manager Jimmy Anderson, now in his 32nd season with Spurs.

The season started with the delayed Kent League Cup final against London Paper Mills in heatwave conditions. With the score at 1-1 on full-time, it was mutually decided not to have extra time in such stifling conditions and to instead share the trophy.

Fleet were always the pacesetters in the Kent League, losing only four times and scoring 125 goals, although the severe weather around Christmas saw both games with Gillingham snowed off. This left another dent in the club's finances.

The title was finally secured in emphatic fashion with a 6-0 drubbing of Sheppey United on 29th April.

With the club again barred from the FA Cup, the two county cups took on added importance. In the Senior Cup, Bromley and Folkestone were beaten before Gillingham edged the semi-final at neutral Chatham. The Senior Shield saw the Fleet go one better in reaching the final only to produce a disappointing display against Dartford where, despite home advantage, they were soundly beaten 4-0.

Despite admission being pegged at 6d for adults and ground season tickets for just 10 shillings, crowds were still lower than the previous season and a deficit of £93 6s 11d occurred in what proved to be the last full season that Northfleet United ever played.

Results 1938/39

Aug 27	London Paper Mills	KLC Final	home	1-1	Trailor
Sep 03	Erith & Belvedere	KL	home	8-0	Revell 3, Trailor 2, Skinner 2, Weston
10	Gillingham Reserves	KLC1	away	2-4	Trailor, Weston
17	Bexleyheath & Welling	KSS1	home	4-2	Skinner 2, Wallbanks, OG
24	Bexleyheath & Welling	KL	away	5-1	Trailor 2, Revell, Hiscoke, OG
Oct 01	Dartford	KL	away	3-4	Revell, Trailor, Evans
08	Lloyds Sittingbourne	KL	home	9-0	Revell 3, Wallbanks 2, Weston 2, Fisher, Trailor
15	Folkestone	KL	home	5-1	Trailor, Fisher, Sperrin, Revell, Weston
22	Ashford Town	KL	away	1-2	Revell
24	West Ham Reserves	Friendly	away	1-2	
29	Bexleyheath & Welling	KL	home	4-1	Weston, Day, Hiscoke, OG
Nov 05	Sittingbourne	KL	away	3-2	Revell 2, Weston
12	Erith & Belvedere	KL	away	2-1	Hiscoke, Revell
19	Maidstone United	KL	home	7-1	Revell 3, Bennett 2, Evans 2
26	Tunbridge Wells Rangers	KL	home	9-2	Fisher 3, Bennett 2, Weston, Coxford, Hiscoke, OG
Dec 03	Sheppey United	KL	away	5-1	Duffield 2, Weston, Collins, Revell
10	Aylesford Paper Mills	KL	home	8-2	Day 3, Duffield 2, Revell, Bennett, Weston
12	West Ham Reserves	Friendly	at Tottenham	3-2	Bennett 3
17	Sittingbourne	KL	home	5-1	
31	Folkestone	KL	away	7-3	Revell 3, Bennett 2, Collins, Weston
Jan 07	Ashford Town	KL	home	3-2	Duffield 2, Coxford (pen)
11	Folkestone	KSS SF	home	3-2	Medley, Revell, Crisp
14	Tunbridge Wells Rangers	KL	away	1-1	Revell
21	Bromley	KSC1	away	4-3	Duffield 3, Revell
28	Gillingham Reserves	KL	home	2-0	Weston, Duffield
Feb 11	Folkestone	KSC2	home	3-1	Duffield, Weston, Revell
18	Gillingham Reserves	KL	away	2-5	Revell, Duffield
25	London Paper Mills	KL	away	4-0	Duffield 2, Bennett, Revell
Mar 04	Maidstone United	KL	away	1-1	Duffield
11	Canterbury Waverley	KL	away	1-2	Bennett
18	Gillingham Reserves	KSC SF	at Chatham	0-2	
25	Aylesford Paper Mills	KL	away	2-2	Revell, Weston
Apr 01	London Paper Mills	KL	home	1-1	Bennett
07	Dartford	KL	home	7-1	Bennett 3, Duffield 3, Weston
15	Dartford	KSS Final	home	0-4	
22	Lloyds Sittingbourne	KL	away	3-0	Bennett, Lown, Weston
29	Sheppey United	KL	home	6-0	Bennett 2, Revell, Weston, Lown, Duffield
May 06	Canterbury Waverley	KL	home	9-1	Bennett 4, Lown 3, Duffield, OG

1939/40

● *Stonebridge Road in the final year of Northfleet's active existence. Although this picture – against Dartford – dates from April 1939, five months later the Darts would provide the final opposition, the day before the outbreak of the Second World War*

The threat of war was casting a large shadow over the forthcoming season as the traditional reds v whites trial game took place at Stonebridge Road. The game proved extremely one sided as the Reds romped to a 13-3 victory with all their goals being scored by just two players. The twinkle-toed Les Bennett scored seven while Jack Browne, an ex-gardener's assistant from Boughton Monchelsea, notched six.

Browne was one of several newcomers alongside Sid Tickridge, who came down from Tottenham at 16 years of age – the very last off the Tottenham-to-Northfleet production line. Ex-Liverpool inside forward Syd Roberts also arrived but even as these players limbered up for the new season, it was highly questionable given the European situation whether they would see it through.

At least it got off to an impressive start on 26th August when Fleet crushed Lloyds Sittingbourne 11-0 with the dynamic duo of Bennett and Browne again causing devastation. Browne scored a double hat-trick and Bennett a mere single hat-trick as they netted the majority of the goals.

By the start of September the threat of war was looming ever closer and what proved to be the club's last game saw Fleet beat old rivals Dartford 4-3 in a

● *Sid Tickridge (below) was the last player to come off the Northfleet-Tottenham production line. He would serve in the Royal Navy in the forthcoming conflict*

thrilling game at Watling Street on 2nd September.

The side was clearly set for another successful season but it wasn't to be. The day before Germany had invaded Poland and the British Government had issued an ultimatum to withdraw or enter into a state of war.

After the game at Dartford, Joe Lingham – who had played for Northfleet in the previous century and presided over so much of the club's history to that point – called the players and management together. With other club officials, Lingham was aware that war was now inevitable and that an announcement to that effect was to be made the following morning by Prime Minister Neville Chamberlain.

He wished everybody good luck in the forthcoming conflict and, as he had 25 years earlier, closed the gates of Stonebridge Road as the storm clouds loomed.

The Kent League was cancelled after this date and resumed as two divisions split into East and West in late October, with fewer clubs. Northfleet, their decision made on the eve of war, were one of those who declined to enter. It was to be their final act.

Aug 26	Lloyds Sittingbourne	KL	home	**11-0**	Browne 6, Bennett 3, Dowes, Simpson
Sep 02	Dartford	KL	away	**4-3**	Roberts, Browne, Bennett, Simpson

1940-46

● In 1951, Tottenham Hotspur would win their first ever English league title. Five of that side learned their trade at Stonebridge Road in the colours of Northfleet United. They included Bill Nicholson, Les Medley, Ron Burgess, Ted Ditchburn and Les Bennett – and were managed by another former Cementer in Arthur Rowe

On the 9th December, 1943, Joe Lingham, the club president and Northfleet United's father figure, died at the age of 73.

He had been the driving force behind the club from the very start in its days as Northfleet Invicta in 1890, first as a player, then as chairman and finally as president – as well as being a high-ranking official within both the KCFA and FA.

At various times of crisis he was always the man to go to, usually by way of his own financial muscle, to save the day. He was the man responsible for resurrecting the club in both 1902 and 1918 and so, with his death, there was nobody to raise Northfleet United from its slumbers after six years of war in 1945.

Early in 1946, the chairman of the club – WJ Treadwell – could foresee no way forward for Northfleet United and on 5th April, 1946 – at the Factory Club, Northfleet, the site of so many past Fleet celebrations of success – he and club secretary Mr RW Smith met representatives of Gravesend United.

They were intent on forming a new 'Gravesend & Northfleet Football Club' and agreed to transfer assets to the new club for the sum of £1,000. An "amicable arrangement" was arrived at since "it was

impossible [for Northfleet] to continue in the present circumstances."

Treadwell and Smith signed off by thanking "all patrons and supporters for the interest shown in the club during its long and successful career and regret that their action has been unavoidable."

Meanwhile, at Gravesend United's football club dinner and dance, their new chairman Mr C Barton was moved to "refer to the fine record of the Northfleet United club" while appealing for "unstinted support for the new club, who would provide a first-class team worthy of the district."

These moves officially ended the activities of Northfleet United, one of the most successful clubs in Kent non-league history. The Cementers as they first became known, and then the Fleet – a nickname that stands

NORTHFLEET UNITED FOOTBALL CLUB
To the Editor.

Sir,—At a meeting between representatives of Northfleet United Football Club and the new Gravesend and Northfleet United Football Club, Ltd., held at the Factory Club on April 5th last, the old Northfleet Club considered that it was impossible to continue in the present circumstances and an amicable arrangement was arrived at, to dispose of the assets on the Northfleet football ground to the proposed new Company.

The Committee desire to thank all patrons and supporters for the interest shown in the Club during its long and successful career, and regret that their action has been unavoidable. They also sincerely hope that the interest and support so generously given the old Club in the past will be extended towards the new Club in its endeavour to foster and maintain a good standard of football in the district.—Yours faithfully,

W. J. TREADWELL
(Chairman),

R. W. SMITH
(Hon Secretary),

to this very day – had given entertainment to thousands in hard and troubled times.

Northfleet's legacy was an excellent ground at Stonebridge Road for the new Gravesend & Northfleet, who also took on the colours and nickname of the old club. And, away from Kent, Northfleet also left a huge legacy for Tottenham Hotspur who ran out for their first post-war Football League game with Birmingham City reaping the benefits of their Fleet association. No fewer than 10 of the starting 11 players were ex-Northfleet men and many went on to form the backbone of a Football League championship side – an incredible legacy left by the now-defunct club.

League Tables (Kent League)

Kent League Division 1 1930/31

FINAL TABLE	PL	W	D	L	F	A	Pts
Tunbridge Wells Rangers	36	29	4	3	150	23	62
Gillingham Reserves	36	27	5	4	103	44	59
Margate	36	24	10	2	99	27	58
Northfleet United	36	23	3	11	125	58	49
Chatham	36	20	6	10	134	65	46
Ashford	36	16	10	10	93	70	42
Dartford Reserves	36	18	5	13	85	79	41
Sheppey United	36	17	6	13	85	92	40
Sittingbourne	36	15	5	16	93	79	35
Canterbury Waverley	36	14	7	15	79	92	35
Maidstone United	36	14	4	18	79	95	32
Grays Thurrock United	36	12	8	16	87	108	32
Bexleyheath & Welling	36	13	4	19	72	99	30
Sittingbourne Paper Mills	36	9	6	21	60	110	24
Folkestone Reserves	36	11	1	24	80	121	23
Tilbury	36	10	2	24	57	112	22
Royal Marines	36	8	5	23	69	112	21
Dover	36	8	4	24	73	142	20
RN Depot	36	6	3	27	57	152	15

Kent League Division 1 1931/32

FINAL TABLE	PL	W	D	L	F	A	Pts
Northfleet United	36	29	4	3	150	23	62
Ashford Town	36	27	5	4	103	44	59
Tunbridge Wells Rangers	36	24	10	2	99	27	58
Margate	36	23	3	11	125	58	49
Chatham	36	20	6	10	134	65	46
Folkestone Reserves	36	16	10	10	93	70	42
Dartford Reserves	36	18	5	13	85	79	41
Canterbury Waverley	36	17	6	13	85	92	40
Gillingham Reserves	36	15	5	16	93	79	35
Bexleyheath & Welling	36	14	7	15	79	92	35
Grays Thurrock United	36	14	4	18	79	95	32
Lloyds Sittingbourne	36	12	8	16	87	108	32
Maidstone United	36	13	4	19	72	99	30
Royal Marines	36	9	6	21	60	110	24
Sheppey United	36	11	1	24	80	121	23
Erith & Belvedere	36	10	2	24	57	112	22
RN Depot	36	8	5	23	69	112	21
Sittingbourne	36	8	4	24	73	142	20
Dover	36	6	3	27	57	152	15

Kent League Division 1 1932/33

FINAL TABLE	PL	W	D	L	F	A	Pts
Margate	34	28	1	5	112	34	57
Northfleet United	34	28	1	5	126	50	57
Gillingham	34	22	4	8	130	44	48
Folkestone	34	20	4	10	114	56	44
Tunbridge Wells Rangers*	34	21	3	10	127	63	43
Chatham	34	17	5	12	95	66	39
Dartford	34	13	7	14	82	64	33
Ashford Town	34	16	1	17	79	76	33
Bexleyheath & Welling	34	14	5	15	65	77	33
Canterbury Waverley	34	14	4	16	82	89	32
Sittingbourne	34	13	5	16	70	109	31
Erith & Belvedere	34	13	3	18	70	97	29
Sheppey United	34	12	4	18	73	90	28
Maidstone United	34	11	5	18	78	105	27
Aylesford Paper Mills	34	11	5	18	79	112	27
Lloyds Sittingbourne	34	10	4	20	62	97	24
Royal Navy Depot	34	9	4	21	64	113	22
Royal Marines	34	1	1	32	32	198	3

* Deducted 2 points for fielding an ineligible player

Kent League Division 1 1933/34

FINAL TABLE	PL	W	D	L	F	A	Pts
London Paper Mills	36	30	2	4	111	42	62
Gillingham	36	26	4	6	118	50	56
Margate	36	23	3	10	94	58	49
Northfleet United	36	23	2	11	122	47	48
Ramsgate Press Wanderers	36	19	6	11	84	58	44
Royal Navy Depot	36	20	2	14	113	74	42
Dartford	36	18	5	13	75	63	41
Tunbridge Wells Rangers	36	16	8	12	76	46	40
Folkestone	36	15	5	16	102	71	35
Sheppey United	36	16	3	17	74	85	35
Canterbury Waverley	36	14	6	16	79	79	34
Lloyds Sittingbourne	36	13	8	15	64	75	34
Sittingbourne	36	11	10	15	57	90	32
Ashford Town	36	14	3	19	72	92	31
Aylesford Paper Mills	36	12	5	19	57	72	29
Erith & Belvedere	36	10	5	21	82	108	25
Bexleyheath & Welling	36	7	7	22	55	93	21
Maidstone United	36	8	3	25	59	126	19
Royal Marines	36	2	3	31	39	184	7

Kent League Division 1 1934/35

FINAL TABLE	PL	W	D	L	F	A	Pts
Northfleet United	36	26	7	3	110	30	59
London Paper Mills	36	24	5	7	95	40	53
Margate	36	23	4	9	110	51	50
Gillingham	36	19	6	11	97	61	44
Ashford Town	36	16	9	11	72	51	41
Canterbury Waverley	36	16	7	13	86	64	39
Ramsgate Athletic	36	16	6	14	69	65	38
Sittingbourne	36	16	4	16	67	76	36
Folkestone	36	17	1	18	81	77	35
Lloyds Sittingbourne	36	12	9	14	65	65	33
Dartford	36	13	6	17	64	76	32
Erith & Belvedere	36	13	4	19	62	90	30
Bexleyheath & Welling	36	11	7	18	74	93	29
Sheppey United	36	12	5	19	50	90	29
Maidstone United	36	12	4	20	58	90	28
Royal Navy Depot	36	11	6	19	81	109	28
Cray Wanderers	36	13	1	22	63	106	27
Tunbridge Wells Rangers	36	9	8	19	49	82	26
Aylesford Paper Mills	36	9	7	20	49	86	25

Kent League Division 1 1935/36

FINAL TABLE	PL	W	D	L	F	A	Pts
Northfleet United	36	26	5	5	158	41	57
Folkestone	36	27	3	6	129	44	57
Margate	36	20	8	8	86	48	48
Canterbury Waverley	36	22	3	11	116	59	47
Gillingham	36	20	5	11	99	58	45
London Paper Mills	36	21	2	13	110	64	44
Cray Wanderers	36	16	7	13	62	83	39
Dartford	36	16	6	14	80	69	38
Bexleyheath & Welling	36	15	8	13	79	75	38
Lloyds Sittingbourne	36	15	8	13	66	71	38
Sittingbourne	36	13	9	14	77	84	35
Ashford Town	36	12	6	18	84	97	30
Ramsgate Athletic	36	12	6	18	61	84	30
Aylesford Paper Mills	36	12	6	18	61	98	30
Tunbridge Wells Rangers	36	12	5	19	82	120	29
Sheppey United	36	10	5	21	63	87	25
Maidstone United	36	9	6	21	63	122	24
Erith & Belvedere	36	9	3	24	57	97	21
Royal Navy Depot	36	3	3	30	42	174	9

Kent League Division 1 1936/37

FINAL TABLE	PL	W	D	L	F	A	Pts
Northfleet United	32	25	2	5	128	29	52
Margate	32	24	4	4	107	41	52
Lloyds Sittingbourne	32	18	6	8	82	61	42
Gillingham	32	19	2	11	81	50	40
London Paper Mills	32	17	4	11	77	52	38
Ashford Town	32	16	5	11	76	53	37
Tunbridge Wells Rangers	32	18	1	13	80	69	37
Bexleyheath & Welling	32	14	5	13	72	54	33
Canterbury Waverley	32	11	8	13	74	63	30
Folkestone	32	12	4	16	79	99	28
Aylesford Paper Mills	32	12	3	17	68	89	27
Sittingbourne	32	9	8	15	68	86	26
Dartford	32	10	5	17	64	77	25
Erith & Belvedere	32	9	6	17	46	85	24
Sheppey United	32	8	6	18	44	80	22
Maidstone United	32	7	7	18	55	100	21
Cray Wanderers	32	3	4	25	55	164	10

● *George Ludford's astonishing record saw him score 101 goals in 1935/36*

League Tables (Kent League)

Kent League Division 1 1937/38

FINAL TABLE	PL	W	D	L	F	A	Pts
Margate	32	24	4	4	103	31	52
Aylesford Paper Mills	32	24	4	4	102	42	52
Northfleet United	**32**	**23**	**5**	**4**	**116**	**29**	**51**
London Paper Mills	32	20	9	3	88	35	49
Canterbury Waverley	32	16	8	8	74	53	40
Gillingham	32	16	3	13	84	63	35
Bexleyheath & Welling	32	14	5	13	68	60	33
Sittingbourne	32	14	4	14	74	64	32
Folkestone	32	12	6	14	78	85	30
Lloyds Sittingbourne	32	11	8	13	69	78	30
Ashford Town	32	11	6	15	67	75	28
Dartford	32	8	7	17	51	89	23
Erith & Belvedere	32	9	4	19	47	79	22
Sheppey United	32	9	4	19	46	108	22
Tunbridge Wells Rangers	32	10	1	21	60	88	21
Maidstone United	32	5	3	24	47	97	13
Cray Wanderers	32	5	1	26	39	130	11

Kent League Division 1 1938/39

FINAL TABLE	PL	W	D	L	F	A	Pts
Northfleet United	**28**	**20**	**4**	**4**	**125**	**38**	**44**
Gillingham	28	20	2	6	77	29	42
London Paper Mills	28	18	4	6	88	45	40
Ashford Town	28	16	3	9	89	59	35
Bexleyheath & Welling	28	15	4	9	67	52	34
Erith & Belvedere	28	14	3	11	77	65	31
Aylesford Paper Mills	28	12	5	11	69	67	29
Lloyds Sittingbourne	28	12	4	12	78	71	28
Canterbury Waverley	28	11	5	12	71	88	27
Sittingbourne	28	8	7	13	60	74	23
Dartford	28	8	5	15	56	90	21
Tunbridge Wells Rangers	28	7	4	17	60	114	18
Maidstone United	28	6	5	17	43	81	17
Folkestone	28	5	6	17	57	85	16
Sheppey United	28	5	5	18	42	101	15

● *Below: Northfleet go on the offensive at London Paper Mills in a 3-1 win in the Kent League in January 1938*

Les Medley

Bill Edrich

THOMAS CLAY

F. & J. SMITH'S CIGARETTES

SUNDERLAND.
C. M. BUCHAN.

R. BURGESS

Percy Hooper

E. O'CALLAGHAN

REAL-LIFE STORIES of LEAGUE SOCCER

FOOTBALL WEEKLY

CENTRES WHO GET ME GUESSING BY JOE JAMES (Brentford)

THE FOOTBALLER FALKIRK FORGOT

"I CROCKED MY BEST PAL!" BY JOE SMITH

"TURF" CIGARETTES

TED DITCHBURN

PLAYER'S CIGARETTES.

T. COOK.

CHURCHMAN'S CIGARETTES

R. IVERSON (ASTON VILLA)

PROMINENT FOOTBALLERS.

W KENNEDY,
WEST HAM UNITED.

E. HANNEY.
P. O. Collier, Photographer.

Albert Ringrose

BUCHAN'S FOOTBALL MONTHLY

JULY. 1954

Vivid pictures and exclusive articles

ENGLAND DISASTER —THE TRUTH BY CHARLES BUCHAN

Northfleet had a proud history of producing future Football League stars and enticing established ones to this little corner of north Kent. The players above were just a handful of the many talented footballers to have played for the Fleet

Chapter Six:
The Fleet files

Opponents: a complete record

OPPONENTS	PL	W	D	L	Goals
Aldershot	6	3	1	2	13-11
Argyll & Sutherlanders	1	1	0	0	2-0
Ashford Railway Works	19	13	3	3	64-27
Ashford Town	20	16	2	2	76-17
Ashford United	4	3	0	1	14-10
Aylesford Paper Mills	14	11	3	0	63-10
Bexleyheath	36	32	1	3	142-33
Bostall Heath	1	1	0	0	11-1
Bournemouth & Boscombe A.	2	0	1	1	0-1
Bournemouth Reserves	6	3	2	1	10-8
Brighton & Hove Alb Reserves	6	2	2	2	12-10
Bristol City	2	0	0	2	3-7
Bromley	12	10	0	2	41-23
Callenders Athletic	3	3	0	0	11-3
Camberley & Yorktown	1	1	0	0	11-1
Canterbury Waverley	23	14	5	4	62-31
Catford Southend	9	8	0	1	39-19
Charlton Albion	3	3	0	0	17-3
Charlton Athletic **	15	5	4	6	16-20
Chatham**	78	30	19	29	142-116
Civil Service	1	1	0	0	8-0
Clapton Orient	1	0	0	1	0-2
Crayford	14	8	2	4	33-14
Cray Wanderers	28	16	4	8	97-47
Croydon Common	4	0	2	2	7-10
Crystal Palace Reserves	8	4	1	3	12-14
Dartford **	99	47	17	35	235-169
Dover	12	11	1	0	47-9
Eltham	9	2	2	5	14-27
Erith & Belvedere	30	28	0	2	105-24
Exeter City	1	0	0	1	0-3
Faversham	8	7	0	1	36-3
Freemantle	1	0	0	1	0-3
Folkestone**	53	33	5	15	152-90

OPPONENTS	PL	W	D	L	Goals
Folkestone Harvieans	1	1	0	0	7-1
Foots Cray	4	4	0	0	20-6
Gillingham ***	76	40	11	25	200-151
Gravesend United	52	24	10	18	102-94
Grays Athletic	4	3	0	1	11-15
Grays Thurrock United	14	12	0	2	59-16
Grays Town	2	1	0	1	3-3
Greenhithe	1	1	0	0	5-1
Guildford United	7	3	1	3	19-14
Holmesdale	3	2	0	1	3-4
Ilford	1	1	0	0	5-2
Kettering Town	6	3	1	2	18-11
KGA Volunteers	1	1	0	0	2-0
Lewisham Montrose	2	1	0	1	6-3
Lloyds Sittingbourne	21	18	1	2	96-9
London Caledonians	1	0	0	1	0-1
London Paper Mills	16	10	3	3	39-13
Loyal Regiment	4	2	1	1	11-4
Metrogas	13	7	2	4	35-25
Maidstone United	56	34	6	16	176-87
Millwall	5	0	1	4	5-20
Millwall Reserves	8	2	0	6	8-18
Margate **	49	21	6	22	86-73
New Brompton Amateurs	4	2	0	2	16-8
New Crusaders	1	0	0	1	2-7
Northampton Reserves	2	0	1	1	2-5
Northumberland Oddfellows	5	3	2	0	16-5
North Woolwich	2	1	1	0	5-2
Norwich City Reserves	6	3	0	3	14-8
Ordnance	2	2	0	0	5-0
Orpington	13	9	1	3	47-17
Peterborough & Fleeton Utd	7	2	0	5	6-16
Plumstead St Johns	2	2	0	0	9-3
Poole	6	3	1	2	14-8

OPPONENTS	PL	W	D	L	Goals
Prices Athletic	4	3	1	0	13-4
Queens Park Rangers	2	0	1	1	2-4
Ramsgate (all teams)	21	10	4	7	55-28
Reading	4	0	1	3	4-5
Rochester	13	8	0	5	36-22
RASC Grove Park	2	2	0	0	8-2
RMLI	11	9	2	0	29-10
Royal Artillery	2	0	0	2	1-4
Royal Dublin Fusiliers	2	1	1	0	3-2
Royal Engineers Depot Batt.	7	6	1	0	28-7
Royal Engineers Service Batt.	3	0	2	1	4-9
Royal Engineers Training Batt.	6	5	0	1	23-10
Royal Irish Rifles	4	1	0	3	6-12
Royal Marines*	15	13	0	2	74-10
Royal Navy Depot	45	38	2	5	170-46
Royal Ordnance	4	3	1	0	12-4
Royal Scots	2	1	0	1	1-1
Royal Warwick Regiment	2	2	0	0	9-2
Royal West Kents	5	4	0	1	19-7
Sheppey United	100	60	14	26	271-146
Shoreham	1	1	0	0	6-0
Sittingbourne	85	55	11	19	218-110
Southampton	4	0	0	4	4-13
Southampton Reserves	6	0	3	3	8-12
Southend Utd Reserves	2	1	1	0	4-3
Star Rovers	2	1	1	0	4-2
Swanscombe	17	6	3	8	30-31
Swindon Town	4	0	1	3	5-15
Thames Association	4	2	0	2	9-9
Tilbury	2	1	1	0	6-1
Tottenham Hotspur	4	1	0	3	3-12
Tunbridge Wells Rangers	48	31	5	12	154-80
Vickers Crayford	4	4	0	0	14-2
Warmley Bristol	1	1	0	0	3-1

OPPONENTS	PL	W	D	L	Goals
West Norwood	1	0	0	1	1-6
Whitstable	2	2	0	0	9-2
Wimbledon	1	1	0	0	4-1
Woolwich	14	11	0	3	59-14
Woolwich Argus	2	2	0	0	6-1
Woolwich Arsenal Reserves	3	0	1	2	6-14
Woolwich Poly	4	4	4	0	13-3
Worthing	1	1	0	0	5-0

KEY

* *This includes both Royal Marines Deal and Chatham, although separate teams results often failed to differ between them .*

** *Includes both first team and reserves as it was not always possible to be sure of which team was playing.*

*** *Also includes results under Gillingham's former name of New Brompton*

● *Sheppey United (stripes) were Northfleet's most regular opponents, with the clubs meeting 100 times in Southern League and Kent League and cup competitions. Dartford were next, with 99 games against the Fleet*

League record by season

Season	League	PL	W	D	L	Goals	Pts	Position	Other achievements
1895/96	Kent League Div. 1	22	16	2	4	85-31	34	1/12	*CCC runners-up*
1896/97	Southern League	20	5	4	11	24-46	14	9/12	*TMC (3rd of 6), SCC runners-up*
1897/98	Southern League	22	4	3	15	29-60	11	11/12	*TMC (4th of 8)*
1903/04	West Kent League	13	2	2	9	13-36	6	8/8	
1904/05	West Kent League	20	7	3	10	37-50	17	8/11	
1905/06	West Kent League	14	5	2	7	19-25	12	5/8	
1906/07	Kent League Div. 1	14	9	0	5	37-19	18	2/8	*WKL (1st of 11)*
1907/08	Kent League Div. 1	16	14	1	1	54-13	19	1/9	*WKL (1st of 11)*
1908/09	Kent League Div. 1	16	13	1	2	52-22	27	1/9	*KSC runners-up*
1909/10	Kent League Div. 1	22	17	2	3	74-31	36	1/12	*KSC, TMC winners*
1910/11	Kent League Div. 1	26	7	4	15	38-64	18	13/14	
1911/12	Kent League Div. 1	28	10	5	13	47-48	25	8/15	
1912/13	Kent League Div. 1	28	14	5	9	58-55	33	4/15	*KSC winners*
1913/14	Kent League Div. 1	30	17	5	8	63-49	37	4/16	*KSC runners-up*
1919/20	Kent League Div. 1	24	19	3	2	70-22	41	1/13	*KSC runners-up*
1920/21	Kent League Div. 1	32	21	3	8	76-40	45	3/17	*KSC winners, KSS runners-up*
1921/22	Kent League Div. 1	28	18	6	4	78-36	42	2/15	*KSS runners-up*
1922/23	Kent League Div. 1	32	17	5	10	88-41	39	4/17	
1923/24	Kent League Div. 1	30	15	5	10	61-35	35	4/16	*KSC, KLC winners, KSS joint winners*
1924/25	Kent League Div. 1	34	29	1	4	114-25	59	2/18	*KSC, KSS winners*
1925/26	Kent League Div. 1	36	29	3	4	172-48	61	1/19	*KSC, KSS winners*
1926/27	Kent League Div. 1	26	15	3	8	76-51	31	5/14	*KSC winners, KLC runners-up*
1927/28	Southern League - East	34	17	7	10	83-54	41	3/18	*KSC winners*
1928/29	Southern League - East	36	17	4	15	87-65	38	9/19	*KSS winners*
1929/30	Southern League - East	32	6	7	19	53-77	19	16/17	
1930/31	Kent League Div. 1	36	23	3	11	125-58	49	4/19	
1931/32	Kent League Div. 1	36	29	4	3	150-23	62	1/19	*KLC winners*
1932/33	Kent League Div. 1	34	28	1	5	126-50	57	2/18	
1933/34	Kent League Div. 1	36	23	2	11	122-47	48	4/19	
1934/35	Kent League Div. 1	36	26	7	3	110-30	59	1/19	*KLC winners, KSS runners-up*
1935/36	Kent League Div. 1	36	26	5	5	158-41	57	1/19	
1936/37	Kent League Div. 1	32	25	2	5	128-29	52	1/17	*KLC winners*
1937/38	Kent League Div. 1	32	23	5	4	116-29	51	3/17	*KSC winners, KLC joint winners*
1938/39	Kent League Div. 1	28	20	4	4	125-38	44	1/15	*KSS runners-up*

FA Cup round reached by season

Season	Round reached	Results
1895/96	2nd Qualifying	*Sheppey United 1-4, Dartford 3-2, 3-3*
1896/97	4th Qualifying	*Millwall Athletic 1-6, New Brompton 3-1, Dartford 4-1, Civil Service 8-0*
1897/98	1st Qualifying	*New Brompton 1-3*
1903/04	Preliminary	*New Brompton 0-2*
1904/05	Preliminary	*Sheppey United 0-2*
1905/06	*Did not enter*	—
1906/07	4th Qualifying	*West Norwood 1-6, Gravesend United 4-2, 2-2, Sittingbourne 2-1, Ashford 3-2*
1907/08	Preliminary	*Bromley 0-6*
1908/09	4th Qualifying	*Croydon Common 3-4, 1-1, Royal Engineers DB 3-1, 1-1, Dartford 5-2, Plumstead St Johns 5-2*
1909/10	4th Qualifying	*Croydon Common 1-3, 2-2, Chatham 4-1, Royal Engineers DB 5-1, Sheppey Utd 6-5, Dartford 2-1, 2-2*
1910/11	Preliminary	*Dartford 0-1*
1911/12	Preliminary	*Ashford Railway Works 1-2*
1912/13	1st Qualifying	*Sheppey United 0-1, Sittingbourne 4-1*
1913/14	1st Qualifying	*New Crusaders 2-7, Ramsgate 4-0*
1914/15	2nd Qualifying	*Dartford 3-4, Sittingbourne 2-1, 2-2, 2-2, Cray Wanderers 3-1*
1919/20	3rd Qualifying	*Sheppey United 3-4, Royal Ordnance 3-1, Margate 7-2, Catford Southend 4-2*
1920/21	3rd Qualifying	*Maidstone United 0-5, Worthing 5-0, Sheppey United 4-1, Whitstable 6-2*
1921/22	5th Qualifying	*Gillingham 1-3, 0-0, Guildford United 1-0, Chatham 3-0, Folkestone 4-2, Margate 1-0, Shoreham 6-0*
1922/23	2nd Qualifying	*Sittingbourne 0-2, Chatham 3-1, 0-0, Folkestone 4-1, 3-3*
1923/24	1st Qualifying	*Ramsgate 2-4, Sheppey United 4-3, 2-2*
1924/25	1st Qualifying	*Chatham 2-3, Ashford RW 3-1*
1925/26	1st Round Proper	*Queens Park Rangers 0-2, 2-2*
1926/27	2nd Round Proper	*Luton Town 2-6, Sittingbourne 3-1*
1927/28	1st Round Proper	*London Caledonians 0-1*
1928/29	2nd Round Proper	*Charlton Athletic 1-5, Ilford 5-2*
1929/30	2nd Round Proper	*Clapton Orient 0-2, Wimbledon 4-1, Sittingbourne 4-2*
1930/31	1st Round Proper	*Exeter City 0-3, Dartford 1-0*
1931/32	1st Round Proper	*Bournemouth 0-1, 1-1, Chatham 4-1*
1932/33	4th Qualifying	*Dartford 0-2*
1933/34	1st Round Proper	*Dartford 0-2, Camberley & Yorktown 11-1*
1934/35	4th Qualifying	*Ashford 2-3*
1935/36	4th Qualifying	*Folkestone 1-2*
1936/37	4th Qualifying	*Dartford 0-5, Callenders Athletic 3-2, Chatham 4-0, London Paper Mills 1-0, Whitstable 3-0*
1937/38	*Did not enter*	—
1938/39	*Did not enter*	—

Full FA Cup record by season

Season	Round	Opponent	Score
1895/96	1Q	Dartford (h)	3-3
	1Q Replay	Dartford (a)	3-2
	2Q	Sheppey United (a)	1-4
1896/97	1Q	Civil Service (h)	8-0
	2Q	Dartford (a)	4-1
	3Q	New Brompton (h)	3-1
	4Q	Millwall Athletic (a)	1-6
1897/98	1Q	New Brompton (h)	1-3
1898–1903		-- No entry --	
1903/04	Prelim.	New Brompton Amateurs (h)	0-2
1904/05	Prelim.	Sheppey United (h)	0-1
1905/06		-- No entry --	
1906/07	1Q	Ashford United (a)	3-2
	2Q	Sittingbourne (a)	2-1
	3Q	Gravesend United (h)	4-2
	4Q	West Norwood (a)	1-6
1907/08	Prelim.	Bromley (a)	0-6
1908/09	1Q	Plumstead St Johns (h)	5-2
	2Q	Dartford (h)	5-2
	3Q	Royal Engineers DB (h)	1-1
	3Q Replay	Royal Engineers DB (a)	1-0
	4Q	Croydon Common (h)	1-1
	4Q Replay	Croydon Common (a)	3-4
1909/10	Prelim.	Dartford (a)	2-2
	Prelim. Replay	Dartford (h)	2-1
	1Q	Sheppey United (h)	6-5
	2Q	Royal Engineers DB (h)	5-1
	3Q	Chatham (a)	4-1
	4Q	Croydon Common (a)	2-2
	4Q Replay	Croydon Common (h)	1-3
1910/11	Prelim.	Dartford (h)	0-1
1911/12	Prelim.	Ashford RW (a)	1-2
1912/13	Prelim.	Sittingbourne (h)	4-1
	1Q	Sheppey United (h)	0-1
1913/14	Prelim.	Ramsgate (a)	4-0
	1Q	New Crusaders (h)	2-7
1914/15	Prelim.	Cray Wanderers (h)	3-1
	1Q	Sittingbourne (a)	2-2
	1Q Replay	Sittingbourne (h)	2-2
	1Q Replay 2	Sittingbourne (neutral)	2-1
	2Q	Dartford (a)	3-4
1919/20	Prelim.	Catford Southend (h)	4-2
	1Q	Margate (h)	7-2
	2Q	Royal Ordnance (a)	3-1
	3Q	Sheppey United (h)	3-4
1920/21	Prelim.	Whitstable (h)	6-2
	1Q	Sheppey United (h)	4-1
	2Q	Worthing (a)	5-0
	3Q	Maidstone United (a)	0-5

Season	Round	Opponent	Score
1921/22	Prelim.	Shoreham (a)	6-0
	1Q	Margate (a)	1-0
	2Q	Folkestone (h)	4-2
	3Q	Chatham (a)	3-0
	4Q	Guildford (h)	1-0
	5Q	Gillingham (h)	0-0
	5Q Replay	Gillingham (a)	1-3
1922/23	Prelim.	Folkestone (a)	3-3
	Prelim. Replay	Folkestone (h)	4-1 aet
	1Q	Chatham (h)	0-0
	1Q Replay	Chatham (a)	3-1
	2Q	Sittingbourne (a)	0-2
1923/24	Prelim.	Sheppey United (h)	2-2
	Prelim. Replay	Sheppey United (a)	4-3
	1Q	Ramsgate (a)	2-4
1924/25	1Q	Chatham (a)	2-3
1925/26	1	Queens Park Rangers (h)	2-2
	1 Replay	Queen Park Rangers (a)	1-3
1926/27	1	Sittingbourne (a)	3-1
	2	Luton Town (a)	2-6
1927/28	1	London Caledonians (h)	0-1
1928/29	1	Ilford (h)	5-2
	2	Charlton Athletic (h)	1-5
1929/30	4Q	Sittingbourne (a)	4-2
	1	Wimbledon (a)	4-1
	2	Clapton Orient (a)	0-2
1930/31	4Q	Dartford (h)	1-0
	1	Exeter City (h)	0-3
1931/32	4Q	Chatham (a)	4-1
	1	Bournemouth (a)	0-0
	1 Replay	Bournemouth (h)	0-1
1932/33	4Q	Dartford (a)	0-2
1933/34	4Q	Camberley & Yorktown (h)	11-1
	1	Dartford (h)	0-2
1934/35	4Q	Ashford Town (h)	2-3
1935/36	4Q	Folkestone (h)	1-2
1936/37	1Q	London Paper Mills (h)	1-0
	2Q	Chatham (h)	4-0
	3Q	Callenders Athletic (h)	3-2
	4Q	Dartford (h)	0-5
1937/38		-- No entry --	
1938/39		-- No entry --	

Kent Senior Shield record by season

Season	Round	Opponent	Score
1913/14	1	Chatham (h)	0-2
1919/20	1	Gillingham (a)	1-2
1920/21	1	Maidstone United (a)	1-0
	Semi-final	Sheppey United (h)	3-1
	Final	Margate (neutral)	0-2
1921/22	1	Margate (h)	4-1
	Semi-final	Folkestone (h)	3-1
	Final	Maidstone United (a)	1-2
1922/23	1	Maidstone United (h)	1-1
	1 Replay	Maidstone United (a)	0-1
1923/24	1	RN Depot (h)	3-1
	2	Charlton Athletic (h)	0-0
	2 Replay	Charlton Athletic (a) *	2-3
	Semi-final	Sittingbourne (h)	2-1
	Final	Gillingham (h) **	0-0
1924/25	1	Sittingbourne (h)	1-0
	Semi-final	Charlton Athletic (h)	2-1
	Final	Chatham (neutral)	1-0
1925/26	1	Charlton Athletic (a)	2-1
	Semi-final	Folkestone (h)	4-2
	Final	Gillingham (a)	7-5
1926/27	1	Chatham (a) ***	1-1
1927/28	1	Sheppey United (a)	0-1
1928/29	1	Dartford (a)	1-1
	1 Replay	Dartford (h)	3-1
	Semi-final	Sittingbourne (h)	6-2
	Final	Sheppey United (h)	5-2
1929/30	1	Dartford (a)	1-1
	1 Replay	Dartford (h)	0-2
1930/31	1	Sheppey United (h)	3-0
	Semi-final	Margate (a)	0-2
1931/32	1	Folkestone (a)	1-3
1932/33	1	Dartford (h)	3-3
	1 Replay	Dartford (a)	1-3
1933/34	1	Charlton Athletic (h)	2-0
	Semi-final	Dartford (a)	2-2
1934/35	1	Ramsgate (h)	4-0
	Semi-final	Gillingham (h)	3-3
	Semi Replay	Gillingham (a)	4-2
	Final	Dartford (a)	1-3
1935/36	1	Margate (h)	3-3
	1 Replay	Margate (a)	1-2
1936/37	1	Charlton Athletic (h)	1-0
	Semi-final	Folkestone (a)	1-3
1937/38	1	Tunbridge Wells Rangers (h)	7-0
	Semi-final	Margate (a)	0-2
1938/39	1	Bexleyheath & Welling (h)	4-2
	Semi-final	Folkestone (h)	3-2
	Final	Dartford (h)	0-4

This competition was by invitation from the KCFA who would rather the top eight teams from the county to compete for the Shield. The exception was 1923/24 when a larger entry was accepted.

*** = Charlton disqualified for fielding ineligible player*
* = Trophy shared with Gillingham
** = Fleet resigned from competition for failing to arrange replay

Kent League Cup record by season

Season	Round	Opponent	Score
1923/24	1	Dartford (a)	1-0
	2	RN Depot (h)	6-1
	Semi-final	Sittingbourne (h)	4-2
	Final	Ashford RW (h)	2-0
1924/25	1	Sheppey United (h)	1-3
1925/26	1	Catford Southend (a)	2-1
	2	Dartford (h)	1-2
1926/27	2	Loyal Regiment (a)	2-2
	2 Replay	Loyal Regiment (h)	5-0
	Semi-final	Margate (h)	2-1
	Final	RN Depot (h)	2-3
1930/31	1	Dartford (a)	2-5
1931/32	1	Gillingham Reserves (a)	6-0
	2	RN Depot (a)	2-0
	Semi-final	Dartford (a)	3-2
	Final	Folkestone (a)	1-1
	Final Replay	Folkestone (h)	1-0
1932/33	2	Canterbury Waverley (h)	5-1
	Semi-final	Margate (a)	2-0
	Final	Tunbridge Wells Rangers (a)	1-5
1933/34	1	Gillingham Reserves (h)	2-1
	2	Tunbridge Wells Rangers (h)	2-3
1934/35	2	Ashford (a)	5-1
	Semi-final	Tunbridge Wells Rangers (a)	3-0
	Final	GIllingham Reserves (h)	3-0
1935/36	2	Folkestone (a)	1-1
	2 Replay	Folkestone (h)	4-2
	Semi-final	Dartford (a)	3-3
	Semi Replay	Dartford (h)	0-1
1936/37	2	Tunbridge Wells Rangers (h)	3-0
	Semi-final	Maidstone United (h)	4-0
	Final	Folkestone (h)	2-0
1937/38	2	Dartford (a)	5-2
	Semi-final	Tunbridge Wells Rangers (a)	3-1
	Final	London Paper Mills (h) *	1-1
1938/39	1	Gillingham Reserves (a)	2-4

Northfleet took part in this competition from its inauguration in 1923/24 up to and including 1938/39, except for 1927–30 when members of the Southern League.

* = Trophy shared with London Paper Mills

● *Sir Gilbert Parker MP was the founder of the Kent Senior Shield in 1913. He was MP for Gravesend from 1900–18 and often championed the cause of Northfleet's neighbouring football club*

Kent Senior Cup record by season

Season	Round	Opponent	Score
1895/96	*Northfleet awarded trophy (as Kent League winners)*		
1897/98	1Q	Dover (a) *	2-1
1898–1903		-- No entry --	
1904/05	3	3rd KGA Volunteers (a)	2-0
	4	Crayford Athletic (h)	1-0
	5	Eltham (h)	0-2
1905/06	1Q	Orpington (a)	2-2
	1Q Replay	Orpington (h)	1-3
1906/07	1	Swanscombe **	0-1
	2	Argyll & Sutherlanders (a)	2-0
	3	Sheppey United (h)	1-1
	3 Replay	Sheppey United (a)	2-6
1907/08	1	Sheppey United (a)	3-3
	1 Replay	Sheppey United (h)	2-2
	1 Replay (2)	Sheppey United (New Brompton)	1-2
1908/09	1	Plumstead St Johns (h)	4-1
	2	Dartford (h) ***	1-2
	3	Gravesend United (a)	3-1
	4	Faversham (h)	4-0
	Semi-final	Sittingbourne (neutral)	3-0
	Final	Maidstone United (a)	2-4
1909/10	2	Bromley (h)	4-2
	3	Sheppey United (h)	3-2
	Semi-final	Dartford (at New Brompton)	1-0
	Final	Chatham (at Maidstone)	2-0
1910/11	1	Rochester (a)	2-1
	2	Gravesend United (h)	1-1
	2 Replay	Gravesend United (a)	1-1
	2 Replay (2)	Gravesend United (at Dartford)	1-1
	2 Replay (3)	Gravesend United (at Chatham)	1-3
1911/12	1	Sittingbourne (a)	2-3
1912/13	1	Ashford (h)	8-0
	2	Sittingbourne (a)	2-0
	Semi-final	Tunbridge Wells R (at Chatham)	2-0
	Final	Gravesend United (at Maidstone)	2-1
1913/14	1	Margate (a)	3-0
	2	Sittingbourne (a)	2-2
	2 Replay	Sittingbourne (h)	5-3
	Semi-final	Chatham (at Gravesend)	2-1
	Final	Maidstone United (a)	0-1
1919/20	1	Royal Ordnance (h)	6-1
	2	RASC (h)	4-1
	Semi-final	Sittingbourne (at Charlton)	1-0
	Final	Maidstone United (a)	1-2
1920/21	1	Maidstone United (a)	1-0
	2	Margate (a)	0-0
	2 Replay	Margate (h)	3-2
	Semi-final	Sittingbourne (at Chatham)	2-0
	Final	Ramsgate (at Maidstone)	1-0
1921/22	1	Ashford RW (a)	2-3
1922/23	1	Tunbridge Wells Rangers (a)	2-0
	2	Sittingbourne (a)	1-2

Season	Round	Opponent	Score
1923/24	1	Chatham (h)	0-0
	1 Replay	Chatham (a)	5-1
	2	Ashford RW (h)	5-0
	Semi-final	Sittingbourne (at Chatham)	2-2
	Semi Replay	Sittingbourne (at Chatham)	2-0
	Final	Dartford (at Maidstone)	1-0
1924/25	1	Cray Wanderers (a)	5-0
	2	Sheppey United (h)	2-1
	Semi-final	Grays Thurrock (at Dartford)	6-0
	Final	Sittingbourne (at Maidstone)	8-2
1925/26	1	Grays Thurrock (h)	6-2
	2	Sheppey United (h)	7-1
	Semi-final	Chatham (h)	4-1
	Final	Folkestone (at Maidstone)	1-0
1926/27	1	Royal Marines (h)	8-0
	2	Dartford (h)	4-2
	Semi-final	Chatham (at Maidstone)	2-0
	Final	Sheppey United (at Maidstone)	1-0
1927/28	1	Chatham (a)	7-1
	2	Margate (a)	3-2
	Semi-final	RN Depot (at Dartford)	4-1
	Final	Sittingbourne (at Maidstone)	3-1
1928/29	1	Erith & Belvedere (h)	7-1
	2	Sheppey United (h)	0-1
1929/30	1	Bromley (a)	6-2
	2	Tunbridge Wells Rangers (h)	1-1
	2 Replay	Tunbridge Wells Rangers (a)	5-1
	Semi-final	Sittingbourne (at Maidstone)	0-1
1930/31	1	Chatham (a)	1-1
	1 Replay	Chatham (h)	1-3
1931/32	1	Margate (a)	1-0
	2	Sheppey United (a)	1-2
1932/33	1	Margate (a)	1-3
1933/34	1	Sheppey United (a)	4-2
	2	London Paper Mills (h)	3-0
	Semi-final	Folkestone (at Maidstone)	0-7
1934/35	1	Sheppey United (a)	2-1
	2	London Paper Mills (a)	2-1
	Semi-final	Folkestone (at Ashford)	1-3
1935/36	1	Canterbury Waverley (a)	2-1
	2	Lloyds Sittingbourne (a)	8-0
	Semi-final	Margate (at Canterbury)	0-1
1936/37	1	Bostall Heath (h)	11-1
	2	Canterbury Waverley (a)	2-2
	2 Replay	Canterbury Waverley (a)	3-1
	Semi-final	Margate (at Canterbury)	0-2
1937/38	1	Ashford (a)	3-0
	2	Erith & Belvedere (a)	2-1 aet
	Semi-final	Margate (at Maidstone)	1-0
	Final	Dover (at Maidstone)	2-1
1938/39	1	Bromley (a)	4-3
	2	Folkestone (h)	3-1
	Semi-final	Gillingham Res. (at Chatham)	0-2

* = Northfleet disqualified for fielding ineligible player

** = Swanscombe disqualified for fielding ineligible players

*** = Dartford disqualified for fielding ineligible players

Other cup competitions

KENT JUNIOR CUP

Season	Round	Opponent	Score
1892/93	1	Star Rovers (a)	2-2
	1 Replay	Star Rovers (h)	2-0
	2	Swanscombe (a)	0-1
1893/94	1	Woolwich Poly (h)	2-1
	2	Swanscombe (h)	1-1
	2 Replay	Swanscombe (a)	0-4
1894/95	1 & 2	Byes	
	3	Greenhithe (a)	5-1
	4	Woolwich Poly (a)	6-1
	Semi-final	Holmesdale (neutral)	6-0
	Final	Chatham (neutral)	2-0

As its title suggested, a competition for junior clubs which meant that Northfleet only took part until 1894/95, when they won it.

CHATHAM CHARITY CUP

Season	Round	Opponent	Score
1895/96	1	Bromley (a)	3-2
	Semi-final	Sheppey United (h)	4-1
	Final	New Brompton (neutral)	2-2
	Final Replay	New Brompton (neutral)	0-2
1896/97	1	Swanscombe (h)	0-4
1922/23	1	RM Light Infantry (h)	2-1
	Semi-final	Chatham (h)	0-1
1923/24	1	Chatham (h)	0-0
	1 Replay	Chatham (a)	1-3

These competitions were very popular around the turn of the 20th century but what was surprising about this competition was that Northfleet returned to it, briefly, after a gap of close to a quarter of century.

SEVENOAKS CHARITY CUP

Season	Round	Opponent	Score
1896/97	1	Swanscombe (a)	4-1
	2	Folkestone (a)	1-1
	2 Replay	Folkestone (h)	4-2
	Semi-final	New Brompton (neutral)	1-0
	Final	Royal Engineers TB (neutral)	2-4

Entered for only one season – the original semi-final with New Brompton was abandoned after 80 minutes due to bad light, with the score the same as the eventual result.

GRAVESEND CHARITY CUP

Season	Round	Opponent	Score
1905/06	1	Rochester (a) *	3-6
	1	Rochester (h)	3-0
	Semi-final	Gravesend United (a)	2-4
1906/07	1	Swanscombe (h)	4-1
	Semi-final	Gravesend United (a)	2-4

Large crowds watched the two semi-finals with neighbours Gravesend United winning both on the Overcliffe ground by the same 4-2 scoreline. The competition was transferred to a junior competition as the fixture list expanded.

* = Northfleet appealed about state of ground, game replayed

WEST KENT CHARITY CUP

Season	Round	Opponent	Score
1904/05	1	Orpington (a)	4-2
	2	Crayford (h)	0-1

FA AMATEUR CUP

Season	Round	Opponent	Score
1903/04	Prelim.	Royal Engineers SB (h)	1-1
	Prelim. Replay	Royal Engineers SB (a)	3-3
	Prelim. R 2	Royal Engineers SB (a)	0-5
1904/05	Extra Prelim.	New Brompton Amateurs (h)	3-4

Playing with an all amateur team after reforming, the club was thus eligible for the above competition for just two seasons but had little success.

ALL CUPS – COMPLETE RECORD

COMPETITION	PL	W	D	L	Goals
FA Cup	88	42	14	32	213-176
FA Amateur Cup	4	0	2	2	7-13
Kent Senior Cup	104	68	13	23	270-128
Kent Senior Shield	49	22	9	18	94-78
Kent League Cup	36	23	5	8	93-51
Kent Junior Cup	10	6	2	2	26-11
Chatham Charity Cup	9	3	2	4	12-16
Sevenoaks Charity Cup	6	4	1	1	13-8
Gravesend Charity Cup	5	2	0	3	14-15
West Kent Charity Cup	2	1	0	1	4-3

● *The Sevenoaks Charity Cup, which Northfleet reached the final of in 1897. Charity and hospital cups were popular fundraisers in the late Victorian and Edwardian eras, with match proceeds going to local hospitals or other nominated charities*

Memorable matches

30th MARCH 1895 • Northfleet 2 Chatham Reserves 0 • KENT JUNIOR CUP
Victory in the Kent Junior Cup gave the Cementers their first ever silverware in a game played at Swanscombe's Rectory Field. Going into the game with 28 wins from 31 matches was an impressive record but the Chats had an even better one with 21 victories from 22 games. The Reds got off to a lively start and H.Moody found Smith in space from a throw-in and he fired past the diving Broomfield from the edge of the penalty box with only 60 seconds on the clock. With most of the 1,000 crowd supporting them it was no surprise when J.Moody added a second goal before the interval and, as hard as Chatham tried, they could not get on the scoresheet.
Team: Flowers; Sands; King; McKay; Ware; Cullen; H. Moody; Wright; Smith (c); J. Moody; Hills.

14th APRIL 1896 • Sheppey United 0 Northfleet 2 • KENT LEAGUE
Fleet travelled to Sheerness on a Tuesday night knowing victory would see them win two trophies on the same night (since the Kent Senior Cup for a short period of time was automatically handed to the Kent League winners) and a point would finally see off the challenge of Woolwich Arsenal Reserves and secure a first major title. There was no way the Islanders would make it easy for the Fleet and a Ferguson goal was all that separated the teams at the interval but a second goal from Grieves soon after the restart gave the Fleet breathing space. And when the team arrived back at Northfleet Station just after 10.00pm, it proved to be the first of many occasions when they were met by a large number of supporters, the Northfleet Silver Band and a fire engine to carry them on the way along Northfleet High Street before the celebrations really began.
Team: Walker; Auld; King; Russell; Ware; Bundock (c); Hills; J. Moody; Grieves; Ferguson; Cullen.

30th APRIL 1907 • Eltham 0 Northfleet 2 • WEST KENT LEAGUE
An ill-tempered game saw Fleet clinch their first of three West Kent titles. They appeared to be coasting at the interval with a 2-0 lead; Humble opened the scoring and Regan deflected a wayward shot from Ted Cannon into his own net. Eltham's gameplan was clearly to become even more physical in the second half and Hubble was the first victim, slipping several tackles before the home side's Hooper, determined he wasn't getting past, stopped him with an elbow to the face that brought about an instant dismissal. Soon after McGibbon – who had already committed several atrocious fouls – attempted a similar tactic on Gray that only partially worked as the Northfleet player retaliated by giving him a close-up view of his fist. To the disgust of the home crowd, only McGibbon – nursing a fat lip – was sent off and a large cluster of supporters and most of the Eltham players surrounded the referee who clearly realised his mistake and then sent off Gray to calm the situation. The desired effect was brief, however, for when Gray reached the pavilion he found McGibbon waiting for him and a further free-for-all began, with the other players leaving the field to intervene. The poisonous atmosphere sadly put a dampener on Fleet's achievement and rather than celebrating, they made a rapid exit at the end of the game.
Team: Bowie; Griffiths; McLauchlin; Mays (c); Gray; Harris; Humble; Williams; Cannon; Neale; Smith.

28th MARCH 1910 • Northfleet 2 Chatham 0 • KENT SENIOR CUP
Following the disappointment of losing the 1909 final to Maidstone by a single goal, the Cementers were back in the county town in tow with their many supporters and the Northfleet Silver Band in a crowd of 7,000. Despite Northfleet's domination, the Chats' defence was solid and custodian and goalkeeper Thomas Holmes was outstanding, "constantly plucking the sphere out of thin air" according to contemporary reports. It wasn't all one-way traffic, however, with Chats twice hitting the woodwork with Bill Jacques beaten. The deadlock was finally broken when William Kennedy headed home Edwin Myers' cross on 40 minutes. The second half continued in the same pattern with the Cementers in command but Chats still dangerous in their fewer attacks. Another goal was clearly needed to clinch the game and Albert Williams achieved it from a Frank Jecock pass late in the game.
Team: Jacques; Quayle; Rogers; Sharpe; Mays (c); Nash; Myers; Jecock; Kennedy; Buchan; Williams.

24th MARCH 1913 • Northfleet 2 Gravesend United 1 • KENT SENIOR CUP
The only time the two local rivals met in the final was a memorable affair, particularly for the Fleet. The usual preliminaries of red coffins carried by Shrimpers supporters, and red and green ones by Fleet supporters, around the Athletic Ground before the match kept the entertainment high. Meanwhile, several supporters who had tried to avoid payment by clambering up surrounding trees gave further amusement when the tree branches broke and deposited them on to the top of the main stand. When the game got under way, the Shrimpers were in early control with Vic Walters twice coming close. Arthur Seccombe turned the game the Fleet's way on 27 minutes with a dazzling run that left five defenders in his wake before firing past John Geggus to score one of – reportedly – the greatest goals of all time in the competition. Fleet extended the lead through Bill Lawrence on 56 minutes before the Shrimpers reduced it through Armitage to ensure a thrilling final 10 minutes. A record crowd and receipts were achieved in a game when north Kent took over Maidstone for the day.
Team: Henry; Mason; Goodhind; Nash; Sharp; Tyler(c); Blackburn; Seager; Lawrence; Seccombe; Myers.

28th MARCH 1921 • Northfleet 1 Ramsgate 0 • KENT SENIOR CUP
A fourth triumph in Kent's blue-riband competition for Fleet was a hard-fought victory. A strong wind and driving rain failed to dampen the enthusiasm of a 10,000 crowd at Maidstone's Athletic Ground and, with the wind behind them, Ramsgate dominated the opening half only to be thwarted by a no-nonsense Fleet rearguard. The roles were reversed after the interval and the all-important goal to break the deadlock came on 70 minutes. It was little surprise that the mercurial Arthur Seccombe claimed it, accepting a pass from George Harber and slipping two tackles before firing past future Fleet goalkeeper George Pleasants to win the game.
Team: Joyce; Barnfather; O'Conor; Daisley; Swayne (c); Ing; Barnett; Seccombe; Layton; Day; Harber.

21st APRIL 1924 • Northfleet 1 Dartford 0 • KENT SENIOR CUP

The brightest things about a generally scrappy game were Fleet's colourful new red shirts with a large white V down the front. In unseasonally hot weather the game got off to an exciting start with both sides having an early chance before Ted Goldsmith got the goal that would win the game after just six minutes, firing in Seccombe's cross. The hot conditions gradually took their toll and the 9,000 crowd had little goalmouth excitement until late on when Cain handled to give Fleet a penalty; Seccombe wasted it, however, as Wright made a fine save.
Team: Hills; Grant (c); Bailey; Todd; Skitt; Houston; Pilcher; Goldsmith; Lane; Bell; Seccombe.

2nd MAY 1924 • Northfleet 2 Ashford Railway Works 0 • KENT LEAGUE CUP

After winning the toss for venue, Northfleet made sure their name was the first on the brand new trophy with a relatively comfortable win. The ever-dangerous Jimmy Bell breached the Railwaymen's defence twice in the opening half and there never looked any possibility of losing the advantage. The margin should have been increased when Harry Skitt missed a penalty – the third penalty miss by a Fleet player in each of the three finals contested during the season.
Team: Pikerman; Grant (c); Bailey; Todd; Skitt; Houston; Pilcher; Goldsmith; Lane; Bell; Seccombe.

13th APRIL 1925 • Northfleet 8 Sittingbourne 2 • KENT SENIOR CUP

A stunning second-half performance saw Fleet defend the trophy in emphatic style but no-one would have predicted this scoreline at the interval, with the teams then level at 2-2. The 12,000-strong Maidstone crowd were amply rewarded after a quiet start. Tommy Roe opened the scoring for Fleet in the 25th minute when his penalty was blocked by Wilson and he converted the rebound. Two minutes later Arthur Sanders added a second with a fine individual goal but the Brickies hit back to level through Whibley and Hill by half-time. Another fine individual goal by Sanders had Fleet back in front and Roe and Jimmy Bell soon put the issue beyond doubt as the Brickies crumbled. Bell went on to complete his hat-trick, with Tommy Pye also getting into the goalscoring act before the end.
Team: Pleasants; Richardson; Bailey; Todd; Pye; Houston; Pilcher; Roe; Sanders; Bell; Seccombe (c).

5th APRIL 1926 • Northfleet 1 Folkestone 0 • KENT SENIOR CUP

The Cementers became the first club to complete a hat-trick of victories in the competition against their Southern League county rivals. The 11,000 crowd at Maidstone were hardly on edge in a dour physical battle in which defences held a vice-like grip on the forwards. What proved to be the only goal of the game came after 17 minutes when Billy Houston placed one of the numerous free-kicks conceded by both sides into the Folkestone penalty area. Arthur Sanders did well to control the awkward bounce and pass it on to Arthur Seccombe and 'little Sec' did the rest with a blistering shot into the roof of the net.
Team: Pleasants; Alton; Bailey; Rowe; Pye; Houston; Pilcher; O'Callaghan; Sanders; Bell; Seccombe (c).

9th OCTOBER 1926 • Gillingham 5 Northfleet 7 • KENT SENIOR SHIELD

One of four victories in this competition, all achieved in the 1920s and this was by far the most memorable. Delayed from the 1925/26 season, Gillingham won the toss for ground advantage. Matters began badly when goalkeeper Bill Moody got a message through that he would be late after missing his train and with no reserve goalkeeper available, Northfleet gambled on starting with 10 men, full-back Alton going in goal until Moody arrived on the field after 15 minutes with Fleet losing 2-1. The teams continued to swap goals in an amazingly open match and Fleet led 4-3 at the interval. But two rapid goals for the Gills after the restart gave them a 5-4 lead before a late surge in the final 15 minutes saw Fleet score three goals without reply to take the game in fine style. Goalscorers were Sanders, Bell and Cooke with two apiece and a single from Pilcher while Gills replied through Dixon 2, Brown (pen), Drury and Bailey (own goal).

18th APRIL 1927 • Northfleet 1 Sheppey United 0 • KENT SENIOR CUP

Fleet kept their grip on the cup with a fourth successive victory and for the third final out of four, a single goal won the day. The Maidstone home ground was covered in red – and not just for the Fleet and their familiar strip – since the Islanders sported red and white stripes, a colour clash that would never be allowed today and perhaps made a suitable excuse for the numerous stray passes in a generally disappointing game. It was decided in Fleet's favour by a 38th minute Albert Evans goal, a fine shot from the edge of the penalty box. For Arthur Seccombe it was a suitable way to end a memorable career by lifting the trophy once again - his sixth winners' medal in the competition.
Team: Moody; Alton; Chaplin; Bagge; Rowe; Pye; Pilcher; Evans; Sanders; Bell; Seccombe (c).

9th APRIL 1928 • Northfleet 3 Sittingbourne 1 • KENT SENIOR CUP

A fifth successive Kent Senior Cup was won against an old adversary. This was an all-Southern League clash and the quality showed with some fine flowing football. Fleet took an early lead when Joe North headed home a pinpoint Wally Pilcher cross but the Brickies showed plenty of their own skills and when Jack Illingworth handled under pressure in the penalty box, Cox came up to slot home a 43rd minute penalty equaliser. Fleet regained the lead on 61 minutes when Jimmy Bell (who along with Wally Pilcher played in all five finals) netted and George Edmonds ensured victory with a third goal on 77 minutes.
Team: Cummings; Illingworth; Chaplin (c); Rowe; Pye; Houston; Pilcher; North; Edmonds; Bell; Alford.

18th APRIL 1938 • Northfleet 2 Dover 1 • KENT SENIOR CUP

After four successive semi-final defeats the Fleet were back in the final for the first time in 10 years. Folkestone and Margate had both beaten them twice but this time Fleet had got the better of Margate by a single George Skinner goal. A crowd of 9,168 filled Maidstone's Athletic Ground and saw underdogs Dover take a surprising 16th minute lead through Baker. Although Fleet were enjoying most of the game, an hour had gone before Alf Day levelled matters. That was how the score stayed until the very last minute when Day created an opening for Charlie Revell to fire home the winner against gritty opposition.
Team: Barron; Roberts; Nicholson; Evans; Coxford (c); Burgess; Revell; Skinner; Trailor; Coulston; Day.

Northfleet United players A-Z

From the first game in 1890 to the last one in 1939, more than a thousand players wore the red and white of Northfleet. It would be impossible to detail them all so we have selected some of the more prominent ones while having to omit others because of a lack of available data. In these days of instant information, it is difficult to imagine that little more than a century ago it was a task to even obtain the Christian names of many players, particularly at non-league level – so where no first name or perhaps just an initial is provided, that is the reason why.

ACQUROFF, Jack (1911–87). Born Chelsea. A Tottenham youngster who never quite made the grade at White Hart Lane, he was nonetheless an outstanding centre-forward who scored 49 goals in his debut Fleet season, including seven in one game against Maidstone. He completed a century of goals over the next two seasons before moving on to Folkestone, Hull, Bury and Norwich. He served in the RAF in the Second World War and emigrated to Tasmania in 1949. In the early 1950s he captained Tasmania against China, who won 11-0! Fleet honours included two Kent League titles and a Kent League Cup.

ALFORD, Frank (1901–83). Born Swindon. An outside left with a few tricks up his sleeve, he enjoyed four seasons at Stonebridge Road having signed at the beginning of 1927/28. He had previously played for Barrow, Lincoln City and Scunthorpe and also made two appearances for Everton in 1921/22.

ALSFORD, Wally (1911–68). Born Edmonton. A half-back sent down from Tottenham for the 1929/30 season, he made a strong impression that led to him returning to White Hart Lane at the end of that campaign. He played more than 80 games for Spurs, winning a single England cap in his time there, and moved on to Nottingham Forest in 1936 before retiring after a season.

ALTON, Charles (1891–1969). Derbyshire-born full-back who played for Chesterfield Town and Doncaster Rovers before the First World War and then totalled nearly 200 league games for Rotherham County and Brentford after it. He signed for Fleet in 1925, playing for two successful seasons and winning the Kent League and Kent Senior Shield in 1925/26 and two Kent Senior Cups (1925/26, 1926/27).

ATTWOOD, Arthur (1901–74). Born Walsall. A forward who started out at his hometown club, scoring 13 goals in 14 games, he turned out three times for Everton in 1928 before longer spells at Bristol Rovers and Brighton & Hove Albion where he scored plenty of goals. He moved to Northfleet for a single season in 1935, firing 10 goals as the free-scoring Fleet coasted to the Kent League title.

BAGGE, Harry (1896–1967). Born Tottenham. As a teenager, he was on the reserves books at White Hart Lane and guested for Spurs during the First World War without ever making a first-team appearance. He played 180 games for Fulham after the First World War and went on to manage Athletic Bilbao and Salamanca in Spain after the Second World War. In between (1926/27 to be precise), he played for Northfleet having arrived with Fulham teammate Alec Chaplin, and helped the club to Kent Senior Cup triumph, though he didn't play in the final.

BALDING, Henry (1884–1962). Born Tottenham. A goalkeeper who had turned out for Bromley before signing for Crystal Palace in 1907, where he played seven games. He moved to Northfleet where a Southern League management committee set a transfer fee of £30 and he replaced Bill Jacques from 1911. However, he broke his leg shortly before the eagerly-awaited Kent Senior Cup final against Gravesend United in 1913. He was well-supported by the club, who paid him a weekly wage as he was unable to work for a time and so could not provide for his widowed mother. The minutes of committee meetings in 1914 show a genuine concern for his welfare and he was provided with a season ticket to watch his former teammates in action plus money from Kent and FA benevolent funds.

BARNETT, Fred (1896–1982) Born Dartford. Fred played local league football for Hawley before being spotted by Tottenham. A clever goalscoring forward he was signed by Northfleet after failing to break through at Spurs and the negotiations helped create the deal that brought so many Spurs youngsters to Northfleet. He won a Kent Senior Cup medal in 1920/21 before returning to Tottenham in the 1922/23 season and, from 1929, going on to play almost 200 games for Southend United. He ended his career at Dartford.

BATTEN, Bert (1898–1956). Born Bristol. An inside left who played professionally for Bristol City and Plymouth Argyle, where he became a consistent goalscorer. This led to his selection for the FA Tour of Australia in 1925. Down under he set a new record for goals scored by an English player on a colonial tour, featuring in 25 of the 26 matches played and netting 45 times, including six goals against South Australia in Adelaide and five against the Australian team. This form brought him to the attention of Everton and, after a delayed start to the following season because of the return voyage from Australia, he was sold to the Goodison Park club for a then-hefty £1,500 fee. He played only 15 games for the Toffees and moved on to Bradford City, Reading and Clapton Orient. His turn at Northfleet came in 1929/30 but it must have been but a brief stay as he is only recorded as having scored one goal in the first friendly of the season.

BELL, Jimmy. Discovered playing local football and signed in 1922. A clever goalscoring inside forward, he would go on to be one of only two players to appear in all five of the club's successful Kent Senior Cup finals between 1924 and 1928. He also collected one Kent League, one Kent League Cup and four Senior Shield titles and he retired at the end of 1929/30 to take over as trainer of Dagenham.

BENNETT, Les (1918–99). Born Wood Green. Bennett, who played and scored in Northfleet's very last game, was a quick-thinking energetic inside forward who made his debut the previous season, helping to win the 1938/39 Kent League. After war service in Burma, India and Egypt, he was a keystone in the Spurs team that became Football League champions in 1950/51, playing 294 times before moving on to West Ham, Clacton and Romford. He scouted for West Ham for a time, managed a caravan site in Clacton and became a security guard at the University of Essex. He also had a cameo role in the 1947 James Mason film *Odd Man Out*!

BOND, George (1910-82). Ilford-born centre-forward who was signed from Millwall in 1934. He led the forward line in fine style, scoring plenty of goals and helping to win the 1934/35 Kent League title and Kent League Cup before moving to Gillingham at the end of the season. In the summer of 1936 he arrived in Malta to play for Floriana. In 1938 he represented Malta itself and had a spell with Sliema Wanderers before, having been interrupted by the Second World War, returning to Floriana in 1943.

BUCHAN, Charles (1891-1960). Born Woolwich. Buchan's initial promise was recognised on his signing for Woolwich Arsenal but he departed after they refused to pay his travelling expenses and signed for Northfleet. A clever, scheming inside forward, he was a key influence in the treble winning team of 1909/10, gaining medals (which were later stolen in a burglary) in the Kent League, Kent Senior Cup and Thames & Medway Combination. He moved to Leyton and soon after that to Sunderland, where he played 380 times, captained England and then moved back to Arsenal. He played in two FA Cup finals (losing in 1913 with Sunderland and winning in 1927 with Arsenal) and gained a Football League winner's medal with Sunderland in 1913. He later became a distinguished journalist before founding *Charles Buchan's Football Monthly* in 1951. A true football legend of the 20th century, he also won the Military Medal in the First World War (see page 61).

BUCHAN, Tom (1889–1952). Charles' older brother, but often mistaken for a younger sibling due to his slighter build and smaller stature, Tom played the season after Charles departed from Northfleet in 1910. He had a mixed reaction from local newspapers, with reviews ranging from scathing to complimentary. Either way, he was signed – like his brother – by Leyton, failed to make the grade at Sunderland, and proceeded into the Football League with Blackpool, Bolton Wanderers and Tranmere Rovers.

BUCKINGHAM, Vic (1915–95). Born Greenwich. Immediately sent to Northfleet on signing for Tottenham in 1934, he spent a season learning the ropes in the Kent League, picking up a league winner's medal and another one in the Kent League Cup. He returned to White Hart Lane in 1935, playing 230 games for Spurs in a 14-year career. He had even better success as a manager, guiding West Bromwich Albion to FA Cup success in 1954 and pioneering the Dutch 'Total Football' approach as manager of Ajax and a young Johan Cruyff. He also managed Sheffield Wednesday, Fulham, Sevilla, Olympiakos and, more famously, Barcelona where he won the Copa del Rey in 1971.

BURGESS, Ron (1917–2005). Born Cwm, Ebbw Vale. Burgess began life as a miner before signing for Tottenham and then being farmed out to Northfleet in 1936. A stylish half-back who soon adapted to the hurly burly of the Kent League, he won that title in 1936/37, together with the Kent League Cup. The following season saw him win the Kent Senior Cup and another League Cup medal before returning to Tottenham where he eventually played 297 times and captained them to the Football League title in 1950/51. Internationally, he won 32 Wales caps – many as captain – and also played for Great Britain v Europe in 1947. He eventually returned home to finish his playing career at Swansea Town, who he went on to manage, along with Watford.

BUNDOCK, Ted (1872–?). Captain of Northfleet's Kent League winners in 1895/96, he played for three seasons and returned after the club's four-year hiatus for a short spell in 1903.

BUNGAY, Reg (1911–86). Born Reading. Another Tottenham youth who was snapped up from non-league while playing for Oxford City in 1932, he was immediately sent to Stonebridge Road. Despite a purple patch around Christmas 1932 when he scored three hat-tricks, the season at Northfleet didn't help his breakthrough at Spurs and he ended up playing small roles for Plymouth, Bristol City and Mansfield Town, where he finally got some regular playing time. He ended his career with Clapton Orient.

CALVERT, Fred (1892–?). A striker who played for the army while serving in the Royal Artillery at Woolwich, he signed for Arsenal in 1911, making his league debut at Liverpool. A handful of appearances followed before he signed for Northfleet at the beginning of the 1912/13 season. A goalscoring start to his career promised much but he seems not to have established himself and, when not playing, was even asked to patrol the Stonebridge Road perimeter and deter spectators who had not paid from watching! He later served in the First World War.

CANNON, Ted (1887–1910). A highly promising centre forward signed from Woolwich Arsenal in 1906, he top scored in helping win the West Kent League in 1906/07 and 1907/08, a season when the Kent League was also won. He moved back to the Gunners but tragically contacted typhoid fever and died aged 23 with a great football career unfulfilled.

CAULFIELD, Tom (1892–1951). An electrical worker signed from Sittingbourne in 1906, he had three successful seasons, two as an inspiring captain, from wing half. He was a Kent League winner in 1907/08 and 1908/09, as well as a Kent Senior Cup runner-up in the latter season.

CHANDLER, Bert (1897–1963). Born Carlisle. A very experienced right back, Chandler signed for Derby County immediately after the First World War, playing upwards of 200 games for them. In 1925 he moved to Newcastle United and a year after that Sheffield United, where he was captain, adding 100 more Football League games to his tally with both clubs. In 1929, having left Mansfield, he turned up at Northfleet after a newspaper advertisement for players and stayed the season, playing against Clapton Orient in the FA Cup. He thereafter played for the short-lived Manchester Central club as well as Queen of the South.

CHANNELL, Fred (1910–75). Born Edmonton. The younger brother of Bill Channell, who played for Northfleet in the early 1920s, he played for Harwich and Haywards Heath before joining Tottenham in 1930. After a spell at Peterborough & Fletton United, he came to Northfleet where he starred at full-back from 1930–33 off and on, before returning to White Hart Lane and making almost 100 appearances.

CHAPLIN, Alec (1892–1986). Born Dundee. A full back signed from Fulham where he made nearly 300 appearances in 1926. He went on to captain the Fleet from 1927–29, twice winning the Kent Senior Cup. In the early part of his career, before the First World War, he played for Dundee Hibernian (later Dundee United).

CLAY, Tommy (1892–1949) Born Leicester. A right back and Fleet captain in 1929/30, the former Tottenham and Leicester Fosse star, who played for both clubs before the First World War, gained four international caps for England and an FA Cup winners' medal with Spurs in 1921 but was in the veteran stage in his time at Stonebridge Road. He coached Den Haag in the Netherlands just before the Second World War and ran a pub in St Albans for a time after retiring.

COOK, Tommy (1901–50). Born Cuckfield. One of the best-known sportsmen from Sussex, Cook's long spell at Brighton as a centre forward gained him an England cap. He also had a long cricketing career with Sussex, playing more than 450 times for his county. His single season with Northfleet in 1930/31 proved successful and he moved back into the Football League with Bristol Rovers. A colourful character, he fought in both World Wars but was severely injured while serving with the South African Air Force in 1943. Unable to cope with life-changing injuries and suffering depression, he committed suicide in 1950.

COVINGTON, Charlie. Goalkeeper whose outstanding performances for fellow Kent League side London Paper Mills attracted Northfleet to sign him in 1934. He helped the club to a double of Kent League and League Cup in 1934/35 and, living just a drop kick from Stonebridge Road in Station Road, matters seemed settled for a long residency between the posts – until he dropped the bombshell in October 1935 of a career change and resigned to join Surrey Police.

COWAN, Billy (1896–1962). Born Edinburgh. An inside forward and a "mazy dribbler", he played for Dundee and Newcastle United who paid a then-handsome £2,250 for him in 1923 and he repaid part of that by helping the club win the 1925 FA Cup. Another £3,000 took him to Manchester City in 1926 before he moved around the country, taking in St Mirren, Peebles Rovers, North Shields, Hartlepool, Darlington and Bath. In between that array of clubs, he – according to two Manchester City sources – joined Northfleet briefly in the late Twenties though there are no other verifiable sources of his involvement with the club.

COX, Freddie (1920–73). Born Reading. A winger who came to Northfleet in 1937 as a 17-year-old, he had an impressive 1937/38 season, winning the Kent League title. He moved back to Tottenham in 1938 and after war service as a fighter pilot, during which he was awarded the Distinguished Flying Cross, he was sold to north London rivals Arsenal for £12,000 in 1949. He played in two FA Cup finals with the Gunners, winning one and losing the other, playing alongside future Gravesend & Northfleet legends Lionel Smith and Jimmy Logie. He later managed Bournemouth, Portsmouth and Gillingham.

COXFORD, Jack (1901–78). Born Seaton. An inspiring defender and captain who used his experience to good effect on his young teammates after signing from Bournemouth in 1934. He helped Northfleet win a lot of silverware, earning the club the Kent League in 1934/35, 1935/36, 1936/37 and 1938/39, together with the 1937/38 Kent Senior Cup and the Kent League Cup in 1934/35, before retiring in 1939.

CULLEN, Pat. A centre-half during Northfleet's formative years, winning a Kent League title in 1895/96. His debut was probably around 1893 and he featured in a resurrected Northfleet's Boxing Day game in 1902.

DABSON, F. A founding committe member of Northfleet Invicta in 1890, he appeared in the club's very first match alongside Joe Lingham. He turns up again in the 1912–14 committee meeting minutes and also in the 1921/22 team photograph, so was presumably a long-term supporter and committee member after his playing days.

DAY, Alf (1907–97). Born Ebbw Vale. A half back who played for Northfleet from 1928–31 after Tottenham sent him down to knock off his rough edges, he was a neat player with a fondness for a passing game. On his return to Spurs after a few games he was moved on to Millwall, Southampton and Tranmere. He earned one Welsh cap, against Northern Ireland in 1933, before he had even made a Football League appearance.

DITCHBURN, Ted (1921–2005). Born Gillingham. Ditchburn moved to Northfleet as an infant and, after following his father into boxing, realised his talents were better suited to goalkeeping. He played for Northfleet and Kent schoolboys and had trials for England schoolboys. Working at Northfleet Paper Mills, he played for their side before being spotted during a trial at Northfleet United and snapped up by Tottenham. Sent back to Northfleet, he made his debut in October 1938 and helped the club to the Kent League title that season before moving to White Hart Lane. He served as a physical training instructor in the RAF, guesting for Dartford and Aberdeen. After the war, he went on to make 452 appearances in goal for Spurs, winning the Football League title with them in 1950/51 and gaining six caps for England. When he left Spurs in 1958 the link between Northfleet United and Tottenham Hotspur was finally severed. He went on to become player-manager at Romford and played in goal for them at Stonebridge Road in a Southern League game in 1961, by which time he had gained legendary status.

DRINKWATER, Charlie (1914–98). Born Willesden. An outside left with Hampstead in 1932, he briefly joined Northfleet in March of the following year, featuring in a handful of games and scoring in a 6-2 win over Canterbury Waverley. A spell at Golders Green earned him a move to Brentford but he didn't make the grade until 1935, this time with Aston Villa, when he scored on his debut against Chelsea. A few more league appearances were earned at Charlton and Watford but the war, in which he served with the Royal Navy, interrupted any further career development.

DUDNEY, George. A member of the Northfleet Invicta side for their first match in 1890.

DURSTON, Jack (1893–1965). Born Claphill. A 6ft 5in goalkeeper better known for his cricketing abilities in helping Middlesex to two county championships and playing as a fast bowler for England. Football-wise, he signed from Brentford and distinguished himself in his single season of 1921/22. He also played football for Royal Engineers (with whom he served in the First World War) and Queens Park Rangers.

EDMONDS, George (1893–1989). Born Holborn. A centre forward, he started out at Watford before the First World War, winning the Southern League with them. Wolves paid £1,500 for his services in 1920 and he appeared for them in the 1921 FA Cup Final. He also saw service with Fulham in 1923 and Watford paid £250 to take him back in 1926. A year later he joined Northfleet and he had two successful seasons at Stonebridge Road, winning the Kent Senior Cup in 1927/28 and Kent Senior Shield in 1928/29.

EDRICH, Bill (1916–86). Born Lingwood. A tricky winger who found greater fame on the cricket field with Middlesex and England, he nonetheless was one of the many sportsmen who excelled at football as well. At 18 years of age, he arrived at Stonebridge Road in 1934/35 and scored 14 goals, including a brace against Gillingham in the Kent League Cup final. He returned to Tottenham the following season and played semi-regularly over the next two seasons. It was his cricket career that really took off, however, though that was held up by the Second World War, in which Edrich made the rank of Squadron Leader as a bomber pilot and was awarded the Distinguished Flying Cross for a mission over Cologne. He excelled at cricket again after the war, starring in the 1946/47 Ashes Tour and playing Test and County cricket until 1958.

EPHGRAVE, George (1918–2004). Born in Reading but brought up on Guernsey, the 6ft 4in goalkeeper started with his local club but was brought to Northfleet, via Tottenham, in 1935 to replace Charlie Covington. Steady performances for one so young brought him to the attention of Aston Villa where he stayed for three seasons, though without troubling the first-team. He played a League game for Swindon in 1939 before the war, during which he was captured in Crete and held as a PoW by the Germans in the Soviet Union. On repatriation, he played for Southampton, Norwich, Watford and Deal Town.

FAIRCHILD, Cliff (1917-74). Born Romford. Plucked from Barking FC by Tottenham in 1936, Fairchild was a full-back who was registered for Northfleet duty on signing. He scored six times in Fleet's third Kent League triumph in succession. Failing to make the grade at Spurs, he played 30 games for Southern League Colchester United in 1937, from where Arsenal signed him for £500 but he didn't get a game in that part of north London either, dropping down to play for Southend, Great Yarmouth and Lowestoft Town.

FERGUSON, W. A member of the Northfleet side that won the Kent League title in 1895/96, he was also a member of the team in the following season.

GEGGUS, John (c1889–1951). A former Custom House goalkeeper, Jack as he was better known made 31 appearances for West Ham United over a two-year spell from 1910–12, after which he joined Gravesend United. He once had to be coaxed back on to the field after taking exception to disparaging remarks while at the Hammers. He played for Gravesend against Northfleet in the 1913 Kent Senior Cup final but was between the sticks for the Cementers six years later as the first goalkeeper of the post-war Fleet side.

GOAD, Dick (1891–1961). A talented local sportsman who served both Northfleet United and Gravesend United in between times as working as a bus driver. He played for Northfleet in two spells, either side of a season at Gravesend in 1911/12, and he was one of six pre-First World War players who returned in 1919 to play for the club again. His war exploits, with the Army Service Corps, also made for good reading (see page 62).

GODDARD, Charles. A useful inside right originally from Lincolnshire who scored 24 goals in 1931/32, winning the Kent League and League Cup double. He was sought by Crystal Palace in the summer of 1932 and played 24 times for them in a two-year period before moving to Fulham in 1935. He also played for Tunbridge Wells Rangers and was seriously injured in a game against Northfleet in 1936, requiring a "major operation" according to newspaper reports.

GOODHIND, George. Known as 'Sonny', he played for Dartford from 1904/05 for several seasons before moving to Crystal Palace in 1910. He joined Northfleet as a full back in 1912 after failing to make a breakthrough at Palace and played in the side that beat Gravesend in the 1913 Kent Senior Cup final. He was wounded on the Western Front during the First World War.

GOODMAN, Bert (1890–1959). Born Dalston. A utility or forward player who played for various local clubs in east London before the First World War, moving on to Croydon Common and Clapton Orient, for whom he featured as a guest player during the war. A short spell at Maidstone in 1919 was followed by 17 games for Tottenham and a move to Margate before he arrived at Northfleet in 1921/22. He was soon on his way to Charlton for three seasons before Gillingham, Clapton Orient once more and Guildford saw him wind down his career. He was killed in a car accident in 1959.

GRANT, George (1891–1947). Born Plumstead. Began his career in local football including a spell at Northumberland Oddfellows before signing for Arsenal aged 19 in 1910. A right half, he made 57 appearances for the Gunners leading up to the First World War and played in the first Arsenal game at Highbury. The Arsenal Handbook of 1914 cites him as being a Chinese international, though it's fairly certain this was a little light-hearted humour on the part of either Grant or the Arsenal handbook editor of the time! From 1919, he was on the books of Millwall Athletic and Queens Park Rangers, from where Northfleet's first manager – Bert Lipsham – signed him in 1922. In 1924 he captained the side to Kent Senior Cup and Kent League Cup glory. By the following season he was more of a bit-part player and ended up at North Shields.

GRANT, John (1891–1974). Born Northfleet. An eventful career that saw him score 11 goals in a single game for Fleet against Catford Southend in 1912 began when he left home as a teenager to play for Cliftonville in Northern Ireland, picking up an Irish Cup winner's medal in 1907. He played in Sweden and then for Southport Central in between two spells at Northfleet. In his first Fleet season, 1908/09, he featured in the Kent Senior Cup final and in his second, 1911/12, he grabbed his 11-goal haul. A powerful, strongly built forward, he was signed by Woolwich Arsenal soon after this spree and scored a hat-trick against Blackburn. In 1912, he was one of several Englishmen spearheading a revival at Italian club Genoa where he spent two years, prior to a short time at Northern Nomads. He joined the Royal Inniskilling Fusiliers during the First World War, rising to the rank of acting captain, and died in 1974.

GRANT, Walter (c1871–1939). A member of the Northfleet Invicta side in their first ever game, he was described as a building labourer in the 1901 census and could well have worked with Joe Lingham's building contracting firm, who had been his teammate in 1891.

GRAY, Bill. Nicknamed 'Rudder', he played for several seasons and was top scorer in 1904/05. He later became trainer to the team.

GRIEVES, T. An 1895/96 Kent League winner who played on for a couple more seasons up to Northfleet's demise in 1898.

HANNEY, Terence 'Ted' (1889–1964). One of three ex-Olympic football gold medallists from the 1912 Games who turned out for the Fleet, Hanney was a tall and graceful centre half who played for Reading before a big-money (£1,250) transfer took him to Manchester City in 1913. In June 1915 he enlisted in the 1st Footballers' Battalion, Middlesex Regiment and, rising to the rank of sergeant, he missed the initial stages of the Battle of the Somme but was wounded four weeks into the campaign. Having taken shrapnel to the face and thigh and a shot to the shoulder, he was abandoned in a trench overnight and, despite his injuries, helped see off three German counterattacks. Invalided out of the army with facial scarring and a torn adductor muscle in his leg, he was unable to sustain a football career at the highest level, though he managed to continue in the game, playing for Coventry and captaining Reading. He moved to Northfleet on 1922/23, his last season before retiring, and scored three times. After hanging up his boots, he coached VfB Stuttgart and FC Wacker Munich before returning to England at the outbreak of the Second World War.

HARBER, George (1894–1960). A key player in the two seasons after the Great War, he was a forward who scored and made plenty of goals, helping to win the Kent League title in 1919/20 and the Kent Senior Cup in the following season. Hailing from Sutton-at-Hone, his brother Ernest played for the Fleet in the 1914 Kent Senior Cup final.

HILLS, Ernie. One of Northfleet's 1895/96 Kent League champions. A decade later, he had a spell as the club's trainer.

HOARE, Gordon (1884–1973). Born Blackheath. A former Bromley and Woolwich Arsenal player, he played in the First Division for the Gunners in 1908 and had a second spell from the end of 1910. In between, the England amateur international played off and on for Northfleet in the 1909/10 and 1910/11 seasons. Despite his good pedigree, he missed out on a place in the Kent Senior Cup final side that beat Chatham in 1910. He rejoined Arsenal at the end of 1910, playing 34 games for them before moving to Glossop North End and, in 1912, playing for Great Britain in the Olympic Games. He scored two goals in the tournament, winning a gold medal. During the war he played for Queen's Park in Scotland, Manchester City and Fulham, joining the Craven Cottage club in peacetime before retiring in 1920.

HOOPER, Percy (1914–97). Born Lambeth. A goalkeeper who made 100-plus appearances for Tottenham after two seasons with the Fleet between 1933 and 1935. At the outbreak of war, he guested for several teams including Brighton and resumed his career in 1947 at Swansea Town.

HOUSTON, Billy. An outstanding club servant for 10 seasons from 1922–32, Houston was a hard-working half-back who was captain in the second half of his career. He signed from Tottenham and soon became a key figure in the Fleet side winning a host of honours including two Kent League titles, four Kent Senior Cups, four Kent Senior Shields and a Kent League Cup. His 11-trophy haul was beaten only by Arthur Seccombe.

HOWE, Les (1912–99). Born Hertford. A half-back who played for Northfleet between 1928 and 1932, winning the Kent League, League Cup and Senior Shield. In 1930, while back at Spurs temporarily, he became only the second 18-year-old to play for the club's first team. He returned to White Hart Lane on a permanent basis in 1932 and went on to earn 182 appearances, playing in every outfield position including emergency goalkeeper. After serving in the RAF in the Second World War, he became manager of Enfield, where he had also played before joining the Fleet.

HOWELL, Harry (1890–1932). Born Warwickshire. A footballer and cricketer, he played for Wolves and Southampton as an inside forward and grabbed plenty of goals while a guest player for Stoke City and Port Vale during the First World War. He turned up at Northfleet in 1921/22, scoring 22 times and playing alongside another country cricketer in Jack Durston. After his single season at Stonebridge Road, he was at Accrington Stanley and Mansfield Town. The cricket side of his career saw him as a fast bowler and batsman with his home county, while he also played in five tests for England. He died in Birmingham at the young age of 41.

HUNT, Doug (1914–89). Born Shipton. A successful centre forward who played for Winchester City and Southampton before being sent to the Fleet in 1932 by his new club Tottenham. Between 1932 and 1934 he gave excellent service, scoring 25 goals. On returning to Tottenham, he found regular football hard to come by and moved on to Barnsley for £1,700 and then Sheffield Wednesday for £3,875. After the Second World War, he played for and was assistant manager at Leyton Orient before taking over Gloucester City and, in the 1950s, Tonbridge as manager.

ILLINGWORTH, Jack (1904–64). Born Castleford. A full-back for the Fleet from 1927 to 1929 after being sent down from Tottenham for further experience, he won the Kent Senior Cup and Senior Shield before returning to White Hart Lane. He signed for Swansea in 1934 and finished his career at Barry Town.

ING, Joe Walthamstow-born half-back signed from Clapton Orient, he played in the 1920/21 Kent Senior Cup-winning team.

IVERSON, Bob (1910–53). Born Folkestone. A 1932 arrival by way of Tottenham, Iverson scored 18 goals as an inside forward as Fleet came up just a little short in the season's end-of-season hunt for silverware. Failing to make the grade at Spurs on his return in 1933, he played for Ramsgate and then had 40 games for Lincoln City which brought him to the attention of Wolves, where he enjoyed two good seasons. In 1937, he moved to Aston Villa, where he would remain – converted to left half – for the next 11 years in the same side as another former Northfleet man, Vic Potts.

JACQUES, Bill (1888–1925). Born Erith. An outstanding goalkeeper signed from Northumberland Oddfellows in 1908 and a member of Fleet's treble-winning 1909/10 side. He moved on to Coventry City before returning south to sign for Tottenham in 1914 where he helped them win Division Two in 1919/20. He missed their success in winning the FA Cup the following season through injury and retired in 1922, suffering ill health thereafter and dying at the age of just 36.

JEWHURST, Fred (1887–1949). Born Hoxton. Jewhurst played at half-back in the successful 1919/20 Kent League-winning side before moving on to Charlton and then Southend before completing his career with Dartford.

JOYCE, John (?–1956). Born Burton. Goalkeeper known as 'Tiny' to supporters, being ironic given his 6ft-plus height. He was formerly with Millwall and Tottenham. At Northfleet he won the Kent Senior Cup in 1920/21.

KENNEDY, William (1890–1915). Born in Grays, he was a schoolteacher when he came to the notice of Northfleet in 1909 at the same time as the great Charles Buchan. He was one of the standout performers of the treble-winning side of 1909/10, scoring in excess of 50 goals – "a diamond in the rough" and "the catch of the season" according to the *Kent Messenger*. He scored in the victorious 1910 Kent Senior Cup final. Considered by many contemporary observers as being the equal of Buchan, who remembered him as one of his more gifted Northfleet teammates in his later autobiography, Kennedy was snapped up by West Ham in 1910, scoring on his debut against Brighton. He impressed the Hammers with a number of goalscoring appearances but suffered a career-ending injury in 1912 in an FA Cup tie against Middlesbrough. A lance corporal in the London Scottish Regiment during the First World War, in October 1915 he volunteered to brave enemy shelling during the Battle of Loos to obtain help for wounded comrades and was killed in doing so, his body never found. See page 59 for more on William Kennedy.

KING, Eddie (1914–93). Born Hackney. A Tottenham signing from Tufnell Park, he played for Northfleet in 1932/33 as an 18-year-old, scoring against Dartford in the Kent Senior Shield, but it was a lean season for the Fleet. He was called back to Tottenham but made just one appearance in 1934 and with a serious injury in 1936, his fledgling career was done with.

KING, Syd (1873–1933). Born Chatham. An early star of Northfleet United at full-back, helping to win the Kent League in 1895/96, he eventually moved on to New Brompton in 1897 and then on to Thames Ironworks (later West Ham United), where he was appointed manager in the 1901/02 season aged only 28. He would remain in the hotseat until 1932, by far the club's longest-serving manager and he led his team out in the historic 1923 'White Horse' FA Cup Final, the first ever at Wembley. After a series of incidents, he was eventually sacked in 1932; this he took very badly and committed suicide shortly afterwards – according to the coroner at his inquest, 'the balance of his mind was disturbed'.

LANE, Bill (1904–85). Tottenham-born centre forward and one of the very first to join Northfleet under the newly negiotiated nursery agreement. He was top scorer in his only season in 1923/24, helping win the first of what would be five successive Kent Senior Cups. He later played for Brentford, Watford and Bristol City and after moving into management with Brighton eventually returned to his old stomping ground by managing Gravesend & Northfleet between 1961 and 1963, taking the club on its longest ever FA Cup run.

LAWRENCE, Bill. A Summerstown amateur in 1906, he was signed by Crystal Palace and made 30 appearances over the course of seven years (in two separate spells) to 1912, during which time he had also signed for Merthyr Town. An ex-England amateur international, Lawrence moved to Northfleet in summer 1912 and scored the decisive goal in the Kent Senior Cup final win over Gravesend United. He returned to the club after the First World War, claiming a Kent League winner's medal. He left for Ramsgate in 1920 and spent several seasons at Dartford thereafter.

LAYTON, Arthur (1890–1962). Born West Ham. A bustling centre forward who was at Clapton Orient before the First World War, he played for Fleet between 1920 and 1922, helping to win the Kent Senior Cup in 1920/21. He moved on to Millwall.

LEVENE, Dave (1908–70). Born Bethnal Green. Spotted playing non-league football by Tottenham, he was despatched to Northfleet in 1930, staying for two seasons in which time the club won the Kent League and League Cup double with a young side. Returning to Spurs in 1932, he played a handful of games until 1935 when he signed for Crystal Palace. He also played in France and ended his career at Clapton Orient, at which point the Second World War broke out.

LINGHAM, Joe (1870–1943). Born Gravesend. Not without reason was Lingham known as 'Mr Northfleet'. He was a member of the very first team in 1890 and later turned to refereeing and administration, becoming a high-ranking official in both the KCFA and FA as well as a JP. He was also an astute businessman owning his own building company at 1-3 The Hill, Northfleet, responsible for construction of projects including Northfleet's Catholic church. He was also chairman of the *Gravesend Reporter*. On several occasions he came to the club's aid with generous financial donations and took a strong role in forming the club in 1890 and reforming it in 1903 and 1919. But for his death at his home at The Mount, Southfleet, he would probably have attempted to restart it again at the end of the war.

LIPSHAM, Bert (1878–1932). Born Chester. Lipsham became Fleet's first ever manager in 1922 in what proved something of a disaster as he failed to last a full season. A qualified accountant and a left-winger good enough to earn an England cap, he played in two FA Cup finals for Sheffield United (or four in reality since both needed replays), winning and losing one each in 1901 and 1902. He moved to Fulham in 1908 and then on to Millwall where he became manager between 1911–18. He later set sail for Canada where he became involved in the development of football.

LUDFORD, George (1915–2001). Born Barnet. Ludford spent three seasons with Northfleet, including a sensational 1935/36 when he scored an incredible 101 goals. Unsurprisingly, he was called back to headquarters at Tottenham where he spent a total of 27 years as both player and coach. As he got older, he played elsewhere in the Spurs team, including wing half and full back. After the Second World War, Tottenham refused a swap deal with a Millwall player for the sole reason that they held Ludford in too high a regard. In 1957 he moved on to Enfield where he had further long spells as both team and later stadium manager. His three-year spell at Northfleet brought him Kent League titles in 1934/35 and 1935/36 plus a Kent League Cup in 1934/35.

McWHIRTER, Douglas (1886–1966). An English amateur footballer who competed at the 1912 Summer Olympics in Stockholm alongside others who would play for Northfleet, Gordon Hoare and Ted Hanney, where they won the gold medal. Having also played for Bromley and Leicester Fosse, he was an occasional Northfleet team member and turned out in the 1914 Kent Senior Cup final, with Fleet finishing as runners-up to Maidstone.

MACKESY, Jack (c1890–1963). An addition to the 1927/28 Northfleet side, Mackesy was a veteran campaigner having joined West Ham from Deptford Invicta in 1910. He played for the club throughout the First World War as an inside forward but by the time he arrived at the Fleet, he was more accustomed to the half-back position. He received two benefit matches from the Hammers.

MARSH, Isaac. 'Ike' played briefly for Northfleet in 1897 – he moved on to West Herts (Watford), his Hornets' debut being an 8-0 defeat at Dartford, and later played in the Football League for Notts County, Doncaster Rovers and Chesterfield.

MAYS, Tommy (c1883–?). A popular, local player who sadly had his career curtailed by injury and later emigrated to Canada, where he had previously been a "fortune hunter". He was a no-nonsense defender who had previous experience at Queens Park Rangers and he weighed in with vital goals from 1906–10, being part of the treble-winning 1909/10 team. Honours included two Kent League titles, a Kent Senior Cup and three West Kent League medals.

MEDLEY, Les (1920–2001). Born Edmonton. An England Schoolboy, Medley arrived at Northfleet as a teenager in 1937/38 and featured in two seasons at outside left where the Fleet ran out Kent League winners. Speedy and with tight control, he was a neat passer of the ball and a natural winger. He returned to Spurs just before the Second World War and played for West Ham on a guest basis during the war before leaving for Canada with the RAF. He was a key figure in the famous Spurs 'push and run' side that emerged post-war, winning the league title in 1951 and gaining six England caps. After 164 games for Tottenham, he moved to Canada for a third time in 1954 (as he had in 1947 for 15 months). He coached in South Africa and returned to the UK briefly before a fourth and final emigration to Canada.

MOODY, Jack (c1868–c1948). A local player who lived on Stonebridge Road before it became a football ground, he was a centre forward in the 1890s, winning the Kent League in 1895/96 and also played when Northfleet embarked on their Southern League adventures from 1896–98.

MORRISON, Johnny (1911–84). Born Belvedere. A forward who impressed with Bostall Heath and Callenders Athletic before signing for Tottenham, he was sent to Stonebridge Road for the 1931/32 season. In that campaign he won the Kent League and scored the winner to carry off the League Cup. He returned to Tottenham and had a good scoring rate of 90 league goals in 134 games. He is one of fewer than 20 Spurs players to score 100 goals in all competitions.

MULFORD, Sid (1896–1973). A forward for Brentford, he was brought to Stonebridge Road in 1924 and, scoring five goals, he contributed to Kent Senior Cup and Senior Shield wins that season, though he played in neither final. He later played for Dartford and Ealing Celtic.

MYERS, Edwin (1888–1916). Born Blackheath. Signed in 1908, the then-teenaged 'Mickey' was a clever winger and popular with supporters. A member of the treble-winning 1909/10 team he moved on to Crystal Palace before returning in 1912. Also an excellent cricketer, he played for Surrey. He died in what became known as the Third Battle of the Somme in September 1916, one of 500 casualties in his battalion, and his name can be found on a war memorial outside The Oval. See page 60 for more on Myers.

NASH, Bill (c1889–?). A tenacious half-back signed from Gravesend United in 1909 and a member of the treble-winning side of that season. Previously with Grays and Southend, he remained until the outbreak of war and later became the first trainer to the newly formed Gravesend & Northfleet in 1946. He won Kent League, Senior Cup (twice) and Thames & Medway Combination honours.

NICHOLLS, J. Played in Northfleet Invicta's first ever match in 1890, staying at the club until at least 1892. A 'Nicholl' was in the 1897/98 line-up but it is unclear if it was the same player.

NICHOLLS, Joe (1905–73). Born Carlton, Nottinghamshire. Having played locally in the West Midlands after leaving the Grenadier Guards, he was noticed by Tottenham and given some time to develop at Northfleet around 1926. He moved back to Spurs in 1927, playing 129 times up to 1936, when he signed for Bristol Rovers and added another 112 games. His brother Harry won a Victoria Cross for heroic action during the Fall of France in May 1940.

NICHOLSON, Bill (1919–2004). Born Scarborough. Two successful seasons at Stonebridge Road did the groundwork for a man who went on to become a footballing legend at White Hart Lane as both player and later as their greatest manager. He was an England international wing-half and a member of Spurs' Football League championship team of 1950/51. His Fleet honours included a Kent League and a Kent Senior Cup. A recipient of the OBE, as manager he guided Spurs to one Football League title, three FA Cup wins, two League Cups, four Charity Shields, a European Cup Winners' Cup, a UEFA Cup and a semi-final place in the European Cup.

NORTH, Joe (1895–1955). Born Burton. A centre forward who scored goals wherever he went, which included Arsenal, Reading, Gillingham and Norwich, he had seen action as a lieutenant in the First World War, winning the Military Medal. He joined the Gunners from Sheffield United where he had played as an amateur in 1919. He made his League debut at Highbury in 1920, moving to Reading two years later. He came to Northfleet in 1927/28, where he was top scorer and won the Kent Senior Cup. He also played cricket for Middlesex between 1932 and 1937.

O'CALLAGHAN, Eugene (1906-56). Born Ebbw Vale. The Welsh wizard, predictably known as 'Taffy', was outstanding in his only season of 1925/26, scoring 49 goals and helping win the Kent League and Kent Senior Cup. A two-footed player, he had a reputation for having a range of passing ability and was part of the Spurs side known as 'the greyhounds' for its speed and style. He went on to play 252 times for Tottenham, moving on to Leicester in 1935, while gaining 11 Welsh caps. After the Second World War, he was on the coaching staff at Fulham.

PHYPERS, Ernie (1910–60). Born Walthamstow. A wing-half who had amateur status at Walthamstow Avenue and Aston Villa before Tottenham offered him a contract in 1933. He played at Northfleet in 1933/34 and at the end of the season headed back to White Hart Lane, making 33 appearances up to 1936. He moved to Doncaster Rovers shortly before the Second World War and played as a guest for several clubs during the conflict.

PILCHER, Wally (1901–73). He began his career at Tottenham, moving to Northfleet in 1922 and was played on the right wing. He took part in each of five successive Kent Senior Cup wins between 1924 and 1928, while also winning the Kent League, League Cup and Senior Shield (three times). He eventually returned to Tottenham for the 1928/29 season but never managed a first-team game.

PLEASANTS, George (1898–?). Born Plumstead. Goalkeeper who appeared for Ramsgate against Northfleet in the 1921 Kent Senior Cup and moved to Stonebridge Road two years later, before returning to his first club – Charlton – in 1926. A veteran of three KSC and KSS wins each, he also won the Kent League Cup.

POTTS, Vic (1915–96). Born Birmingham. A full back who started out at Tottenham, he was given his chance at Northfleet in 1933/34 but it was a disappointing season. He enjoyed a better second spell in 1935/36, winning the Kent League in the side that contained hotshot George Ludford. He moved to Doncaster Rovers and then guested for Aston Villa during the war alongside fellow Northfleet player Bob Iverson. This led to a contract with Villa in 1945 and he played 62 times in four years, retiring through injury in 1949.

PYE, Tommy. Signed from Fulham in 1924, he gave Fleet four seasons of solid service at centre-half winning three Kent Senior Cups, the Kent League and two Senior Shields.

REVELL, Charlie (1919–99). Born Belvedere. A prolific goalscorer with Callenders Athletic, his exploits brought him to Fleet's attention and with them he won the Kent League in 1938/39 and Kent Senior Cup in 1937/38. After the war he played for Charlton and Derby County, retiring as a professional in 1952.

ROBERTS, Syd (1911–?). Born Bootle. An inside forward who broke through at Liverpool in 1929, he made his senior debut in 1932, playing almost 60 games up to 1937. He had brief spells at Shrewsbury and Chester before arriving at Northfleet in the summer of 1939 with war already on the horizon and there were just two games for him to play in before the curtain came down on the club and, presumably, his football career.

ROE, Tommy (1900–72). Born Evenwood. Roe started out with local side Durham City before Tottenham signed him and sent him to Northfleet in the very first intake of youngsters in 1924. An inside right, he was top scorer in his only season with 35 goals, winning the Kent Senior Cup and Senior Shield.

ROWE, Arthur (1906–93). Born Tottenham. An outstanding half-back who was at Stonebridge Road between 1925 and 1929. He won plenty of silverware at Northfleet and on returning to White Hart Lane he provided long service as both player and manager, steering the north Londoners and their ex-Northfleet players to the Football League title in 1950/51, a year after winning the Second Division.

SANDERS, Arthur (1901–83). Born Edmonton. A brilliant two-footed forward – and English teacher – who moved to Northfleet from Peterborough in 1924 after failing to make the grade at Tottenham. His outstanding displays helped win a host of Kent silverware until his return to Tottenham in 1928, where he played 13 league games. He later played for Clapton Orient, retiring in 1933 and resuming his teaching career. He was a headmaster at a school in Enfield into the 1960s.

SARGEANT, Fred (1912–48). Born Islington. He played for a single season in 1934/35 on the right wing, winning the Kent League and League Cup before returning to Spurs where he was a regular – recording 109 appearances – until the outbreak of war. An aggressive runner with the ball, he played in several wartime leagues until breaking his leg in 1940. He cancelled his Tottenham contract by mutual consent in 1945 and ended his career at Chelmsford. While in Essex, he died from a stomach ailment aged just 36. Spurs played Chelmsford in a friendly to raise money for his widow and a crowd of 7,659 watched the match, making £1,389 for the player's wife.

SCOLLARD, Alfred (1885–1928). A half-back who starred in the 1904/05 season, getting a few goals to his name including against Cray Amateurs in Northfleet's then record win (11-0). He also played for Maidstone and Croydon Common before going to Scotland and playing for a number of sides including St Johnstone. He served with the Royal Artillery in the First World War.

SECCOMBE, Arthur (1893–c1972). Born Woolwich. A club legend who scored more goals and made more appearances (450) than any other Northfleet player. Normally on the left wing, he sometimes played inside forward and made his first appearance in 1912 after signing from Plumstead St Johns; this despite Football League interest after some outstanding performances for Woolwich Schools. Already a regular – alongside his brother Henry – when war broke out in 1914, he joined the Royal Artillery and came through unscathed – unlike, alas, his brother who was killed in 1916. He returned to Northfleet after the war and played for another eight years, winning Kent League, Senior Cup, League Cup and Senior Shield honours. Curiously, for such a club legend, little else was heard of him after retirement though a record matching his exact name and birthdate shows him as having died in Barnstaple, Devon, in 1972.

SHOTTON, Ned. A member of Fleet's first side in 1890. A local man, he maintained links with the club throughout his life. A 'Shotton' was back playing for Northfleet in 1903/04 (it is unclear if it was the same player) but what is for certain is that he stumped up funds to help resurrect Northfleet after the First World War, following a meeting at the Factory Club in 1919.

SIBLEY, Eric (1915–96). Born Christchurch. A Tottenham youth who arrived at Fleet in the summer of 1934, he picked up Kent League and League Cup medals in his first season playing in defence. He had another spell at Northfleet in 1936/37 after a season back at White Hart Lane in which he failed to make a breakthrough. He moved to Bournemouth in 1937 and then Blackpool later the same year, playing 78 times in a 10-year spell that included the war years. Moves to Grimsby and Chester followed, where he retired in 1950.

SKITT, Harry (1901–76). Born Portobello. A half-back sent from Tottenham, he quickly showed his potential winning the Kent Senior Cup, League Cup and Senior Shield in the 1923/24 season. After just one season at Stonebridge Road, he returned to White Hart Lane and made more than 200 appearances for Spurs, gaining interest from the England selectors in his early days. He departed north London in 1931 and travelled up to Chester for their first season in the Football League, where he added a further 100 appearances to his record.

SMITH, Bert (1892–1969). Born Higham. A local player who turned out for Metrogas and an Army side before joining Huddersfield just prior to the First World War. Back in peacetime, he transferred to Tottenham, being part of the 1921 FA Cup-winning side and playing almost 300 games for them. He won two caps for England and in 1930 came to Northfleet in a player-coach role. He later held coaching positions at Young Boys in Switzerland and at Stevenage.

SMY, Jimmy (1907–97). Born Edmonton. An inside forward who played for Hampstead Town on leaving school, he signed for Tottenham in 1926, becoming professional three years later. Although at the White Hart Lane club until 1931, playing 38 times, he didn't establish himself and signed for Northfleet in time for the 1932/33 season. Two seasons in north Kent were followed by a spell at Sittingbourne where he was club captain. He emigrated to Australia late in life and died in Brisbane.

SWAYNE, Bill (1897–1988). A centre half signed from Tufnell Park, he was an England amateur international who spent two successful seasons at Northfleet from 1920 to 1922, winning the Kent Senior Cup in his first season.

SHARP, Don. Formerly of Tunbridge Wells Rangers, Leyton Reserves, Maidstone and Metrogas, Sharp was a stiff tackler and known as something of a tough opponent. He had two spells at the club and was runner-up in the 1910 Kent Senior Cup final. He played for Gravesend for a single season, returning to Northfleet in 1912 and won the Kent Senior Cup at Gravesend's expense in 1913. His wife was a keen follower of his career, once going so far as to write to the Northfleet committee demanding to know why her husband had not been selected for a game.

SMITH, P. Captain of Northfleet's first ever side in 1890 and he must have presumably been instrumental in setting up the club to have attained such a position from the first kick-off.

TICKRIDGE, Sid (1923–97). Born Stepney. A full back and England Schoolboy who became the final player to roll off the Tottenham to Northfleet conveyor belt. He made his debut as a 16-year-old in 1939 and played in Northfleet's last ever game. After the war he played 100 games for Tottenham, departing for Chelsea in the same season Spurs won the First Division title. He ended his career at Brentford.

TRAILOR, Cyril (1919–86). Born Merthyr Tydfil. A Welsh Schoolboy international, Trailor came to Tottenham's notice and played for their junior side. After a season playing mainly for Northfleet Reserves in the Kent Amateur League, he took full advantage when given his chance as an inside forward with the first team, scoring 46 goals, winning the Kent Senior Cup in 1937/38 and the Kent League in the following season. After serving in the Royal Artillery in the Second World War, he added to his Tottenham appearances, playing 118 times. In 1948 he joined Leyton Orient for £600, moving on to Bedford Town where an ankle injury put paid to his career. He moved back to his hometown on retiring from the game.

TYLER, W. Signed from Crystal Palace in 1912/13, he was a "clean and clever" wing half who captained the side the following season and returned after the war. After winning the Kent League and Kent Senior Cup in 1920/21, to add to his KSC medal from 1912/13, he signed for Charlton.

WALKER, J. The Fleet goalkeeper in the successful Kent League-winning side of 1895/96, he returned for the first few games of the rejuvenated Northfleet in 1903.

WARE, Bill A member of the 1895/96 side that won the Kent League, he was one of the founding committee members in 1890 and served at the club in later life in various administrative capacities, playing occasionally in the early years of the 21st century. His son was killed one week before the armistice ending the First World War.

WESTON, Reg (1918–98). A young centre-half, 'Buster' Weston played in the last-ever Northfleet United side. A Greenhithe local, he had joined in 1937 and got among the goals in the 1938/39 season, picking up a Kent League medal on the way. Wartime service in the Royal Navy brought him to Pembroke Docks and he was spotted by Swansea while playing locally. He was a regular for the Welsh side, winning the Division Three South title with them in 1948/49. After 229 games, he left for Derby County in 1952 and four years later dropped into non-league as Burton Albion's player-manager.

WHATLEY, Bill (1912–74). Born Ebbw Vale. Another Welsh International, full back Whatley moved to London as a child, but it was only when he returned to Wales to play for Ebbw Vale that he came to Spurs'

notice. He played a few games for Barnet and came to Northfleet as teenager for a single season in 1931/32, helping to win the Kent League. After a long spell with Tottenham (254 appearances) either side of the war, during which he served with the army in India, his career was ended by an ankle injury in 1948. He returned to Stonebridge Road in 1954 as manager of Gravesend & Northfleet, an appointment that sadly was not a success.

WILLIAMS, Albert. Inside forward signed from Sittingbourne in 1906, having previously played for Grays, he scored regularly for the next six seasons before becoming a fringe player in the last two seasons before the war. Speedy, skillful and intelligent, three Kent League titles, two Kent Senior Cups and a Welsh Kent League medal were a fair return for his years of service.

WILLIS, Arthur (1920–87). Born Denaby. The Yorkshire youngster was something of a schoolboy prodigy with offers from Barnsley, Sunderland and Tottenham on the table. He worked as a miner on leaving school and then landed a job in the south of the country, allowing him to accept the offer from Spurs and play for their junior side. In 1939 he was sent to Northfleet but it was an ill-fated arrangement that saw him contract gastro-intestinal ulcers that threatened to end his career in the game. He had better luck playing non-league football for Finchley, plus wartime guest appearances, and Tottenham gave him a second chance in 1944. From 1946 until 195- he played 160 games, winning a Football League title in 1950/51. He earned a single England cap and in 1954 signed for Swansea City.

WITCOMB, Doug (1918–99). Born Ebbw Vale. A Welsh international in the 1940s, Witcomb was spotted by Tottenham playing for Cwm Villa and sent for a brief time to Northfleet. He played for Enfield before finding professional success at West Bromwich Albion, where he enjoyed 10 years from 1937, broken by the Second World War. In 1947, a move to Sheffield Wednesday rejuvenated his career and he totalled 224 games before a season at Newport County in 1953/54.

WRIGHT, A. A member of the 1895/96 side with whom he was issued a Kent League winner's medal, Wright's Northfleet career began in 1894 and he played through the remainder of the 19th century, including the Southern League years, until the club's original demise in 1898.

YATES, Bill (1903–78). Born Bolton. A goalkeeper who played in Northfleet's final Southern League season of 1929/30, he was Bolton's second-choice custodian in 1925/26 until moving to Watford where he got 47 games over the next two seasons. He retired at the end of his first season with Northfleet and took up a coaching role in the Netherlands, where he stayed until 1940 when he was forced to flee following the German invasion of the Low Countries. also played minor counties cricket for Buckinghamshire.